As You Seek So Shall You Find

A Souls Awakening

Barbara Knapp

authorHOUSE®

AuthorHouse™
1663 Liberty Drive
Bloomington, IN 47403
www.authorhouse.com
Phone: 1 (800) 839-8640

Published by AuthorHouse 12/28/2016

ISBN: 978-1-5246-5614-0 (sc)
ISBN: 978-1-5246-5612-6 (hc)
ISBN: 978-1-5246-5613-3 (e)

Library of Congress Control Number: 2016921280

Print information available on the last page.

This book is printed on acid-free paper.

NASB
Scripture quotations marked NASB are taken from the New American Standard Bible®, Copyright © 1960, 1962, 1963, 1968, 1971, 1972, 1973, 1975, 1977, 1995 by The Lockman Foundation. Used by permission.

As We Seek So Shall We Find

A Souls Awakening

My motivation behind this information is to provide you the understanding as a Spiritual seeker that there is more to life then what we have thought in the past. You will begin to understand the mystery that we sometimes ask ourselves: "WHO AM I?" The purpose is to inspire those who are seeking find their answer. It is intended to be a path towards your journey into the light, but it is up to you to choose the best path for you to walk upon. Each of us must awaken and find our own truth. This book as well as many books have been written that serve as a steppingstone for those who are ready to awaken to their true essence. It is not meant to offend anyone's beliefs just to open your eyes to a new way of thinking. This is the start of something new! My goal is to bring this information to you in the most pleasant and positive way possible so you will see the truth for yourself. Just remain open to the possibilities and follow where your heart leads you. This is how I understand the Awakening of the Soul!

May all who read these words be encouraged and inspired to let go of your old way of thinking and trust your intuition with an open mind and open heart to follow you higher self, in order to answer the ultimate question: "Who Am I?" Pray for guidance as you search for your truth. Pray for courage to embrace it, and ultimately know how special we really are! Be open to receive the simple answer: which is "I AM THAT I AM". But what does this mean? *"You don't have a Soul. You are a Soul. You have a body." C.S. Lewis*

IT IS TIME TO WAKE UP AND REALIZE THE HIGHER TRUTH OF WHAT IS GOING ON.

Life is much more than you think it is. Our experiences from the past and present will be carried over into the future. Who are we and where did we come from? What species are we and why did we come to this planet during this time line? Have we been here before? Who is the creator of this system and how does it function? What is reality? Look at creation as we know it, the billions of Universes, galaxies, planets and beings. What is the intelligence factor that drives this whole system and how does this all work? Questions like these have been asked by many of us for years. Until now the answers were not available to us at the Universal level. Up until now the general belief is that GOD/GODDESS/ SOURCE is the direct creator of all. This is true at the ultimate level as Source is the Creator of everything that exists. We live in a multidimensional world with every kind of spirit force one could imagine. As we process through this great awakening there are major portals opening, and we have undergone sequential events that have radically shifted our Universe. These openings link celestial bodies, constellations, and stars with our planet. With each portal opening, membranes that used to separate realities are collapsing, and more beings are sharing this space with us. There are new levels of support for those of us on the path with this understanding. During these activations the energies allows us to communicate with the intelligent living matrix of other Star Systems. This network of communication is intended as a support

2

for the Star seeds, and Light Workers that work the grids in service to the Cosmic Sovereign Law. We are entering potentially explosive timelines with extraterrestrial disclosure, which open into this year and ongoing into the future. As we learn more about multiple species agendas, we must improve energetic discernment of the variety of forces that we interact with. There are both seen and unseen forces that may try to take advantage of our lack of awareness. What we hold as our intention in our personal thoughts is what we hold as our focus.

As we seek and learn about things we have never thought of before, we walk down many paths in life encountering just what we need to help awaken us to a higher destiny. Our journey can cover many lifetimes as we gather many experiences that will help us expand and evolve. The most important issue is not to allow ourselves to become rigid and closed minded in our thinking. This is a common human issue which causes many people to shut down the gates to further exploration, settling comfortably within the confines of one's outdated belief system. Our Universe is expansive, vast and never ending and mostly unknown. You will learn that anything is possible when you open your mind and realize that there are a lot of things you have not had experience with and are now beginning a new path and a new way of thinking. We are all connected!

Many SOULS are experiencing what we call the wakeup call. The cause of this call is for us to realize that our lives are no longer working in the way we set them up to be. This is due to a shift that is occurring inside ourselves as well as the larger shift that is currently affecting all of humanity. This change is happening at an increased rate which makes it difficult to understand and predict what our future brings. Many of the old ways of thinking and being in this world are no longer applicable, yet we still try to hold onto them even though we feel out of touch with the old reality. We try to justify that this is how it supposed to be and we close ourselves off, never searching for a new way. The shift we are undergoing now is about recognizing ourselves as being more than human. WE are multidimensional beings, having a human experience. We are beginning to realize that the life we originally planned in our limited concepts no longer works. Our needs have changed not only for our bodies but for our Souls. This realization may occur slowly for some and for others it is a sudden jolt into a new reality. Finding what works for each person is the key to integrate ourselves within the shift. You may need to allow the change to happen slowly or you may feel compelled to make changes that before you could not have dreamed. Any way you choose know that this process is a natural sign of growth and that we are all going through it, just trust in the journey and let it guide you to your awakening and start living the life of your dreams.

Most humans are unaware that our thoughts form a vibrational quality and force, as well as the energetic consequence of the thought form substance created, and that is has an impact on the self and others. This has an impact on our entire energetic signature with the collective consciousness of the entire planetary body. What we observe today in the global scape is the result of every single person's individual thought forms. Our thoughts make up the collective consciousness body of the earth. When we pay attention to what is happening on earth, we can see the glimpse of the vibrational quality of the average collective thought forms, or what human beings are really thinking. Look around is what you see positive, we all vibrate on a frequency and the level of frequency is determined by your emotions. Positive thought create positive experiences as well as negative thoughts create negative experience. If your life is not progressing as well as you would like, and you are not thinking with a positive mind, change your thoughts and your world will begin to change.

THE GRANDER PLAN, AND HOW ARE WE CONNECTED AND AFFECTED?

For some time now there has been a group of Souls who began an unprecedented process of Spiritual evolution referred to by many as **"Ascension."** It was decided at the highest Soul levels that it was now time to wrap things up here on Earth, release and reclaim every form that we had infused our energy within for eons of time since the very beginning, and start completely over by creating a very New Planet. This is the time we have been waiting for, to connect to Source.

This miraculous and extremely challenging process created many bizarre, confusing, and at best, unusual experiences of opening to a higher level of consciousness and a greater connection to Source and to our own Souls, as we were returning home. **"Am I part of this plan and process?"** you may wonder. **"And how would I know?"**

In recent years and months you may have felt you were being stretched far beyond what you had the capacity to endure, with many emotional ups and downs, strange physical aches and pains, many losses in the form of friends, jobs, family, and finances. Experiencing dizziness and vertigo, neck and back pain, an intolerance for lower vibrating energy, and abdominal weight gain and or bloating are some of the symptoms that many experience. Do you wonder who you are looking at in the mirror feeling like you lost your identity, not recognizing who you are anymore? Maybe you left your means of employment and are now looking for another job, not understanding that you are now being asked to do something else. Do you experience short periods when you are very cold and cannot seem to get warm or you had hot flashes and night sweats? When you go out in public or to an event, do you feel as though you are acting? Have you had a serious medical situation in recent years that left you feeling hopeless? Have you had periods where you wake up at exactly the same time every night? Have you had anxiety, panic, or what feels like depression? Do you at times have strange and disturbing dreams? Have you had periods of time when you continually saw repeating numbers, whether on digital clocks, license plates, or other places? Have you had times in your life where you felt like you do not belong here? Do you continually have short-term memory loss and at times cannot remember things that occurred only yesterday or even a moment before? Have you experienced periods of what felt like low blood sugar forcing you to eat every two hours whether you wanted to or not? Are your emotions out of control from time to time sudden weeping and sadness, or are you just plain over-emotional often time feeling lost and alone? Do you at times feel that there is nowhere left to go that remotely fits you anymore and that the only way to stay sane is to be home in your own personal sanctuary? Do you have a strong sense that you are here to accomplish something, but are not yet aware of what it is? You may feel ungrounded and spinning out of control at times but not at other times and you feel that you are missing something but are not sure what that is. It may become difficult to be in crowds, large stores or certain locations due to the fact that you are no longer vibrating on that frequency and need time to adjust to the new energies evolving in you. Many will experience energy pouring through the top of your head, or may hear ringing in your ears, or energy pulsating through their bodies. It can be increasingly difficult to spend substantial amounts of time around individuals who seem dis-connected, or ego driven. You may just want to run away from life because you no longer feel that you belong in this world the way it is and begin to co- create a new world one that feels more like home.

These are the most common of the ascension symptoms and experiences. Many of us have had these strange and common occurrences as a direct result of our Spiritual expansion process. When we begin to vibrate higher and begin to embody more light than ever before we evolve higher and higher in our Spiritual evolutionary process, and these experiences begin to lighten up. These internal changes are necessary, purging and releasing the old and lower vibrating energies. As we process through this period we align ourselves with new and higher vibrating energies, bringing us into a new and higher way of living and being. It is then that we know we are ready for our next level of awakening. This marks the turning point in the ascension process. Up until this time, we evolved in small and continual steps, although at times it did not feel like it! In this way, we released much of our old lives and old selves, and always moved into another phase of our evolution. The ascension process involves many periods of waiting for others to catch up until we can ourselves progress onto another rung. As we take our next step on the ascension ladder everyone will move up into a higher level of existence according to where they had been residing before. This is a monumental time in our Spiritual evolutionary process. WE have been making great progress and it is a time for an entirely new dimensional shift to occur. Some people have progressed far and are very tired of waiting! When we are waiting, it can feel that we are trapped, boxed in, or perhaps surrounded by darker and denser energies knocking on our door. But now the waiting is over. This is what we had been waiting for a very long time indeed! This massive first phase has brought us to a new beginning which is now here. We are evolving into what we were created to BE!

During the Ascension Cycle, many of us have come here to finalize, complete and end these imbalanced energetic cycles and their negative influences upon our genetic history, DNA record, astral recycling, and the patterns recorded in the family of origin. When we make progress with personal ancestral clearing, our clearing efforts will extend to cities, nations, and the global grid work for the entire human race. This means many of us have the Spiritual purpose to clear unresolved conflicts and Spiritual issues of our patriarchal, matriarchal and ancestral bloodlines and timelines. The process of healing the Ancestral DNA is called Genetic Path cutting, and is the main spiritual mission of many of us Indigos and Star seeds. Many Star seeds incarnated purposely in different Soul groups, known as the "False Parent" family lines. In the early stages of Spiritual awakening, all of us must address and clear ancestral issues, whether we are aware of this fact or not. Ancestral issues are inherited in our DNA record and they will manifest as specific archetypes and patterns throughout our life experiences. When we are unconscious, we will repeat these same patterns many times as we only knew a certain way of being, because they are directly inherited ancestral behavioral patterns. If you are looking for the direction or path you need to follow, you can begin by looking to see the path that led you to this now moment. What put you where you are right now, without judgement of either good or bad just reflect on all of your life experience so far. See how far you have come and then you can begin to identify with the path that will lead you to where you are destined to be. Judgement, blame, criticism, resentment, control, jealousy, blame are all characteristics of the ego. The Soul's expression is that of love and light, compassion, understanding, forgiveness, trust, self-love and self-acceptance. The Soul is a streaming flow of consciousness from its Source that is unique for each of us. The purpose of the Soul is to fully realize and recognize itself in every moment. Its seems that most people are searching for something, joy, material abundance, love, anything that will make them feel satisfied for having obtained it. This is often times not enough as the ego will always drive to obtain more and do more and be more. The Soul has the potential to realize its cosmic self and begins to manifest itself in many forms. As you liberate your Soul you begin to unleash the divine light and start to live from a higher state of consciousness.

We are living in extra-ordinary times. Not only are we as humans going through this great shift as it is often referend to, our planet is going through ascension also. The Divine energy is pouring new energies and providing extra support to the planet right now to help raise the vibration of the earth and create a new golden era, by the opening of new energies to the planet. We are beginning to experience this cosmic moment and momentous shift in the future of our planet.

This is a higher level of universal truth provided in simple form to those that are ready to accept and comprehend it. If we are to wake up, it is important to explore the possibilities and reach further to know who we really are. By exploring and remaining open, it is always possible to reach beyond ourselves for guidance, higher wisdom and enlightenment. Here is a window of opportunity that has opened up for you. Wisdom hides itself everywhere. It is sometimes seen in hide sight but it was always there for Soul growth. Each day as we wake from our sleep a new day presents us with our windows of opportunity as we learn to ask how I will use this day, and how may I serve others today? Everyday gives us the opportunity to make the best of the moments given to you by your Creator. This is an opportunity for you to be a blessing to others and at the same time bring more light in to the planet which only strengthens your Soul. It is up to you to make the moments count, all that we have is NOW this is how you will contribute to your own maturing Soul as you begin to feed others with love, light and kindness. We have been told that the ultimate goal for each of us is "Enlightment", but some may ask: What is Enlightment? The definition of Enlightment is: Spiritual, insight or awakening to the true nature of reality, the independent use of reason to gain insight into the true nature of our minds.

It literally means "awakening" and "understanding". Someone who is awakened have gained insight into the workings of the mind which keeps us imprisoned in craving, suffering and rebirth, and has also gained insight into the way that leads to their bliss and the liberation of oneself. There are no accidents only synchronicity and everything happens for a reason. Everything in your life is linked from the past, present and future. "Your purpose in life is to find your purpose and give your whole heart and Soul to it" Gautama Buddha

AWAKEN YOUR INNER LIGHT, GIFTS AND TRUE POTENTIAL

Each of you is a gifted Soul. You are mind, body and SOUL. You came to this planet in order to learn and grow, as part of your Soul's development, this is why you have challenges and problems to face. You also came to the earth to help others, and contribute to building a better world. For some of you, this may be through simple ways, such as giving love and support and encouragement to others in your daily life. For some of you, it involves much more. Some of us are advanced beings, with unique qualities and gifts, and have an important role to play in the healing and development of the world. There are many gifted Souls who are awakening fully to their light, revealing their special gifts, and higher purpose, and the true reason for being here on the earth. It doesn't matter where you are on the path, as long as you make progress every day to awaken and explore and develop your path of light, joy and abundance

In these special times of transformation in the world, the angels are calling many of us to awaken, connect with them, find and develop our true paths, and play our part in the healing and transformation of the planet. The call may come in many ways: Ask yourself am I being called? You may find that you have an awareness in things that before you knew nothing about. The calling may present itself in many ways. Do you have a feeling or a knowing that deep inside there is something more that you are supposed to do with your life? Do you love helping others and desire to make a difference? Do you find that you need to make a fresh start and are bored with the way you are in this world? Rather than ignoring the calling, resisting and struggling on with our lives as they are, even though it may feel safe, it is far better to open to the Divine, to allow the Universe to guide us to a better path. We will end up far happier, more fulfilled, richer in every sense, if we allow the angels and the Divine to guide and bless us. WE are all children of God, Spiritual brothers and sisters. Many of us are gifted Souls with advanced abilities and gifts, who have chosen to incarnate during these times to assist the transformation of the planet. Deep in your Soul you will sense whether you are here to live a simple "normal life", or you have a need to one day awaken your higher gifts, to bring healing, an light energy, and to help others. This year is a good year to decide which path you are on. Many of us are Earth Angels, old Souls, gifted, Enlightened Ones, and Masters. Some have not awakened yet, or are just beginning to realize that they are the light-workers too.

Understanding that there are no two seconds that are the same in our lives could help you to recognize just how exciting your life is. Try to take a few minutes to notice that everything about you today is slightly different from yesterday from your conversations with other people to the clothes you are wearing. Even your body has changed, replacing and transforming you from deep within your cells, nothing in our lives is ever the same. Sometimes we are so conditioned to the habits of our routines that it can often feel as if our lives are fixed on a set path. Looking more deeply into the nature of our humanity, however, helps us recognize that the only constant in our lives is, in fact, change. There is no way we can truly repeat our thoughts, words, and actions no matter how hard we try. By seeing the variety that exists even within the ordinary aspects of your life today, you will realize the freedom you have and the excitement of the ever-changing wonders of your life.

Our perception of humanity as a whole is, to a large extent, dualistic. We may judge some people as not like us, as different, and only sharing our opinions and our attitudes with others that are like minded. Our commitment to values we have chosen to embrace is often so strong that we are easily convinced that our way is the right way. We may find ourselves frustrated by those who view the world from an alternate vantage point and make use of unusual strategies when coping with life's challenges. However we believe that these people would be happier and more satisfied following our lead, but we should resist the temptation to try to change them. Every human being has been blessed with a unique nature that cannot be altered by outside forces. We are who we are at any one point in our lives for a reason, and no one person can say for certain what another should be like. Our creator has assigned each one of us a role to fulfill its Soul's journey. Since we are made in the image and likeness of this one energy. Your understanding of this will help you find you mission and allow you to fully embrace the reason why you came here at this time. You have chosen to be here at this time before your incarnation. Allow your heart to lead the way and you shall find your mission in this life time. When you accept this, things will begin to change just by letting go of what was and the fear of the unknown you will begin to see life as an exciting adventure of light and love no matter what has happened in the past.

The reasons we try to change one another are numerous. The potential we see in the people who are a part of our lives will never be precisely the same as our own, so we do these individuals a disservice when we make assumptions about their intentions, preferences, and goals. Our power lies in our ability to accept others for all their flaws and differences and to let go of the need to control every element of our existence. We can love people for who they are, embracing their uniqueness, or we can love them as human beings.

To have any kind of relationship that is growing, whether it be human or Spiritual, requires you to look within and see what is real and what is not. From the spirit world perspective, nothing is hidden who you are and what you are" IS". There can be no deception. Humans wear many masks and hide behind many fears, and so honesty the self becomes buried beneath layers of self-importance and fears of being exposed for who they really are. This illusion is, made up in the human mind, and delays the progress of the individual, and so the only way to evolve is to move forward and to grow the Soul, which is the reason you have come into being. It is time to stop pretending and become real with your inner self, and ask yourself some probing and revealing questions in complete honesty about who you are and how you hold yourself in the world.

A good place to start is to ask, what am I afraid of? If our greatest fears were to be realized, what is the worst thing that can happen to you? First and foremost, the bigger picture is that, life is eternal, so if you choose to live your life as a child of the Creator Father, then nothing can prevent an honest and sincere Soul from achieving eternal life. In light of this, there is nothing really to fear in life. Life in the universe is a school where you learn how to love. God will not allow any person to keep you from your destiny.

Your sense of self-worth is the single most important determinant of the health, abundance, and joy we allow into our life. To some degree we doubt our worthiness, we limit or sabotage our efforts, and undermine our relationships, finances or health. We get in our own way with our negative thoughts or lack of self-worth. Why do so many seem to self-destruct or why do some people continue to accept less for themselves? No one else can give you an improved sense of self-worth. It exists as a fact of life, just like the air we breathe and doesn't need to be raised, revitalized, or earned. By acknowledging your role and responsibility in your current life, you find the power to make different choices. The choice to stay in dysfunctional relationships may point to low-self-worth. This is not about blame, but it is about acknowledging our role or responsibility, which leads to the power to change. It is unacceptable to continue to take abuse from anyone. Why some people lose their tempers is their need to control you, taking your power from you. Once you stop allowing this type of behavior and accept that you deserve respect you begin to take your power back. Look into the mirror, this is the journey of the Soul how each one of us fulfills a special and unique requirement in the development of the Supreme Being, that part of the Infinite God that is becoming and growing in experience along with the evolving space-time Universes. There truly is a reason for your being and a purpose for your life that is priceless, cherished, and irreplaceable. See yourself and see the value you attach to your own worth. There is nothing more beautiful, more precious, more loved, or more cherished than who you are and what you are becoming.

Discovering your unconditional worth can help you expand fully into the world. It begins with a first step. Our lives are shaped by the choices we ourselves make, and the actions we take. Your awareness of the problem is the beginning of the solution. Sometimes bad things happen, and we may feel that we are a victim of circumstance. We can only make the best of those circumstances and learn from them and grow stronger. So if life isn't going well, maybe it's time to look in the mirror and take another look. You have to start making the changes you wish to see. We don't always get what we deserve in life; we get what we believe we deserve. So the problem is not your actual worth, but our perceived worth. Most of us have lost touch with our value and goodness, and often allow our worth to be covered over by memories of the past real or imagined, so that we feel only partly deserving of life's blessings. We can end the self-sabotage game only by taking responsibility for the choices and actions that created it. Only when we stop blaming others, or circumstances, fate or God can we change our lives and say with conviction, I chose these circumstances and I can make other choices.

Our sense of self-worth, or deservedness comes from many influences, beginning in our early years. How we were treated by parents or other caregivers as judgments, placed upon us by others become internalized. Abused children, as well as people from stable and loving households, but with extremely high standards, may both grown up with self-worth issues. Self-Worth is a subconscious self-assessment of your perceived value, goodness, and deservedness. You allow yourself to receive only those people, experiences and blessings that reflect your sense of worth. Bear in mind that you have been subconsciously rating yourself since childhood. Now we bring it into the light, and consider how this self-perception has shaped your choices and your experiences. Self-worth is you subconsciously choosing or allowing into your life the level of people and experiences both positive and negative that you believe you deserve. Until you come to realize that life is full of choices and you start making new choices you will continue to repeat the same experiences again and again. "Rain or blessings may pour down from the heavens, but if you only hold up a thimble, a thimbleful is all you receive."

In any moment, you are free to choose the high road, by being kind to others, working hard, finding supportive people, and following good role models. Through your choices, your sense of self-worth influences whether you choose to learn easy lessons or more difficult ones, to strive or to struggle. These choices are not conscious. Some of us get in our own way and block success or abundance. Success involves talent, effort, and creativity and passion and a willingness to receive. We may start something but don't finish it or don't allow ourselves to ride the wave and enjoy it in perspective. Coming to appreciate your innate worth has nothing to do with entitlement or putting yourself above others. Rather it involves a basic recognition of your essential value as a human being, realizing that you have done the best you could and made the best choices you could see at a given point in your life. More important, unconditional worth does not have to be earned; it belongs to you just as it did when you were a young child. Most of us would gaze into that infant's eyes and know that this beautiful Soul deserves only the best in life. You were that child once too. We may start thinking that you do not deserve the best in your life, because we made mistakes and may not always have been kind or may have had slips of integrity. Understand that if you were already perfected, you wouldn't be living on this planet now. It's time you recognize that you've done the best you could each day of your life, taking into account your own baggage, information, limitations, wounds, and struggles. You made the best choices you could see at the time. And now the time has come to appreciate your innate worth and choose the higher roads of life. It's time to forgive yourself and others from the past and begin to understand that the past is what made you the person you are today. If you don't like who you are in the present moment you have a choice to begin the change for the future, begin one step at a time, knowing that with intention and determination you will begin a journey into your future and your life is changed for the best. Maybe the journey is not so much about becoming anything but really about unbecoming that which is not you, so that you can be who you were created to be in the first place. WE come into this dimension as a beautiful Soul waiting to experience love and life.

As you gaze into your bathroom mirror each morning, ask yourself, how much love am I capable of today? Because that's how much love and light you'll allow in. Let your imagination drift to a better life. You are the star in your life and you will no longer have to let others tell you where to go and what you can or can't do. You become the director, the writer, and the star. Most of us have been our own "worst enemy" sometime in the past. We can all recall a choice we made or action taken that we now see as a subconscious act of self-sabotage. What lesson have we learned by our past and what awareness can we bring to our lives so that we may create a better future for us and the other people in our lives.

All sentient beings in the Universes want to be loved and love is of the highest vibration. Why is it that so many feel alone and unloved? It is because they haven't figured out how to feel love in a way that will manifest the experience of love. To feel love and to attract love into your life, you must embody the vibration of love. If you cannot imagine or induce a feeling or state of love, then you must pursue the steps that will lead to that feeling you must do something. Improve the condition of your mind so that you can become love. Begin to take little steps that can bring you into the feeling of love, and when you feel love you will attract it into your life. If you feel unattractive then you will be unattractive. Switch the gears, and feel how you want to be, feel attractive. If you cannot imagine feeling attractive, then do something to get you there. Healthy is attractive so get healthy! When you feel good inside, you will exude the vibrations of vitality and become attractive outside. This is not something only for others to experience it is for you, for Our Creator has made it so! Once you learn to feel it you will become it. This works for everyone. Now that you are aware of it start attracting the kinds of experiences, you wish to see in your life. Only you can do something about it. Try it and you will see! When you are alone, in quiet moments as odd as it may feel every once in a while, open your arms wide and say to an imagined person, or to life itself: "Yes! Thank you!" And let this be your approach to living from now on, and as you continue through this journey we call life.

The Universe will send you message by the events that are unfolding in your life. Whenever you are synchronized with something you truly want to manifest you are likely to meet that experience. This principal draws to you an experience; a state of being; condition, or person of like mind when you match the vibration of that desire which you seek. This effect has been built into the fabric of the Universes by the Universal Father to bring His created children full-circle and into His Presence. It has everything to do with becoming whole, to attract those experiences, persons, and teachers needed to learn and become. There are many of you who would like to change the circumstances of your life, yet you feel stuck, defeated, or unloved. When you feel this way, the vibration that you are sending out will continue to bring to you those experiences that match the vibration of your state of being. If you wish to change it, then change how you feel. Emotion is the engine that drives us and when you feel stuck, defeated, or unloved those feelings set up the vibration that magnetically draws the experience to you. Not only do you need to change your thinking, but you must change how you feel and this is where your God-given power of imagination works for you. If you are not feeling it, then imagine what it feels like and focus on that. If you cannot imagine it, then focus on the steps needed to bring the feeling to life and move in that direction. The higher the vibration, the faster you bring the matching experience. The stronger the signal or vibration that you hold the more you will see those events unfold for you. There are no coincidence, by understanding synchronicity and seeing things not as ordinary and committing to creating a deeper connection with your inner sync allows you to open the channels to let the Universe bring these things to you. This is the time to start changing your thoughts and watch your world change. This is the law of attraction!

Don't wait for time, Make it, Don't wait for love, feel it, Don't wait for money, provide values and earn it, Don't wait for the path, Find it, Don't wait for opportunity, Create it, Don't go for less, Get the best. Don't compare, be unique, don't fight misfortune, Transform it, don't avoid failure, Use it, don't dwell on mistakes, learn from them. Don't back down just go around don't close your eyes open your mind, don't run for life, Embrace it. Dare to Be Awesome.

We're in a time of awakening, it's easy to imagine being swept up in a force greater than you. It's the lifting of veils that reveal illusions that traps us into believing that we have to be part of a system that no longer works for all the people. The radical social changes in the 1960s happened when the conjunction of the planet Uranus occurred. This is a planet ruled by the sign Aquarius and the coming New Age. This event represents the changes needed for the Age of Aquarius, liberating US to seek new ways of living. When does the Age of Aquarius begin? And what is the Age of Aquarius? The Age of Aquarius is not part of astronomy. It's an astrological age, which occurs because of a real motion of Earth known as the precession of the equinoxes, which, for example, causes the identity of the pole star to change over time. The cycle of precession lasts 25,800 years, and there are 12 constellations of the Zodiac. So, roughly every 2,150 years, the sun's position at the time of the March, or vernal, equinox moves in front of a new Zodiac constellation. The Age of Aquarius begins when the March equinox point moves out of the constellation Pisces and into the constellation Aquarius. When will that be? There's no definitive answer. Various interpretations give different answers to this often-asked question. Some astrologers say the Age of Aquarius actually began in 2012. That's because they believe the star Regulus in the constellation Leo the Lion marked the ancient border between the constellations Leo and Cancer. This star moved to within 30° of the September equinox point in 2012, meaning that Regulus left the sign Leo to enter the sign Virgo in that year. Presuming equal-sized constellations in antiquity, that places the border of the constellations Pisces and Aquarius at 150° west of Regulus, or at the March equinox point. This started the Age of Aquarius, in 2012.

If this is the dawning of the Age of Aquarius, where's the peace and love you may ask? The first time I heard of the Age of Aquarius was in the 60's by the group the 5th Dimension and it sounded really cool and made sense to me. In 1969 the song Age of Aquarius became a very popular song. I then started listening to the song over and over again trying to understand the meaning, but at that time I was young and really had no way of understanding these lyrics. It was many years later that the song still stuck in my head began to take meaning. I didn't know at the time that this was real. It is hard to understand the words without the meaning behind them. Today this song has revealed it meaning to me finally. The Beatles also were very popular in the 60's and many people understood the message they were channeling in their lyrics. Listen to any of these songs and you may be surprised that they have so much more meaning today then you may have noticed before. There are clues everywhere.

For the next 2000 years we will be in the Aquarian Age. We have been in the transition from the Piscean Age to the Aquarian Age for the last 50 years. The official beginning of the Aquarian Age is November 11, 2011 or 11/11/11. Some people have set this date as December 21, 2012. Considering that this is a 2000 year cycle, no matter which date you accept, we are in for lots of change in the near future!

Why is this so important? Many people go their whole lives not caring or knowing if they are a Pisces, or a Gemini, or a Taurus, or an Aquarius, etc. or what their moon or rising sign is. They may have heard something's about astrology but never really look into what it all means. WE sometime find ourselves so wrapped up in what society tells us we have to be that we may not look beyond for answers. This change to the Aquarian age is so important because it changes the astrological conditions for the entire planet. **Every person on planet Earth has been and will be affected by this shift.**

The Piscean Age has been dominated by hierarchy, and power. The key phrase for this age was "To be or not to be." To make a successful and happy life, you needed to resolve this question. The key to the astrological sign Pisces is "I believe." During this age, in order for you "to be," you needed to find someone or something to believe in. This thought may have come from your upbringing or your beliefs so when you found that thing, you attached yourself to that thing and were guided how to live. This could be a religion, a political ideology, society ideas, work, etc. This created vertical hierarchies as a result, and it was essential to find your place. The keys to life were hidden and secret to those in power. You didn't need to know these secrets, only to follow leaders and guides who did. This has been the foundation for human consciousness for the past 2000 years. Everything that you have learned from your parents, and they from their parents, going back 2000 years, has been colored by this Piscean frame of reference. And now that is all changing.

The Aquarian Age will be dominated by networks, and information. The key phrase for this age is "Be to be." The key to the astrological sign Aquarius is "I know." This is the age of information. Nothing is secret anymore. All information is available at your fingertips. Where the Piscean age was organized in a vertical, up and down structure of hierarchies, the Aquarian Age is organized in a horizontal network, opening the world up to true equality.

During this age, the focus is no longer on your identity and existence "to be something or not to be something", but on accepting yourself as a whole person who does not need to believe in something outside of yourself. You are ready to accept that you have the knowledge and wisdom within yourself. It is no longer necessary to attach to something outside yourself, but to become a leader for yourself. It is your responsibility to stay on your path and to keep moving forward.

With this understanding, it is easier to comprehend what has been happening in the world over the last 50 years. On the inner level, since the 1960's, there has been a huge movement towards personal transformation: self-awareness, self-improvement, yoga, meditation, alternative healing, and clean living. There has also been a major increase in depression, suicide, anxiety, stress, and drug use, both pharmaceutical and recreational. In the outer world, we have seen the rise of terrorism and racism but also the amazing changes in civil rights, environmental consciousness, women's rights, gay rights, and global consciousness.

This shift is bringing out the best and the worst in mankind. Some people are preparing for this shift by opening their hearts and minds and embracing this new age, and some people are intimidated by the changes that they don't understand and want to return to a "golden age" in the past, or trust only those who are like themselves.

Transformation is never a painless process. When you fast or cleanse to purify your body, at first you feel worse, because toxins get stirred up in order to be eliminated. Once these poisons have been cleared, you feel lighter and more energized. Now imagine that every person on planet Earth is going through this shift. We are heading into a time of radical change. It is a time of great potential growth and expansion, but it is also a time of great potential pain and suffering. The more that you understand what is happening, the more that you can go through all of the changes without losing your balance and stability. There are several things that you can do to help you through the transition into the new age of information and consciousness. Begin by having a daily Spiritual practice. This can be many different things like yoga, meditation, prayer, contemplation, exercise, journaling. It is not important what you are doing, but that you do something almost every day, and do it with an intention to let go of your blocks and focus your consciousness. I have found that meditation works for me, but everyone must find their own pathway and use whatever tools work for them. Meditation can be as simple, it doesn't always require rituals, it simply is allowing your mind to relax and release your thoughts, so that you may clear your mind to receive. Sometime just sitting quietly and listen to the sound of your own heart beating is very soothing. Don't give in to fear, despair, or anger. There is so much happening that can trigger these emotions. If you understand that these emotions are all symptoms of the Aquarian shift, then you can go through them without losing your center. You have the power to change your life. Don't give that power away to anyone through blame or resentment. You are responsible for your happiness and grace. Don't buy into any view of reality in which you are not 100% responsible for making your life work. The Aquarian Age is all about empowerment and consciousness. Be a source of light for others who may be in a dark place. Shining our light helps others see their way through these dark places. The more people who consciously choose to embrace the Aquarian shift, the easier this transformation will go for humanity. It is a Spiritual truth that a small percentage of people who have shifted their consciousness can influence the rest of humanity. Some changes may appear as negative on the surface but you will soon realize that something new is being created for your life. Eventually you will end up where you need to be with whom you are meant to be with doing what you should be doing. Believe in what you want so much that it has no choice but to materialize.

The major part of the change began in 1987 at the time of the Harmonic Convergence. A transition began at this time heralding increased Spirituality and harmony among people. The Aquarian Age points to the direction of our own evolution in consciousness. We are each being asked to make a choice. We can cling to the old outdated values or adopt the new evolving ones. Our happiness and peace depends on our choice. The Age of Aquarius is causing great turmoil, to make room for the new values of love, brotherhood, unity and integrity. Everything with any other values is being exposed and taken down. This includes governments, corporations, individuals, and even personal relationships. Many call this a disaster, as the world appears to be falling apart, but is it? Prophesiers such as Edgar Cayce called for a "gradual change". He also hinted that it's up to us through our actions and choices as to how much pain this change will bring. The intensity and end result of the cycle change depends on how we handle challenges in our lives RIGHT NOW!

Both the Aquarian Age and the Mayan Great Cycle appear to have begun at the same time, around 2012. Scientist today confirmed the galactic alignment as the Mayan predicted. In fact, many scientists believe we should be paying closer attention to what the Mayan predicted for our own sakes. Hidden in their hieroglyphic text is the key to our own salvation, but we must open our minds eye to see it. The Mayan calculated to the day the historic alignment on December 21, 2012 over 2,000 years ago. This is the shift from one world age to the next. In fact the Mayan did everything they could to inform us of the great "window of OPPORTUNITY for Spiritual growth" opening to us with this historic alignment of the earth, the sun and the galactic center of the Universe. The Earth is now experiencing an activation coming from the Galactic Center. The Age of Aquarius mimics the ancient Mayan prediction for the next Great Cycle. The rapid changes in technology we've seen in the last number of years was orchestrated by the universal forces or the Divine to prepare us for the next new age, the Age of Aquarius. Our technological boom is all a part of the universal plan to prepare us. This coming new era should usher in a period of group consciousness. Maybe we'll finally learn to work together for the betterment of the "whole" world as a unified unit. Now that's progress, when everyone, and everything wins!

This is a time of the merging of the opposites, the masculine and the feminine. These two energies "within" each of us will once again work together to know its source, and they will act on Divine inspiration, bringing messages from the Divine to manifestation in the world. In this new and developed consciousness everything will be given freely on demand to meet a need. Aware individuals will not conceive of lack. What we give out of love grows, not diminishes. We will become "Spiritual Beings having a human experience," instead of human beings having a worldly experience. Spirit and matter will merge and function as one.

It will be the feminine, the receiver of Divine inspiration, and the masculine, the acting it out in the world, uniting as one unit, unquestioning, without altering messages from the Divine. It would be the end of selfish desire and the beginning of selfless free expression of the Soul of humanity.

IT'S A TIME TO UNDERSTAND THAT WE ARE THE SPIRITUAL MASTERS WE HAVE BEEN WAITING FOR.

As we think so shall we create! It will be a time of truly living instead of just surviving. We will have access to deeper knowledge a knowing that we haven't been aware of before. But some believe the Spiritual teacher will come from within. Christ will come to awareness within those who seek the inner teachings. He has always been within us all, but will be KNOWN innately, by those who truly seek him with devotion. Christ seeded us with grace and with a bloodline thru his children. This has been hidden from us but is now coming into the light. All humanity is to decide which direction we take in the coming new age, the Age of Aquarius. It's in fact a choice a personal one, as well as a collective one. Change always starts with the individual. So don't take your personal direction choices lightly. A positive move towards the Divine, compounds and has far more effect on the collective consciousness of the earth than a negative stand.

God after all in his infinite wisdom gave us Free Will. So, will we allow ourselves as a whole to be swallowed up in hate, greed, and prejudice? Or, are we tired of this yet? The other choice is to reach for the light and go in the new direction represented by the coming new age of "love, unity and integrity. Will we learn to live and work together for the good of the whole planet? Or, will we continue on the road of self-destruction we've been traveling now for some time? I know some of you are thinking you are helpless to steer the change.

But you're wrong! It can happen. All it takes is for you and me and another to change our thinking and values to align with the new energies coming in right now. Once the synergistic ball starts to roll, it will be unstoppable.

The past is over. Old and out dated values are being wiped out causing unprecedented change and upheaval in our lifetime. And, we're not done yet. The values of money, power and control are being replaced. They do not resonate with the values of the new great cycle. We are encouraged to look beyond the five senses and experience true living by relying on our guidance from within. This will be an Age when we truly realize that the love we show towards each other is the love we feel towards ourselves. This represents the oneness of all things which fosters unconditional love.

Science and technology will be used to improve human and environmental situations on earth, and not for monetary gain. We will finally know the true meaning of progress. In the process we will represent decisions or activities where ALL things and people gain from the change. This may sound impossible by some people but it's not.

We will finally KNOW we are not victims of circumstances, but the creators of our experiences. We are also the ones to change our earthly situation. The focus will be on making our lives a Heaven on Earth, opening a window to further our Spiritual understanding. Now that this is taking hold, we just may come to know we are the one we've been waiting for. This is one of the gifts ancient people have known for thousands of years. Our ancient ancestor revered the higher powers and made understanding their existence their daily focus. They accepted the unknown and respected the Divine. In fact trying to understand the cosmos and how they affected them was their lives. Our ancient relatives understood the effects of cosmic alignments on the earth.

Modern scientists run everything through the senses and the scientific method. If it doesn't pass the tests it isn't real. But that's changing. Quantum Physics doesn't follow the rules, because energy changes depending on whose doing the experiment and what they were thinking about at the time. When the Mayan Great Cycle, which coincides with the Age of Aquarius, changed on or around December 21, 2012, the world age Shifted towards a rise in Spiritual Consciousness. It has also been a very Spiritual age for many who started on the path back to our Creator. This searching will come to fruition and the greater meaning of things will be known. We are all experiencing these trait changes now as we travel the path.

The Indigo, Crystal and Rainbow Souls are here to help us move towards these values of love, unity and integrity. These Souls possess increased Spiritual sensitivity, and have stronger ties to the upcoming values. We think we are so much more advanced than our ancestors. WE still have a lot to learn as we embark in this new age.

The present cycle must be cleansed before we can move full force into the next cycle the close of our Age has been anticipated from the Hindus to the Mayan as an era of war, suffering, excess and inequality. While these descriptions sound ominous, there is a bright side: although the darkness appears to be necessary, it also appears to be brief. The darkest moment is just before the dawn. We are in the darkest moment right now. But, after this dark period, the sun will shine again and we will be like new born babies in a changed world. Darkness fears one thing and that it is the light, because within the light darkness cannot exist. If you are reading this, then you are most likely one of the pioneers here to help humanity move from the old age into the light. Find a way to spread your light in your everyday lives. If you know something teach it, if you are a healer work with those who may need healing, and create community networks, that serve and act fully in the state of love. Welcome to the Aquarian Age! You could see that many changes were coming that were associated with the shift to the Aquarian Age, and it is time for people to have the tools they would need to transition from the Piscean Age that we had been in for 2000 years, into this new age.

The collapse and chaos we sometimes experience in our lives is part of the process of awakening. It's an ongoing part of the "ascension" process to find ways to liberate human consciousness. In a very real sense, the times we are now in seem to be the fulfillment of what was first put into motion years ago. The negative energy will rear its head in your life and reveal things that you never saw before. Your eyes open to a new way of existing in the world. It's not the end of the world. It's the end of the old world. This is referring to those that want to stop human Spiritual evolution. There is evidence that we've been denied the truth because of other people's agendas. Look into the many others who have tried to bring this information to the public and have been received by some as crazy, or "out there", this is because they were. We all have the ability to connect to other dimensions and may be in touch with other beings. Open your mind to this concept, trust me it is possible. When you realize that other dimension exist you'll never think of life, or death, or yourself in the same way.

It's clear that we're in a volatile time, and this time in our evolution is going to test our faith. On one hand, there are amazing discoveries being made that open our eyes to our true power as Divine beings. And on the other hand, it's hard to see how there could be a happy ending the way things are going. What's being torn apart is making room for the new energies coming in to this planet, though at the time it feels like the world is ending. The systems of control may tighten, but the momentum for evolution can't be stopped, just like you can't hold back a surging ocean that's threatening the shore. It's a time when fast changes are possible, when the right innovation is put forth. And the vibe of awakening can move through the masses, changing everything in an instant. This is just a taste of what's to come. A great change is upon us, "the end of the world" is the phrase used in the Bible. We have come to understand that this not some vision or warning of a great, horrifying apocalypse, or even of Judgment Day. This great and ordered change in the energies available to us is the next step in humanity's evolution.

With the arrival of the Aquarian Age, humanity begins its "entrance into heaven" the Spiritual Kingdom. During the Age of Pisces, the truth of our essential duality body and Soul was revealed. The sign itself shows the linking of the two fishes, as our Soul and body are linked. The evolutionary work of this age has been the lifting of our lower physical nature to that of the Soul. Christ, has shown the way for us to follow the fusion or blending of Soul and form to produce the incarnate Christ in all. This is what we call Christ Consciousness.

The energies of Pisces will not suddenly stop but they will recede, as did the energies of Aries some 2200 years ago as we moved into Pisces. We as conscious beings, must be aware of this great shift. It is quite another experience to have an awareness of what is happening. Such awareness will allow us to prepare and work with these potent energies, opening the door to our evolution in the new age. Let us open our hearts, our minds, and our very beings to these inflowing new energies. These energies can and will cause humanity to identify with the group Soul, as we rise from the Human Kingdom to the Spiritual Kingdom. The qualities that are the hallmarks of this evolution and our "entrance into heaven" are, unselfish service, group work and selflessness.

This great cycle of the ages is like the cycle of the seasons, meaning winter in reality does not necessarily end on a given day, but is part of a larger cycle. The energies of winter gradually recede as those of spring become enlivened. We have naturally come to understand how to work with the seasons and their rhythms. We must understand and become attuned to the energies and rhythms of the life. Attuning to the cycle of the seasons can produce optimum growth, and on this grand scale a conscious alignment with the energies produces optimum growth or evolution for humanity. This is up to us to move past our limited thoughts and become part of the transition.

Be aware of the new innovations that will bring radical change to society, and expand the vision of how the Universe works. Seek to widen your vision, and opens doors to the cosmos, with new perspectives. There could be more interest in out-of-body experiences, lucid dreaming, alternative timelines, and meetings with higher beings. The current interest in ancient wisdom could expand and be integrated to fit the 21st century. With minds open to the far out we could see more interest in life beyond Earth, new energy technology and more interest in the workings of the mind. The theories about the origins of humankind may start to be intergrading in the mainstream. The buzz about UFO's is growing. And this may be the year that we're ready to have our minds blown. The question must be answered are you ready to be exposed to other realities, the answer may be that some are just not ready to handle it. Humanity must take leaps forward by accepting others ideas until they take hold at a deeper level. The truth opens the door to surprises with the awakening of the people, and a drive to find solutions for what we're facing now. We'll see the expansion of practical idealism, so that what seems to be far out ideas are brought down to Earth and applied to the urgent problems of today. We could see an abundance of new ideas that serve the common good. All this is reason to be optimistic.

You might ask yourself, what can I do to help? Anything that you have experienced in life that is true, beautiful, or good can be communicated to other Souls. Use your co-creative powers of imagination to reach out to others. Continue to seek those things that interest you and always remain a learner, for this is the way of a universal citizen and this is how you will ascend the grand Universe. All can benefit from peace, love, and understanding, therefore go and learn and teach and stand for the moral values of life, growth, and equality for all peoples. Until the vested interests that profit from war and the treatment of preventable illness see profit in peace and growth for all peoples, little shall change on our world, and this is where the teachers of truth can and are making a difference with the upcoming generations. We are students on the path that are learning about the sacred value of life and what it means to be a universal citizen. This sacred knowledge and wisdom must be passed on to others in ways they can understand, and this is the challenge to all of us. As you learn, grow, and become wise, so shall we teach, nurture and lead. It is not for you to make others think like you, but to inspire others to see the potentials for truth, beauty, and goodness in themselves. On our world where life is so intense and relatively short in duration, it would be beneficial to all to have access to higher thought and education. If only we would make it a priority to educate all people, regardless of their social and financial status, we would see our planet emerge in light where we learn universal unconditional love. Our positions as an enlightened soul now is to ask for what you need to do this work to learn and teach and it shall be given. Therefore use and value your time here wisely, and together we can make a difference in the quality of the lives of all Souls. As you awake to this truth you grow and ascend the Universe schools of perfection, as students and teachers knowing this dual role is the key to your passage into a greater existence here on Earth and beyond. The Universal Father requires that all the time-space Universes become perfected along with the consciousness of all sentient beings and so it becomes imperative to have this student/teacher relationship between all creatures, for without it, all progress would cease. "When the student is ready, the teacher will appear". This is especially important on our world as it struggles to free itself from the chaos of rebellion and emerge into the enlightened era of Light and Life.

During your entire lives you have all been so influenced by material desires that a life without them may seem inconceivable. When we talk about material desires, we are not talking about those basic human needs like, food, shelter, rest, and clothing. Those needs will always have to be satisfied and they will continue to play an important role in your life on this world. The material desires for those things that have no eternal value and don't provide true and lasting happiness, riches, fame, power, and one's physical appearance. These are the things that vanish once mortal life is over, and they are not needed in order for you to live a fulfilling life with great prospects of Spiritual development. Life has been designed by Source so all can enjoy the same opportunities to grow and become the best they can be. Everything you need to achieve your purpose is already within you to bring a new awareness to the consciousness of the people of this planet starting first by awakening those we call, The First Wave. This 'wave' will grow and build in size and energy. The first wave leads the second, and the second leads the third, and so on as more and more people become aware of their Spirit, their purpose, and a deeper meaning to life itself. Spirit is the tidal force from which these successive waves will be nurtured and strengthened. Some of us have been students on the path most of our lives and are part of this First Wave, and many of you have been gifted with extraordinary God Fragments which are your on board spirit guides of great experience and ability. We are the ones who shall blaze the trail making these first vital connections with Spirit, then with others of like mind and purpose, then with those on the fringe of the second wave, which wave are you riding on.

WE are one of the first groups of human teachers, in our generation, on a world approaching Light and Life and it is our purpose as Spirit teachers, to awaken, nurture, and strengthen others. Perhaps many of you have never thought about yourselves as teachers, but, consider your experience. Think about the journey you have thus taken, and how you came to know the Spirit within and all those extraordinary experiences and synchronicities that led you to the truths you now know. Those experiences can be shared, and this is how you build a wave. Start today to enjoy your Divine heritage, right there where you are, doing what you do. The realization of this profound truth will elevate all your tasks and activities to the category of Divine service and will make you a reflection of the love of the Creator to your peers. This is how humans become Divine, by accepting their parts in the Universe and keeping alive their desires to know more. Seek for those of kindred spirit and exchange information and express and explore the creative force that is within you with great passion. Work in groups and find a need in this world, for there are many, and create something that will serve as a beacon of light that will awaken those in the second wave. Spirit alone cannot do this for you, we need to work together to transform this world into a planet where quality Souls can be nurtured and given opportunities to grow and find meaning and purpose in life.

It is important that your work as teachers contains the information that will create a 'Spiritual Map' for those who are seeking and who are hungry for the meaning of life and purpose. This map will lead them to the truth about the Spirit within, about Gods Plan, eternal life and ascension, and how cherished and unconditionally loved each person is by our Creator. Some teachers will first need to lift the self-imposed illusions of bondage this world imposes on the mind of their students before these higher truths can be revealed, and Spirit will be here to assist in this process. You also have the ever-present Christ consciousness, the Spirit of Truth, to guide you as you work and nurture other students. Consider your role as teacher, you have more to offer than you may think. The time to be about the Father's business is now. If only you can awaken just one other Soul, you initiate the wave effect, and can observe how one changed life affects another. There are many possibilities. This is a message to all of us, for it matters not whether you are a man, woman, or child, all who have ears to hear, let them listen. Everything you see around you, all life and all matter in the Universe the sky, the stars, the trees, are all a part of your reality created from the infinite and eternal Super Intelligence which is the One WE call 'God.'

This God is the original parent and pattern for all realities and living beings both physical and Spiritual. Source is the Original Personality, for all other personalities could not exist were it not for this first personality to create there from. There was none before, Source is perfect and has all knowledge, is all wise, all powerful, and everywhere present. God is Spirit. God brought into existence the finite Universes and set in motion all matter and material as the theater for the desire to have experience, this energy desires to know and explore itself in each one of us.

We are the living experiencers that fulfill the desire of the Creator to have all experience. The Universe monitors your experiences by giving you a fragment of itself some call the Spirit, or Over Soul. You were all made imperfect, intentionally, by His perfect plan and designed so that you would evolve and grow more perfect through experience. The Source Energy presence that lives within you is there to guide you through the Universes of time back into His presence in perfection. Because you are His Children and a part of Himself, it is

His intention to grant you eternal life should you decide to continue on with the experience. This is your purpose to be the eyes, ears, hands, and feet of Source in your realm wherever you find yourself in the multiverse. Since we cannot become perfected in our short terrestrial lives on the worlds of time and space, God has a plan for the continuance of your identity and consciousness beyond this world and into higher realms where we can experience new and greater things. As you grow more like the Creator, you are given greater capabilities to work with and co create with the Universe energy and your mind and consciousness is expanded to comprehend the sublime and astonishing experiences as you ascend toward wholeness.

His Great Plan for us as his children is that we would become perfect by learning and experiencing greater levels of Divine love. Love is the condition for which all consciousness develops and evolves toward perfection, for without love there is no forward movement no life. What you understand of love now in our earth life's is only the very small percentage of Divine love which will expand with your ascension toward perfection.

You are loved full strength by God, yet some people only comprehend a very small part of that love. As we explore our lives and diversify our experiences, keep in mind this Great Plan, and open up to experiencing greater levels of love in this world, which will carry over into the worlds of light. In this world of light you will continue a deeper exploration of love. See yourselves as explorers who are just starting out on a great adventure. We are citizens of the Universe and it is time for everyone to grow up and see life as a continuum that spans eternity. How truly blessed are we, all Souls of this Earth.

Everything in the Universe is created from the pure light electrons known as the body of God, Source, Heavenly Father and Heavenly Mother, or Prime Creator, any name that feels right to you. The understanding that everything in the Universe is energy and that all energy is at different levels of vibration and frequency, indicates that all planets and their inhabitants vibrate at different levels. Planet

Earth is a third dimensional planet with fourth and fifth dimension activity in progression. Currently the beings on the planet Earth are estimated to be mostly in the third dimensional plane, and some in the fourth and the fifth. We are here to be the keepers of the 3rd Dimension. We are here to bless the earth not to destroy her. We are wired to access all dimensions. You need to clear your negative emotions and create the portals into the higher dimensions. Without reaching towards these other dimension you will never experience true Bliss or Nirvana. Your Souls may go through periods of transitions before you have access to the higher dimensions.

The planet Earth is currently going through a dimensional ascension, moving from third to fourth with eventually being in the fifth. For individuals to shift with the planetary ascension, they must individually focus on raising their vibration or frequency level. As vibration levels are raised you release the blockages in the physical, emotional and mental bodies, and the shift in frequency uplifts the person to the higher dimensions. To fully evolve into the fifth dimension the person must open up to unconditional love, expand his/her inner light quotient, be fully forgiving under all circumstances and not generate negative harmful thought patterns. When you original temple has been restored you will begin to anchor in more light and have the ability to hold the higher vibrations, then offer that light to others.

You have the chance to co-create with Spirit creating a new and better future for you and the world, one that leads both you and others forward to a glorious new future. It's through your Spiritual growth, raising of your consciousness, and by making a difference in service to others, you are playing your part in lifting up humankind and the planet. As thousands around the world lift their own energy, and find new paths, each Soul can help to lift the energy and shift the future of mankind and the planet as well. Large numbers of Souls are incarnating on the planet now, to take advantage of these special times and the opportunities for exceptional Spiritual growth that they bring. What an opportunity we have here.

Where do you start? Start where you are, and sense or seek guidance about your path. Start conversations with others if you have questions or need direction. There are many Souls who have already been through the many stages of awakening. They have had many experience that you may find helpful in your current situation. We have the access to the higher ream once we begin to look inside yourselves, you already know the answer. Listen to the small voice you hear trying to get your attention, that is your higher self, that is you at the center of self. Whether your life is good, bad, or wonderful already, you can make it even better with a little help from above. Life was not meant to be a trial. Life was not meant to be an unpleasant learning experience for any of us. Our lives were planned by Prime Creator to be open, free, joyous and enjoyable. Our Creator is distressed to see generation after generation of humans living in a world of suffering, sadness, illness, violence and hatred. We humans are born into this less-than-perfect world. And since the pattern is set, humans just keep repeating the same old mistakes, lifetime after lifetime. But now the time has come for change. That is what **Ascension** is all about.

All human beings are part of a process happening on planet earth called Ascension or The Shift. We have been on the planet living in the third dimension for many eons of time. We are being asked to raise our consciousness level, to raise our frequency, in order to rise above the past limitations on our planet. As part of this Shift, we will be moving spiritually to a new dimension. We are now moving into a higher dimension awareness. This is about the opening of our hearts. This means that the heart and the mind are joined and everything from that point onward becomes based on Love. Without love you understand nothing, when you understand love you will find peace. In peace you will find inner strength and through that you find serenity. The ego looks on the outside to find peace but the Soul know peace lives within. Love is the spirit of joining, sharing, manifesting, and flowing. This step requires humans to raise their consciousness level, and to raise their vibratory level. Many of you are probably aware of some of the current situations on earth. There may be some truth that people are acting and reacting against the flow of the new Ascension energy. But elements of the Ascension energy process began to play out years ago. We are already well into the Ascension process. There is no way to stop it. It is an integral process happening within, and it is happening on a Spiritual level. The world needs this process more than ever at this time. There is nothing that can be done to stop the process of our evolution as Spiritual Beings.

You may have noticed how time flies by. This is to help humans wake up, to boost their awareness, and to begin to raise their frequencies. Be aware that you may experience that your consciousness is receiving updates or downloads. Similar to the way that your computer receives updates, so are humans receiving updates. This is interfering with the energy levels of many human beings. In the past, humans lost some of the DNA structure that they had received at the time of Creation. They went from 12-strand DNA to 2-strand DNA over several thousand years. Now humans are being updated to the original structure. The updating takes integration. This is tiring. Many humans have been fatigued on and off for the past several months for this reason. These updates are strengthening human knowing and intuition. Sickness has been occurring at higher levels with the raising of consciousness, old issues that were buried deep in the emotions, deep in the human tissues, have been coming up for release. This has been happening at a higher rate since the shift began. This has resulted in more illness such as flu, colds, infections and general fatigue. Many individuals are experiencing confusion, dizziness and brain fog because of the rise in consciousness, life does not seem normal for many of us. Change is often disruptive to one's old habits. There are new ways of thinking, new ways of acting. And if a person is not aware that changes are taking place, it is even more disorienting. Humans who are overwhelmed by these changes are often falling ill. The elderly are succumbing to dementia and Alzheimer's at record levels. Many individuals are "checking out" because the changes are too much for them. Yet others are experiencing a Spiritual renaissance many individuals are flowing with the new energy. They are raising their consciousness levels and they find the new energies exhilarating. They are alive and interacting with their new found higher energies. Several Energy Portals or star gates have been opening up each month bringing in some new energy. These portals brought in new energies, and many people are aware of these portals. This is an opening to the higher dimension allowing our Ascension. Each person experience will be unique. This is the path to multi-dimensional consciousness. Imagine for a moment if you woke up one day and realized that you had dormant abilities that were just waiting to be unleashed. Imagine a stream of white light coming into the top of your head. This column of light is your light body. It runs down through your body right into the core of the earth. If you can, try to expand this pillar of light and see it grow. Surround yourself in this light this is you, your higher self. Ask this light what information it can provide you with. You are beginning to connect to other dimensions don't be afraid just take your time. It has always been with you and it is there to help you on your journey. This is a transitional period when we will be evolving into a brand new race. We're growing up, and we're being helped by our star families. What we're all experiencing now are growing pains, which is a natural part of this transition.

THE ASCENSION PROCESS

The Ascension Process is basically about all of us raising our level of consciousness. This is a transformative process. Whether or not humans are interested in the process, it will affect all human beings living on planet Earth. The entire Universe is in the process of raising its frequency. This New Cosmic Cycle that we are now part of has been awaited for by many of us and is now beginning to take light. How humans got stuck in the lower frequencies of dualism (right/wrong) and life on planet earth is a sad story. We were programmed. The fact is that it is over. All the humans who have KNOWN intuitively that their heritage and their "BEING" abilities were of a higher level were correct. Humans, by nature, are not used to suffering, pain, sadness, loss, death, separation. It is not the way we were created. Humans were created as Children of a Divine Source. We have already lived at the level of our Divine heritage. We know what it is to feel deep inner peace. We know what it is to live in enormous amounts of joy and what it is like to live a pain-free existence in a huge flow of endless happiness. We are now in that process of evolving back or returning to that wonderful Source Energy state where we started. That is what the shift and ascension is about. Some will resist it. For some, change will always be resisted. In time, they will move forward. The rest of us will show the Way. And we will be shown the Way, inwardly and outwardly, by Source. The Loving Universe is one of those outward sources to help you to see your own new light. This source is our God Source itself that will be more present with you day after day as you allow its presence to feed you from within. Accepting our Divine Source will be encouraged by your higher self. This is a mystical gift that is being offered to us as a higher path than we are used to. The past fifty years have brought us many wonderful gifts of new Spiritual literature, new Spiritual teachers, and new inspiration to prepare us for this Path of Ascension. We are now at the beginning of this New Cosmic Cycle and it is a time for rejoicing and celebration. The future of peace and Love is just waiting for you. Question is will you be awake to recognize it?

The higher energies of 2012 and beyond have a twofold effect. We have been stuck in a Universal Time Matrix System that has been disconnected from the higher dimension frequencies for thousands of years. Ancient Earth history shows manipulations of the planetary grids by beings from other more advanced systems of Orion, Sirius, Pleiades and the Annunaki. Who were the Annunaki? They were the Watchers, assigned to earth to watch over Gods Creation in the Garden of Eden and Earth. They were created by God as perfect Angels. Their name comes for the old God of the sky "Anu". These Watchers rebelled against God and their assignment and they abandoned their mission to oversee humans and began to defile the women of the earth by having offspring with them. This led to a defect in the DNA of the offspring and an eventual almost complete contamination of the human DNA. By the time God destroyed the world with a flood because of this contamination, only one family on earth was left with pure human DNA. But even after the flood, the Watchers kept revolting and even more were punished and cast out of heaven losing their first estate and habitation, as they continued to defile women and human DNA (Genesis 6:4) This hybridization and corruption of the human DNA is still very much a part of our world although some of the defects has been corrected and most hybridization goes undetected. We can no longer be silent about UFOs, Aliens, and abductions. The Annunaki are not our creators. As you can see they themselves were created beings by God in heaven and were assigned to watch over the earth. They do still reside in the first and second heavens and inhabit other planets and star systems visiting Earth.

These Annunaki are also known as Nephilim, and several other names. These angels were the Sons of God who rebelled against Him. The Book of Enoch was taken out of the Scriptures to hide this worldwide hybridization and the truth as to who these aliens are and what they are doing. Zecharia Sitchen claimed that the Annunaki visited Earth during the time of Ancient Sumerian. The Sumerian society invented writing and had advanced knowledge of mathematics, science and astronomy. According to these writing the Annunaki were Angels. They came from the plant Nibiru in search of Gold. The Annunaki needed workers to mine the gold and therefore genetically engineered a slave race of humans. Human Civilization was for a time overseen entirely by alien forces.

The Universal Time Matrix system we are in is being manipulated. The energies of 2012 and beyond are coming in to give each one of us the opportunity for a faster ascension. The few that are waking up are being pulled/pushed by their higher aspects to seek out methods to become free from these restrictive energetic programs being activated on this planet. Through opening your higher chakras your third eye also referred to as the six sense, makes the connection to the in between, shifting your awareness. Medical science has established we have 2 strands of DNA and 10 strands of junk DNA but they have little understanding of this junk DNA. Recent information knows it has a higher purpose which is to support a multidimensional consciousness. That is our true nature. We can realign and reconnect and active the other stands. We are multidimensional, our physics abilities can be reawakened and we can develop a network at the etheric level. Within this network you have the access to connect and communicate with others. Once you begin to reconnect and activate those higher energies and realign with your life force energy the energy will begin to flow through it again via your crown charka. This is your Merkaba antenna tuning into giving you the ability to receive messages from other dimensions. Messages are received through frequency as thought forms. Many of these messages come as a sense of emotions or sometimes pictures, or visions, or even by you hearing words intuitively.

This opening occurs with the release of DMT into your body. DMT-Dimethyltryptamine is produced in your Pineal Gland. The pineal gland is considered part of your higher brain. This release causes your third eye to open to a doorway. Within this doorway is your connection to your higher self. Within this space you find you can be at Peace and Love, it is you! The mind is energy and has the power to change matter. Know that matter is simple the physical manifestation of energy. Awaken and realize the Divine nature of yourself. WE all have the ability to awaken to this start of consciousness. Every day we must make the choice whether we choice to connect to this light energy or if you choice to walk without it. In reality it is the Pineal gland is considered the Spiritual third eye. This is the inner eye that is spoken of as the gate that leads within the inner realms and space of higher consciousness. This is considered the seat of your Soul. It is located in the geometric center of the cranium. This is a natural part of everyone and consist of all the senses and the mind working together as a larger more powerful sensory organ.

Higher frequency energies being transmitted by the forces of light (Light workers) onto this planet allow individuals that are open to receive the newer higher frequencies, through opening their beliefs and mindset to activate their higher Chakras 7 to 15, this opens our central channels Universal Kundalini, raising our frequency and activating our DNA. Light workers are a certain type of Soul that has incarnated here to help enlighten humanity. We are here to guide or teach where we are needed. Some Light workers may have forgotten who they are or what their purpose for coming here is. They have a Divine purpose and a mission. They have been gifted with Divine assistance to help humanity access the higher dimensions and are here to help rebuild the love and light on this planet by sending energy into the core of the earth. Those that do not raise their frequencies energies will not be able to ascend to the higher dimensions. The DNA of most people on this planet has already been mutated. That is why only some of our DNA strands are inactive. Most of us know that DNA is our blueprint of life and is located in our cells. There is a lot going on in this planetary system that people are not being made aware of. The higher Earth frequencies will allow beings on this planet with higher frequencies activated in their system to ascend to Dimension 12 and higher Universal Time Matrix systems. The distortion of this planetary grid system thousands of years ago caused a mutation in our DNA structure. The original human had minimum of 12 DNA strands, 12 fully activated higher senses, 5 lower and 7 higher, full access to the higher Divine mind and memories of life experiences in all time lines. The average human being today has only 3 to 4 DNA stands active, 5 functional senses and no memories of who they are and why they are on Earth. We have been told that we have junk DNA, yet what we really have is DNA that is not fully accessed. Scientist acknowledge that we currently only use about 3% of our current DNA. As we make the shift into higher consciousness we must raise our frequency to have access to the higher dimensions. Your brain functions will start to become more active especially your pineal glad. This allows you to connect to your Divine source. It allows you to feel at one with your creator. We are all one being and one consciousness and everything exists within this one consciousness energy. We are a piece of that energy we call source but have forgotten who we are.

Our journey here is about us individually reuniting with our original GOD SEED., by means of our over Soul and higher aspect of being. We have been trapped in this system for thousands of years this is our journey home. It is in knowing the higher Universal Truth that will help us go forward in the ascension process. Seeking the highest level of Universal Truth in our distorted and manipulated system is the biggest challenge as this information has purposely been hidden to stop beings from ascending. Things need to be brought back into balance. Yet a lot of people at the top do not want to see this happen. Some of the information that we were taught is false. This may be hard to understand but as you read on you will see that there is a lot of information that has been held back from us. Awareness brings realization which causes an awakening that will bring you to an in lighten state. In the light you will find your truth and finally you will know that the power is within you. Go beyond where they tell you that you should not go and you will begin to see what you did not see before. Love is the essence to all things. Many of you have forgotten who you are and why you came here.

Those that are awakening are seeking higher level answers and processes to activate their higher DNA strands and raise their frequency. How can we raise our frequency and activate our higher DNA strands? We must clear all past issues, releasing all negative energy patterns in our physical, emotional, mental bodies. By generating more loving thoughts for ourselves and others, and expanding our restricted belief systems and opening our minds. This allows the Universe to initiate the basic process of opening ourselves to receive our full power. Activation of the pineal gland opens the higher heart center our sacred heart. This begins to open the higher Chakras, raising your frequency levels and opening to the higher paths through the central channel Kundalini, reaching our higher level of consciousness. Activations are available for those who are ready to access the higher dimensions. Just Ask, Believe and Receive!

If we do not love ourselves, we will not be able to fully support and provide the level of love and optimism needed to bring this planet and its human civilization back onto the path of Light and Life. This clearing of our chakra seals allowing us to reset our original blueprint and infuse and expand our inner light. Activating the higher DNA codes, develops our light bodies, opening us up to the higher Dimension frequencies and re-activating our connection with your Soul. Your kundalini channel is in the lower part of the body your root charka and it runs up to your crown chakra. This needs to be open through the Pineal Gland or your third eye. This allows the shift to begin, it an opening to the in between, the higher states of consciousness. Experiencing this unique aspect of yourself opens this path beyond your wildest imagination. People with fully assembled fifth dimensional and higher frequencies activated in their DNA will be able to ride this ascension wave. Many of us have waited a long time for this opportunity to ascend to the higher dimension time matrix systems. If we are to truly understand who we are we must be in touch with all aspects of ourselves to fully understand this concept. Our Creator has made us as an extension of itself!

RAISING LEVELS OF CONSCIOUSNESS

Who are you? How can you connect with the universal mind? Why are you here? Where did you come from? What is the 5th Dimension? What is the meaning of Heaven on Earth? Upon asking these questions and seeking answers you begin the journey towards knowing the truth about planet Earth and why you chose to come here during this ascension period.

In recent years I've done a lot of Soul searching and spent extended periods in many challenging situations. I've had many amazing experiences, met many amazing people and shared many magical moments. Being in both positive and negative environments has also been challenging at times, it's been interesting to witness Gods love through all of the Souls I meet, to understand why I am here and what that all means. During my times of expansion I have been asked to see things differently and became aware that God has chosen me to help shed light on this. If we're to move to experiencing more love we obviously need to be more open, accepting and understanding. Understanding is obviously most challenging when there's something you feel at odds with, perhaps something that feels painful, confusing, offensive, with your principles, or beliefs. Understanding means to stand under something and view it with a wider perspective or a broader sense of awareness. We learn to understand that everyone you meet is there along to the path to guide you or teach you something. There are no such accidents you have invited these people into your life to show you something about yourself that you may not have know before. If you keep asking" why" you will begin to experience an opening, lighter perspectives, a sense of understanding. Ask yourself why did YOU create or allow the experience? This is the most important question. Is it a hidden shadow aspect within you being projected and coming at you from the outside. Perhaps it's a challenge with a gift attached that will help you develop greater strength, compassion, resolve, healing, self-love, forgiveness, discernment. Asking alone gets the focus back on you which in itself is valuable. Accept and forgive yourself and others. Seek empathy. Take responsibility and compassionately own any shadows, accept and forgive yourself and allow this healing gift, be it deeper awareness or any other gift of greater self-love, letting go, freedom, strength, whatever it is that wants to come through the experience.

We must lift ourselves out of separation and judgment and raises our level of consciousness back into the Light. Light is information and dark is lack of information. It is part of a Spiritual practice, and when we develop Spiritual discipline, we develop inner-strength, inner-peace. This helps us forgive and release negativity towards others and ourselves, and sets us free from the past allowing us to heal. When we align ourselves with Divine Consciousness we are connected to the one true Power, the Light, the Love and the Truth, out of darkness and negativity, back into the Light. As we connect to our Higher Self, Divine Consciousness opens up to the presence of Spiritual Light and Power in our Life. We feel safer and become more trusting, more relaxed, more receptive, more prosperous, more successful and more compassionate, loving, lighthearted, courageous, enthusiastic, and peaceful. When we are aligned with our Higher Self, we receive direction, clarity, guidance, and protection, and we find peace of mind, and healing. When we connect to the Divine Father-Mother's energy of unconditional love, it assists us in staying in our heart, and opens our hearts to receive her blessing. Connecting to this our Source helps us neutralize and transcend negativity. That space is replaced with compassion, mercy, forgiveness, love, healing and liberation and deliverance from the past. We are then liberated from judgment, from karma, from the ego and from lower vibration people and situations. That is when we can ascend to higher levels, and surrendered to the Divine, connecting us to this power, and merging us with the Light. Releasing of the old negative patterns clears blockages of past issues and replenish us with new vibrant higher frequency energies. This will open you up to more love, joy, passion, prosperity and enthusiasm to live your life to its full potential.

Daily practice of meditation helps open and align the kundalini channel. This is the first stage to developing your connection to the higher dimensions. It expands the consciousness. This state of relaxation releases many core issues and clears negative thoughts. It radiates more light, which brings more love and clarity onto a person's path. Its benefits are without limits. It will open the path for those who want to work in the higher levels of consciousness. Once you enter a deep relaxation meditated state you can focus on activating your creative force fulfilling your purpose for being here in this life. This is your place to connect and receive your upgrades.

When you start out on the Spiritual path, you may be seeking something. Perhaps the urge to make sense out of life is what put you on the path, and this can happen at any age during your life. From that time on the Soul will most often choose to be led by its inner spirit, often unconsciously at first. During this time it depends to a great extent on the prevailing circumstances how a willingness to be led develops. At times this is very gradual, but sometimes we have to be brought to our knees, and made to realize that there is more to life than being addicted to thoughtless work or and easy living. It is very much a matter of where conscious or unconscious attention is placed on the plane on which the person lives. Therefore, if one lives on the surface of life, everything is superficial and mundane, but when one begins to think more independently they begin to question the true purpose of life, and starts seeking the deeper meanings and values. The person develops a hunger to look behind the veil into eternity. The immature Soul will begin to grow and will seek to be fed and nurtured. This urge and search to belong does not stop until the eternal God is found, indeed, until the Soul realizes that it always did belong to God, because it simply cannot exist without God, for everything is inclusive with God. God gave us the gift of free will. It is up to each and every one of us to choose to do the will of God and live in that consciousness of mind to figure out what it all means, to then start acting on the leadings and the prompts of the God-Fragment within. Think what it means to you personally, to do the Will of God. You were created with a definite purpose, as an original idea in the mind of the Creator. Some day you will fulfill that intended purpose, and you will reveal entirely the intent of the Father through your existence, your life and your actions. In this way our Creator reveals himself more fully. Even if this purpose may not be clear today, you can begin to work towards its expression. Little by little you are being guided to be what the Father desires for you to become, and you only need to learn to follow the guidance of the Divine Fragment within you. Our destiny is unity, to become one with God, to be an extension of his will, and to be a co-creator of realities. Those who work alone may achieve small things. Those who work in unity with the energy that sustains the Universe which is Divine love, know that nothing is impossible and they can achieve anything. Every action then becomes connected to the Divine will. You learn to enjoy every moment as make the most of your time here. Nothing is ordinary, and everything becomes extraordinary.

When you are living in the now moment, without fantasies about escaping reality, or being somewhere else, you are living the will of our Creator, which has placed you in a particular situation. Being at peace with your current situation and being self-satisfied are very different things. Being self-satisfied implies the mistake of believing that there is no more progress to be achieved, this is a sign of stagnation, and even regression. Those who live in the present moment do not pursue stagnation, nor do they desire inertia. The desire of escaping reality comes from your mind. Many times it is the result of various external influences. It may be what others consider as normal, or as success. They are the materialistic tendencies and the whims of the ego. It is to want things that in reality won't add any value to your life. Living in the present moment which is the gift we receive along the path is a desire of the Soul. It is to realize that we are here for a reason and with a purpose. It is to take responsibility for the consequences of our decisions and for our destiny. It is the knowing that our Creator is in charge, and for us to progressively let ourselves be guided by His hand.

Living in the present means to pay attention, and to always be observing students, capable of reading in the routine events of life the gifts and opportunities sent by the Source of all things. Those who focus into the present moment know that every second is a gift that can reach into eternity. Those who live their life in this way are truly in harmony with the will of the Creator, basing their decisions on it, and learning with every opportunity that life brings them. These are the ones who are not desperately looking for a way out, but see life as an adventure and a journey full of surprises that will bring them precisely what they need to grow and be. You must learn the difference between conformity and inertia, between living in the present and forgetting to listen to the voice that inspires you to be better. Avoid dramas and cultivate an attitude of living in the present, of doing the task in front of you in the best way possible, because maybe that is what our heavenly Father has placed in our hands today. Understanding this unity with the will of God you will always triumph. Those who desire and are working for peace today will be victorious, because on each day love is spreading more into the hearts of the people of this world. We have come to bring light in this world have worked toward this goal, and so our efforts are not in vain. To turn a primitive world into a sphere of light is the most amazing miracle that can be observed in a Universe. Every forward step by each single creature does bring this goal closer to reality. You are the creators of the miracle, and this is just a small example of what you can achieve when you combine your co-creative efforts. Together, all the children of God will be His hands throughout eternity. Making Miracles is hard work; some people give up before they happen. We are the Light workers and gatekeepers, the builders of this new reality. For everyone to open themselves up to this level of experience allow each one of us to grow closer to the light. We hold the door open to those waiting to step into the light and serve humanity. As we build this bridge we begin to build the way to heaven, ultimately bring "**Heaven down to Earth**".

VIBRATIONS AND FREQUENCIES

Meditations activate your higher Chakras and expand your light quotient. A person's vibration or frequency level is indicative of their inner light capacity. The lower your vibration or frequency the less light capacity you can hold in your system. The higher vibration levels allow you to expand your inner circuitry to receive the higher capacity electrons, which expand your inner light quotient. This creates awareness of you as a Spiritual being and expands your limited beliefs, releasing your stuck pain, suppressed emotions and stress, empowering your thought process, overcoming fearful issues like worry, and anxiety. By expanding your heart this new energy fills you with greater flow of Love and compassion to gain more confidence, self control, focus and direction which opens up your Spiritual body: Aura, the Chakras, and higher energy channels. You then can develop clarity of vision for your Life path with greater creativity using the creative GOD force, giving you a more open and direct relationship to your higher GOD source. You see your life from the higher perspective, allowing you to accept all life experiences with a better understanding. This makes you a better person, feeling more joy, love, and peace in your life. Awakening your Soul require the expansion of your existing beliefs beyond the restrictions of your programmed belief system. You came into this planet knowing the Universal Truth. As you grow up you were disconnect from the Universal Truth and inherited your family's belief system. Your parent's beliefs usually end up being the foundation of your beliefs. The foundation of this belief creates your restrictions. The Universe has no restrictions. You create the boundaries based on your beliefs. These boundaries limit your Spiritual growth and inner development. Through our inner awakening we receive the answers and begin to teach, and help others directly opens up the processes that raises consciousness to higher levels which allows higher dimensional frequencies to assemble into their DNA. This journey to self-awareness and the Soul awakening requires that your intentions are in line with what your life's purpose is. You must expand you existing Spiritual beliefs with a deeper hunger to perseverance to know the Universal Truth. You must open your mind to receive teachings and healings from the heart without interference from the Ego-Mind. As you become more aware you learn to let go of your negative ego your wealth, status, job title, these are all illusions. It's NOT YOU. You open up and are able to bring more Love in your system. This sometimes creates humility which provides a higher perspective to life. This is understanding your Self as a being of energy existing with multiple subtle body layers, and that you create with your thought forms and feelings. Positive thought forms create positive energies and negative thought forms create blockages in your system. Clearing all blockages from all your subtle bodies opens you up to the higher frequency energies. The higher frequency energies speed up your development. Expanding your pillar of Light. Once you open up your sacred Spiritual heart you allow yourself to open up to the pure love GOD consciousness energy and develop your direct connection to the GOD source. As you expand your awareness you activate your higher DNA strands. Develop your life to this 5th Dimensional Plane is the beginning process of creating Heaven on Earth. The ultimate goal of awakening your Soul is to open up to the higher dimension realities and to truly know your true self.

This phenomenon of Self-transformation is a process that has been available to every living Soul on this planet through our advanced Spiritual masters, to aid us in expanding our consciousness. As you begin to receive a deeper understanding of your Whole Self, the energies within and its relation to vibrations, frequency, and density and varies dimension you begin to align with your higher self, the part of you that is your Soul.

In this school we call Earth we learn about our journey and purpose on this planet, as well as the laws of polarity and how this effects us with its positive and negative cycles, the laws of fear, love, forgiveness, gratitude and acceptance. Learn the importance of living in the present moment and how this creates your life. This makes you better understand how reality works and the most effective and direct way of opening up to the Universal Source. Upon connecting with and transmitting the higher Universal love and light energy frequencies, your co-creative abilities are empowered. This awakens you to the cosmic reality and teaches you the Universal laws of Gratitude, Love, Cause and Effect, and the Law of Attraction. Manifesting a prosperous life full of love, joy, freedom and perfect health is now within your reach with the higher Universal love and light energy.

Everyone goes through lifecycles of good and bad times. Every situation in a person's life is self created by their own individual thoughts, words, emotions and deeds. Hoping, worrying and being anxious without action is not positive, and creates stressful depressive states. Realizing that all of life's situations are lessons that require mastery makes a person accept all situations. This teaches you to 'be' in the present without the worry and anxiety. It makes you realize your lessons in every situation and the process of overcoming the lesson and moving forward. To understand the Universal truth, ask your masters, teachers, guides, or GOD (within) "WHO AM I" and contemplate on "what is my role on the planet right now. There is much more to life than living through the routine daily rat race issues. Doing God's Will means overcoming the lower instincts through self-discipline to self-mastery. To live as a master means to be whom you are as a Soul in a body and to express your Soul alignment with Spirit in everything that you experience and manifest on Earth. This path is not easy, but it builds a strong character, which can withstand temptations, and is not easily swayed by others. God's will simply put, seeking the way with the most love in it, and with respect to all others. In short, it means living the golden rule, as in doing unto others as you yourself, would like to be treated.

Jesus lived an exemplary life on earth by living according to the golden rule and thereby always being obedient to the Will of his Father in Heaven. The golden rule is to be found in all religions, yet it is not practiced to the extent that it could be practiced. Jesus always taught His followers to 'love one another'. Well, look around you! The time has now come for each person to take responsibility for their thoughts and actions, ask what God's will is. It will be a path filled with love and goodwill towards all others. One person at a time, that's how the world will be changed, as the vibration of love will be spread all over the planet. Ascension requires turning inward to discover one's own God-Goddess within. In so doing, one becomes one's own savior and one's own champion to continue to transcend in the journey of ascension.

Understand that all Earthly GODs, masters, teachers that are prayed to through religious beliefs came upon the Earth plane to teach the beings on this planet to connect directly to the Universal GOD source by going within and connecting through their inner Self. The masters came on this planet to give you love and connect with God to receive the love and guidance, with the purpose to help you ascend. Listen and implement the deepest message to open your heart to feel love for yourself and others, release your negative ego, fully forgive yourself and everyone and connect directly to the GOD source from within. You are from the same energy as the GOD source, this is how we are all connected at the higher level. True self transformation is a deep connection to your Spiritual Soul an extension of your inner light, connecting you to receive the higher Universal love and light energies. Your ultimate purpose is to raise your frequencies, live in joy, expand your consciousness, and realize your truth and develop unconditional love for all beings by opening your Spiritual heart and prepare for the ascension gateway. As the gateways are opening step across the threshold and claim your place with the higher dimensions of light that are being offered to you. God will not close any door without opening a window. Don't give your power away, you will need all your power to raise your frequencies to this higher level of understanding, therefore allowing yourself the time needed. As we improve our lives and relationships, we become a better people here to fulfill our destiny.

There are several people who we call Channeler's. They are scholars, artists, businessmen, truck drivers and PhDs, scientists and grade school dropouts, business executives and housewives. They come from all races, nationalities, cultures, and creeds. Some are atheists (initially); others are religious. They attune to the spirit realms or higher dimensions to bring in certain information. They are simply willing to tune into another place, another time and receive information. Many humans have always had the capacity to do that. There will be some that will actually take that chance and put it out there for others to partake of. Channeling is a form of communication between humans and other beings, usually from higher dimensions. These beings could be angelic beings, nature spirits, spirits of departed loved-ones extraterrestrial entities, or even animals and pets. A channeler can choose who or what they want to channel. If the other party has an interest in communicating, the link is made and the channelings can begin. There are different ways of channeling. In order to channel, the medium usually doesn't have to go into a deep trance state, or surrender their body and or mind to the entity. They just focus their senses and attention on the entity they are channeling. But there are also channelings where the Soul or Spirit of the medium either steps aside or leaves the body. This makes room for the other energy to enter and use the body for a specific period of time. This shift of energy can take seconds or minutes, and those capable of seeing auras, can see the shift. Some people fear channeling because they don't understand the process, or they think that a negative or dark entity can come in. But the channeler always has the choice of who or what they want to channel. The channeler can insist on knowing the name and origins of any entity who wants to communicate with them. Experienced channelers understand that just because an entity wants to communicate doesn't mean the entity is necessarily enlightened. The channeler should discern for themselves the level of enlightenment of the entity, and the value of their information. Some entities just like to chat, others can have an agenda. But many are of the Light, and also have a desire to provide enlightened guidance and counsel overseeing all information that is shared during the process of Ascension that we are now in. This serves the higher-dimensional ascended masters, Galactic's, and celestials who has gathered around the Earth at this time to assist her inhabitants to enter a new and golden age a world that works for everyone. The planet is shifting her focus of perception to a higher dimension. Some people can only hold the thought or believe that only what can be perceived by our physical senses is real; the beings who reside on this planet will find their consciousnesses gradually shifting from third dimensionality to higher dimensions, for many, 4th and then 5th Dimensionality, and for some, higher. Much information that come thru these channlings are meant to begin awareness to light so that certain messages are being passed down. The higher aspect of your Soul want to communicate with you and sometimes this is done through channeling. Our friendly star brothers and sisters who've helped our planet since her inception will make their presence known to some people. These higher-dimensional beings, have been watching over this planet since its beginning. In fact they're humans like us and seeded Earth in the first place. They come from star systems like the Pleiades, Andromeda, and Sirius, as well as many other places within the Universe. Andromeda is the keeper of the 7D and the message coming from there are to begin to take control of your own mind. They also have much beneficial technology to contribute to us. The planet has reached the point where it will accept their presence without moving into fear or alarm is nearing. They have no unfriendly intentions toward us because they to serve the same One God in all things as we do. They obey universal laws much better than we do because they understand the laws of karma and free will, which some people here have forgotten. We have little or no understand of the love that they are capable of and can only benefit from contact with them. The Galactic's are ascended masters, although we don't think of them as such. We more often think of our own sages as ascended masters, like Jesus, Buddha, St. Germaine, etc. These ascended masters are busy at this time attending to elements of the Ascension scenario also. They're bringing in new energies and are working to heal us and teach us what we need to know for a smooth shift in consciousness. Our Creators plan is brilliant, beautiful, and perfect, constant delight and amazing as it continues to unfold just as was intended.

For some on the Earth plane, engrossed in their illusory reality, it is and will remain totally beyond comprehension in fact, the vast majority of you are unaware that a plan even exists. Your guides, mentors, and channels in the Spiritual realms have been keeping you up-to-date on the aspects of it that affect you directly. So pay attention, listen to their advice and guidance, take it to heart and act on it. Part of the Divine Plan is apparently for us to be bathed in successively more intense energies of love that will lead us to draw together in sacred partnerships projects. The Divine Mother said "The plan has always been one of union and reunion." The plan is designed to teach us unity consciousness and to reconstruct society by first having us reunite with parts of ourselves.

Eventually, we will all become the Light at the center of creation, which is God or Spirit or whatever name you choose to call it. As we evolve, gaining wisdom and true understanding about our real essence, we begin to open up to more Love, and to feel our connection with one another and the Universe. In the Earth realm, Love is only experienced and known at a low level compared to all that truly exists. The God/Spirit frequency is beyond anything we know. It is pure love and Light. As we strive and come closer to that center of creation, we will know Love completely and be totally in this light. Your Soul knows this light and desires to experience it again.

It is your sacred light that you'll choose and you finally are seeing and recognizing, and accepting and cherishing yourself. It begins small and it continues to expand out. It is really a very simple plan. The plan is for the entire group of humanity to fall in love. Listen to your heart. You are being divinely guided and inspired. Now, there will be many situations what you would think of as simply synchronicities and meetings. For those of you who are aware and open to it, that is how it occurs. And it is occurring every single moment, all over your planet. How will we get people to ascend? Through love, freedom, and through the desire to be together. So, do not avoid each other. Engage as you see fit, your guides and your guardian angels are working to guide you to open you up to Love.

This drawing together is happening at an unprecedented rate, and it is happening in terms of union of friendships, of groups, of what we would call partnerships or sacred unions. Even family members are beginning to recognize one another. But strangers across the lands, across the continents, are realizing, I need to be working. I need to be talking. I need to be playing. I need to be in a form of relationship with that person, or with that group of people. This is only going to intensify, because you are willing to stand there ethereally naked and be seen. The importance and the readiness is in the now moment to step forward so that our sacred partnerships would serve our missions and purposes in being here. You are seeing that in the sacred unions that are being formed, that are bringing people together in partnerships that conjoin not only the hearts, complement the minds, the emotional fields, but also intersect on mission and purpose. This is the way that you intended it when you designed your part of the plan in conjunction with yourself, and with each other. We are to lay the foundation for those who are to come and to point the way. As you acquire enough information to accelerate your own evolution you will become the new starseeds of this realm, now awaken to begin your mission. If you find yourselves in a position to lift someone up, do it. We start passing the torch to all that are ready to receive it.

Our sacred partnerships and circles will be fun. We are going to play, we are going to laugh, we are going to work, and we are going to continue on and create Earth. This will not be equal to the past it will be better than before. This begins with the Light Worker community as more people join in, Earth becomes one family serving the light. That is the way. Love will sweep you and the planet, and in many ways, that is Ascension. Light workers are here to show the way for everyone and they carry the torch holding the light and have come here to help the planet shift into higher consciousness. They are extraordinary beings and that have incarnated at this time to fulfil their Light Workers mission. Light Worker carry this light within their Souls to enlighten and illuminate the world. Most Light Workers are healers and how they heal things is completely up to them. When a Light Worker comes into the physical world they often times struggle to find their light within. Often they forget their mission and purpose and often their light is put out. When their light is turned on the Light Worker will go on a journey to of self-discovery and try to heal themselves. The dark side is also present for them until they begin to find their light again and then they become powerful again and resume their mission. Light Workers all have different mission but they main goal is to help people through their shadows and help them find their light. Most are accountable for balancing the energy of fear with the energy of Love. Light Workers are great at manifesting and most often create things with just their thoughts. They have special unique ability to heal and make others feel comfortable and safe when they are around them. Being very intuitive they are very sensitive to energy and are in tune with their psychic ability. Often you will meet a Light Worker during hard times or during your awakening phase. They help people realize their life purpose in life. They have the ability to read energy and frequencies and can feel what others are going through that is why they sometimes will stay away from crowed places. Alone time is very pleasing to them for they need time to recharge their energies as they take on the vibrations of those around them. Light Workers have an open heart that is felt strongly which is why many people share their secrets with them. They often hear how after a conversation with them that the person feels so much better them before. Light Worker are always being exposed to the problems of those around them without judgment. They have the ability to listen and guide others through difficult moments while navigating with divine wisdom. Many have had near death experience, disease and have overcome obstacles in their lives. Their journey has allowed them to let go of the illusions that death is final. Because they accept that life is transcendent. Our job is not to change anyone but to accept their choices and assist to bring forth the Divine light. They are considered to be warriors of the light here to help with the shift to higher consciousness and our own Spiritual evolution.

We can no longer live in the old realm, that way has not worked in the past and the time is now to ride the wave of light and love. You explode and you feel all the energies of the Universe. And then, because you are becoming attuned to that feeling, that ecstasy, it steps down, and then you anchor it within your expanded field. Each time you make the connection, it expands you more and more, and your capacity to love, to create, to do, to be, to connect, more and more until there is no memory, no experience, of separation. It was an illusion! What you see around you is not what it seems to be. The world that you are now living in is the world that has been built by your own higher selves, and has indeed been predisposed to changes which have occurred. So both the building of Earth and our Ascension itself are to be achieved by this coming together of concentric circles of unions, Spiritual partnerships, then Sacred circles, and finally Light Workers united in project to build our new Earth. The time has now come for a new state of evolution for the human psyche and the human beings. For years prior to arrival on this planet, many of you have had a link to an interconnection sphere where all of you have decided to create a world where you would completely and fully immerse and be in amnesic state and the real link to your Divine selves would be lost, in order to experience the veil of forgetfulness. In order to prove to yourselves that indeed you can find your way to Divinity through the labyrinth of amnesia. And so we dwell at this very moment in time, we have volunteered to take part in this experiment, and to see and experience the Divinity. Many of us Light Workers were the volunteers who have first stepped foot onto this planet, many of us are now remembering who we are, and seeing our selves standing in front of the Great Pyramids and the Temples of Atlantis. We are the pioneers who have come to planet Earth and have built a beautiful habitat for other Souls to dwell in. Some have left this planet to allow the Souls that have chosen to incarnate into fully formed human vehicles to participate in an experiment of a cosmic significance. They have vowed to return in the future in order to illuminate that which was lost to the beings who have decided to stay on Earth. We are able to illuminate the way for humanity, guiding our children and our own selves back home, to our Divine selves which is our birth right and that is Divinity and our power. There are many who have been brave enough to descend into human bodies, brave enough to conceal your wisdom and understanding of life, and the cosmic gateways of truth, the time has now come, for you to fully utilize that which you are, to fully manifest that which you wish to experience on this planet. As the gateways open you have the choice to step across the threshold and claim your place in the higher dimension of light.

Understand that you are not here to make anyone follow your footsteps, you are here to simply show that IT IS POSSIBLE to be a powerful being in a human body, that the body that you are incarnated into is not a limiting force, but on the contrary a force that is to assist you in creating that which you wish to see, it is a magnificent vehicle that is designed in accordance to the universal truth. Never before has any Soul had the opportunity to transcend duality in an amnesic state of being. And so find your own force within; find the way back home to your true selves. Understand that there is nothing and no one that you are to wait for, understand that although there are others here assisting you in this quest for knowledge, in this quest to end the duality of your being, in the quest to know who you are, YOU ARE THE ONES THAT ARE HERE TO CHANGE AND INFLUENCE YOUR WORLD.

Each one of us carries the light and power within our own selves. That is something that cannot be done for you, for until you find your own being, for until you find your own truth and fully and truly comprehend that which you are. You cannot do it for someone all you can do is wait for them to, listen to their heart beats, as it sends out the codes into the Universe announcing the moment that you truly will be ready to find the portal within, and finally see this world for what it truly is, a magnificent experience, a magical journey from the mysterious to full understanding of THE SOURCE.

In assistance of such manifestations you have been receiving a variety of messages from other beings and your own higher selves about various events that are to occur in your near future. These events will occur and that is something that has indeed been preordained by all of you. Each and every single one of you are not to wait for anything, but go deep within and find the truth of the cosmic laws of attraction, cosmic laws of manifestations and cosmic laws of love, peace, harmony, health, joy and abundance. You are to find your balance, and you are to announce to yourself that you are ready to build that which you wish to see. By working in groups, you can intensify this energy by focusing on that which you wish to occur and manifest in your daily lives.

Ask for guidance, and open your mind to these other dimensions and allow yourselves the opportunity to tune into the higher dimensions beyond your wildest imagination. Time & space are illusions because matter is energy and consciousness and we are made up of the same stuff. When you surrender and realize your true essence that you are inside the particle we call GOD-Source, your power is turned on and you begin to manifest amazing things in your life. You exist with in this realm because that is where you came from and you are the one with the source energy relying on your guides to show you the way. Your imagination is the key to unlocking this power and manifestation with your new upgrade light body, or higher consciousness. First there is the initiation, then there is activation and then there is integration. These are stages you will go through as you transform into your higher self.

OPENNING YOUR MIND

The enlightened mind is the gift acquired when one transforms desire into Spiritual aspiration. In the early lives desire rules the thought life, coupled with the bold determination and strong will needed to acquire that which is desired. A cornerstone of his teaching, the Buddha's 4 Noble Truths, is how to handle desire and gain liberation from the suffering caused by desiring anything. A wonderful mantra is "giving it up to the Universe," learning to surrender to the greater Will of Spirit and giving up control of the little personal will.

When your body has been purified completely, then the light does indeed shine through. Only when the desire is mastered and forces are controlled can the Soul progress towards initiation. Eons of time and many incarnations are needed to raise our frequencies to this level this will ultimately transform into aspiration eventually leading to light and illumination. When the eye of the bull is opened (the Spiritual third eye), "thy whole body shall be full of light," as Christ stated in the New Testament (Matthew 6:22). This single eye takes the place of the two eyes of the personal self, as the attention becomes focused upon Spiritual attainment. When the Soul acts as the controlling factor, and not the desiring personality, then the whole body becomes full of light. Jesus taught his disciple "If you become of one eye then you will know my kingdom of God. If you attain one eye then all bliss will be yours".

The MIND IS ENERGY and has the power to change matter. Understand that MATTER is simply the physical manifestation of energy. Go BEYOND where they tell you that you should not go and you will begin to see what you did not see before. Just as there are people that live in foreign lands and remain unknown to you there are also beings that live in other realms and other worlds. Many of you have forgotten who you are and why you are here. Your blinders will be removed. You will see the truth for yourself. All that is asked is that you remain open to the possibilities. Follow where your heart leads. Open your mind to the possibilities. Without LOVE, you can understand nothing.

Our mind becomes greatly expanded when we see ourselves as universal citizens, rather than just a mere resident, who runs over the same ground day after day, month after month, and year after year. The Universe is our playground, our destiny, and we were born into the primary system where life begins for so many new Souls. You are not so unlike these people of Light, for you have a similar capacity for understanding, and it is very likely that if you were taken at birth and transported to one of these worlds, raised by another family, that you also would know and understand how to live and work as a universal citizen on a world settled in Light and Life. Every single one of you has direct access to the energies that are being sent down. These beings will come to you with Love and purpose, and do not claim to have the ultimate truth, but are here to help shed light on the truth. Their intent and desire is to awaken you so that you may realize the Divine nature of yourself. They came long ago from the stars as Star seeds and now have evolved and exist in another realm.

We all have energetic blocks that need to be removed from our record. This will be done instantaneously in Spirit. However, to manifest these changes in the physical world you will need to update your subconscious files. Understand that you are not imagining anything, for you truly are all seeing that which you did not see prior, for now, at this moment in time we can inform you that indeed the veil has been lifted for you!

It has still not fully lifted for others, and that is why it is so important for you to spread your light, it is the light force and the light energy that you infuse into your surroundings that change others' understanding of life. In this understanding is that each moment is a magnificent one to behold, the understanding that you create that which you see, feel and experience. You are all here to co-create.

The time has now come to put everything that you have learned thus far into a way of being, into a new creation of your own journey, to restore the peace, restore the harmony, restore the link to your Divinity and the understanding of ONENESS. Evolution involves ascension. The Divine Plan is for us to evolve in consciousness until we realize to the fullest extent our essential nature as God. When we do, we return to Source.

Awareness brings realization. Realization causes an awakening. Awakening brings us to an in-Lightened state. In the Light, you will find your truth and finally you will know the power is within YOU. There are three levels of enlightenment Spiritual awakening (when the kundalini reaches the fourth chakra), cosmic consciousness (sixth chakra), and God-realization (seventh-chakra).

It has been said that 'God is Love,' but do you really understand what that means? Even to an atheist who does not recognize the equation 'God = Love' still has an idea about the concept of love and therefore it is his or her highest understanding for the quality of life itself. Because you are human and your spirit is encased in a material body, you have varying degrees of understanding about what Love is. Your unique personalities attach different meanings and ideas about what it is, and you each express that idea differently. The varying interpretations and the expressions of Love make up the diversity of all sentient life in the Universes. Love is the very gravity by which God attracts all Souls and collects all diverse experiences in the grand Universe. Because Love, in its purest form, is perfect and absolute. One can only understand it and express it in a relative and imperfect form, yet as you expand your consciousness, Love becomes something that can be expressed and applied to all the circumstances of life and relationships and can illuminate and make all experiences more meaningful and valuable. This is what is being asking of each and every person on the planet to consider and apply to their daily lives. Consider first, your highest concept of love, and then expand it through imagination, your inherent God-like ability, and see it as something that could be a real part of your life. Whatever it is that stirs heartfelt emotion in you should be something you feel and explore every day of your life. Let these heart felt thoughts fill your mind more and more and become a part of your expanding consciousness, for these are the very thoughts that expand consciousness! "A better world starts with the thoughts of each individual. Practice having better thoughts even though you may be in difficult situations. If you are feeling overwhelmed try to just relax and think of one positive thought. Now hold that thought and you can remember that there is still hope. Every experience you are going through is worth one positive thought. Love lifts the Veil! Listen to the lyrics of a beautiful song, not only hear the words but tap into the emotions you are experiencing. Music has a way of touching our emotions sometimes really letting us know what we feel when you resonate with a certain song. There are many ways to bring more of these feeling into our lives. It is up to you to decide what those experiences are because no one but you know what they are.

There are many different kinds of love. Firstly, there is the love of things, such as the love of chocolate or a warm bath. This is often more of an expression than a true emotion. Still, good chocolate, or anything we love, can put a smile on our face and make us feel good, like our gardens, our hobbies, our quite time or whatever can take us out of our heads and into our hearts connecting you to something special. Then there is parental love. The love of a child is a very powerful thing. The desire to protect him / her, nurture them, see them happy, help them lead good lives can bring out the best in us. We speak of our hearts bursting with joy and pride at a child's smile, first steps, or small achievements. This is a selfless and good love. The passion and desire to be with another is called Romantic Love, your heart yearns to be with them again, and how it flutters with excitement when you meet again, this is intoxicating. It can move us to do things we never dreamt of before, the heights of generosity and devotion, or of foolishness! It drives us mad, but we love it! Next comes mature love. When the passion of romantic love has burned away, it can evolve into a deeper love, the love of a Soul mate, a companion to walk with through life. A best friend, your rock of support, someone who is there through thick or thin. You love them, flaws and all, for you appreciate the good qualities in them. Their faults and weaknesses may even make them more endearing to you. This is a mutual love, a love of togetherness, through time. Friendship is also a form of love. You can love your friends, feel camaraderie, kinship with them. They allow and encourage you to be yourself. A good friend will also tell you your faults, they want what is best for you, to see you happy. Again this is a good kind of love, focused on mutual happiness and support, and wanting what is best for the other person. Unconditional love is in essence to want the best for the other person, regardless coming from a loving place for them, a perspective of Spiritual love for them as a Soul, and acting accordingly. It means transcending lower emotions (anger, hurt, frustration, or whatever) and behaving in a loving way, that would make God, Jesus, or other Spiritual Beings proud of us. It focuses very much on trying to be loving at all times, or at least as much as possible. It is how we would ideally behave, all of the time, if we could and were perfect. We admire those who display such qualities most of the time as being wise, loving, advanced people. The blissful phenomena we call "being in love" is a narrow heightened state of awareness brought on by several conditions in the mind, body, and spirit of the individual. When two people come together in the compliment of being they are vibrating at near the same frequency, they are in alignment. They are attracted together by a near equal amount of light. Through God's Spirit, present in the mind of the individual, this light, this reflection that attracts, is the magnetism that moves the Soul into alignment with the Will of the Universal Father. This practical experience of discovering love draws two people together.

This first encounter we experience with 'love' between two people is, in reality, a first glimpse into what it is to know the love of God. There is always a pattern in life on the material worlds that is pointing, teaching, and demonstrating moving you along this path that brings you to the awareness of God's integral relationship with the Soul. The mind begins to put the pieces of the puzzle together and recognizes these correlating values as being of Divine origin. God knows that before His very young children can understand His infinite Divine love, they must experience human love in a way they can comprehend from their finite perspective of living in a material body and having their first intimate encounter with another person.

As you live, you mature, grow and the Soul expands, and you make decisions based on the wisdom of past experiences. In the journey of the Soul, when you compare the moment to moment experiences of your life up against the memory of these first experiences of love, in all prior relationships (all sources, friends, family, lover), you begin to make decisions that, incorporate those values experienced by the reflection of light that makes your own understanding of love more complete. The more we love, the more we understand God's love, and so by mutual attraction to both the love of others and the love of God, the Soul expands and we move closer to unity with God and in knowing ourselves we then know our Source.

It is the dysfunctions of this understanding of love, or the absence of real love, that confuses so many who are disconnected from spirit or our separation from God (reality). The ego compensates for the absence of love and attempts to protect the heart by making the self-important. We need to love everyone on this planet, for it is not only in alignment with the Will of God, but it is the one thing that draws the Soul into unity with God. To move a whole planet into Light and Life requires a greater understanding of love by all of us. To love is to understand, and to understand is to know the character of God to know His character is to 'be' the light of love to others.

The next level of love is Universal Love. This may be a slightly new concept for many people. Whereas unconditional love could be said to be a human behaving in high and loving ways, universal love is about being connected to God and the Universe. It is a sense of awe and oneness that we can experience when we see a beautiful sunset or a rainbow after a summer rain, a butterfly fluttering around and appreciating the love, beauty and majesty of God in all things. It is about acting out of love for the world and the whole of humankind, and nature with a desire to serve God for the highest good of all. It is about being in tune with the Universe, acting regularly from Divine love and guidance. When we appreciate that we are powerful Spiritual beings, part of the One, linked to God, here to serve the planet, feeling God's love and guidance flowing through us, then we act with Universal Love. It is a higher, more experiential state you cannot 'think' your way there, you have to feel the connection. That is the tip of the iceberg, so to speak. It is a greater, awesome, all-encompassing Love for the planet. The Universe understands energy and speaks to us in frequencies.

Finally we come to Angelic Love. If you have ever felt the love of the angels experienced an angel hug (their wings wrapped around you), or felt energies flowing from them to you, or received messages from your angels, you will know the depth and strength of their love for us it is deeply touching and moving, often overwhelming. They have such a powerful, deep, never-ending love for us that is beyond human love. People often describe it as a feeling like no other feeling they have every experienced. Angels are expressing God's love for us, so you would expect it to be powerful and awesome. Everyone has a Guardian Angel who has been with us through all time, and loves us completely, no matter what we have done in this or previous lives. We also have Earth Angels, Archangels, Masters and Beings of Light with us, who long to connect with us, demonstrate God's love for us, help us, take us by the hand and lead us forward. They long for us to stop and listen. Ask your Angels and Beings of Light to wrap you in their love, to shower you with loving blessings, and to show you signs that they are there, and are guiding and helping you. They are many Angels available to you every moment all you have to do is connect and ask them for guidance. That is all that is require for they cannot help you unless you ask them because they value your own free will. Angel Michael is considered the Master of light. He is the Angel of Love, Light, Wisdom, patience, protection and infinite blessing from Heaven. Call upon him anytime you feel the need. Raphael is the Divine healer, he guides those who seek healing showing you how you can help heal yourself. Uriel is consider the Angel who brings humankind the knowledge and understanding of the Divine. He helps us interrupt our inner voice and our dreams. He guides us to take more responsibility in our lives, to fulfill our potentials as creative spirits. There are many more Angels available to you all you have to do is open you heart and mind and call on them for help. You may see them as Hugh or you may see them as small but they are right by your side you and will hear you whenever you call. You can trust them to care for they are you Guardian Angels and they will always be there.

We are Divine beings, children of God, with the spark of God's energy in each of our hearts. As you attune to the energy of love and the Angels, you open the portals to greater Divine assistance and miracles in your life. Focus on being heart centered loving beings. If all humanity moves to living this way, the Earth will be transformed. Notice when you are NOT being a heart centered loving being, towards yourself or others for example, when you are 'in your head', or caught up in emotions, this is when you need to re-center yourself again and connect to your heart. Do this is small steps each day, to move you towards being a more loving heart centered being, and you will be amazed at the changes in your life, and how it helps your Spiritual development, for the good of you and others and the world.

May your Angels love you and guide you, and may you pass this greater love on to others, seeing the benefits for your life. Together, let's make this an even more loving world, one person, one day, one loving action at a time. You are here to play your part, and the vibrations of a thousand loving actions each day by all of us can transcend your world, like a ripple in a pond, touching all of humanity. Ask your guides and Angels to show you simple ways in which you can improve the relationships you have, or attract love into your life.

Ask yourself what steps can you take today, tomorrow and over the next few weeks? You may receive messages in the form of words, pictures or sounds. Take note of them and reflect on what meaning they have for you. It's really important to sharpen your listening skills. Actually, listening involves both the head and the heart. The heart being the most important as feeling and discernment are lodged there. So if one has a desire to advance it can greatly increase the connections through continued right thinking. The fact is that over time, the more you turn within, the more the quality of listening improves. It is the inner focus which matters, so the outward noises become less intruding, and even when a sudden noise erupts on the outside, you will no longer be startled by this, because your habit of concentration has become so established that it has become second nature to you. This will be accomplished over time. Pay attention!

Ask for signs and look out for Divine signs that will show you the right path to take. Often simple signs like feathers, cloud formations, visions and sounds are indications from your guides that you are doing the right things. You may even notice a strong sign around a particular person guiding you towards them. Trust your Intuition. The first step in Angelic connections is learning to understand your intuitive feelings. Some call them 'gut' feelings, but actually these feelings are given to us by our Angels. Sometimes your intuition will tell you that something is NOT RIGHT. You may get the feeling of discomfort or dread. But you'll also notice positive intuition that is saying YES, this is the right choice, path or person. Understanding your intuition and what tells you will begin to align you with your life path. Develop the right state of mind, our feelings and emotions are the core of how we are seen by others. If you feel miserable all the time, you will never attract love into your life. Use your meditations and Angelic connections to develop a happy, positive state always with the belief that love is just around the corner. Each and every person you meet will see that positive energy and be attracted to you even more! The Angels are here to bless and help you in all aspects of your life but especially in creating deeper, more meaningful and passionate relationships. If you call on them for help, they will respond.

Meditation is an excellent discipline to quiet unruly and restless minds. God has bestowed upon us many gifts, which as yet lay dormant in our minds, and can only be actualized into perfection in eternity, if one chooses immortality. The mental, emotional and physical are ruled by the Spiritual. As a man or woman thinks, that he or she becomes. Therefore, sharpen your listening skills by taking time to turn within and learn to listen with focused attention. The benefits accrued over time are enormous.

Make room in your minds for this new way of thinking and being. Unload all the dysfunctions of your past and step up to be counted as the first ancestors of Light and Life. Work with your Angles and Guides, for this is what it is to be a universal citizen to live with purpose and to see life beyond this world; to participate and anticipate your role and be responsible for the energy you carry. You have been given many lessons by your experiences, which are all good and healthy for the mind and Soul, and yet, only reading the lesson does not guarantee that you fully understand it or know how to apply it in your daily lives. It is therefore necessary that you prepare your mind to open the layers of the mind for input from your inner Spirit assisting you in understanding and applying those lessons. This process takes time and conscious effort to expand your horizons, extend your minds, ignite your Souls, and become citizens of the Universe. There are many worlds out in the greater Universe that are settled in Light and Life and its citizens enjoy and experience a very different kind of life because each one has been educated from birth about Universe realities; their relationship to the Creator and to their fellows; and their co-creative role. Be aware of the Divine Fragment in your life. This is a framework of the Great Plan preparing your role in a co-creative role in the Universe. See life beyond the terrestrial world and know that we have the opportunity to live eternally and participate in the Great Plan. Those who believe without seeing live with the reality of Divinity in our midst. WE are the first-wave; the game changers; and you can be the first of many to expand your minds and live as Universe citizens and participate in the reclamation of this world.

You have the capacity to become like those enlightened ones and enjoy a much different life than you have today. Gods Spirit is the Master Operator, which knows you so intimately knows how your unique mind works, and truly knows the most effective way to reach and to teach you how to digest and use the information in Spiritual messages. Because you have free will, you can allow or ignore this highest form of Spiritual input, yet we know many of you want to learn, discern, and allow your guides to work within your mind and help you grow. It is in these Souls that the individualized aspects of Spirit in form has awakened to the One Truth, and find themselves consciously aware and on a path moving inward toward the center of the One Truth. They are experiencing life and expressing the Will of this One Truth in imperfect form, yet learning and gaining wisdom along the journey as a way to make perfect and achieve equilibrium with Source. For it is in the journey knowing this One Truth, that we fulfill the desire and the Will of that which we call "God," that we become integrated with its light and become like Him. There is no purpose more vital in our world than to know the One Truth and your connectedness to that Truth. Be the expression of this truth and help awaken our sleeping planet. Anything that brings joy, happiness and Soulful satisfaction to the individual, originates in the Divine Intelligence, guiding the growth and development of the personality. Everything that you can see, touch, hear, taste, and smell, is a part of this One Truth, it pervades all realities both seen and unseen. There is nowhere you can go in all of creation where this energy is not present. All consciousness is a part of this One Truth and it is the very core essence of all meanings, values, and universal principals. Everything that is true, beautiful, and good is derived from this energy, and all that is false, ugly, dark, and evil, stands apart from the light.

This energy is present in life itself. It is in the pattern of all life and in nature. Its signature is written in the code of life. The One Truth is perfect and complete, and all that is imperfect and incomplete is drawn to it. All love, compassion, and mercy, are universal characteristics of the One Truth. It is the Will and desire of Source to create, to explore, and to know itself by experiencing life in creative form. All that is alive and animated by Spirit is an individualized aspect of this energy seeking equilibrium with the Divine Will. Since all spirits are aspects of this One Truth and intimately connected through its consciousness, there really is no separation from it, only your beliefs, denial, or ignorance of this connectedness creates the illusion of separation and so we view ourselves as alone.

Only those who ask questions will receive answers. As the Master said, "Seek and you will find". Forget the idea that talking with the Creator is impossible. In reality, it is the simplest thing in the world. Even when the communication doesn't happen with words, you will always receive what you need and the real desires of your Soul will always receive answers and guidance to achieve the goal of human life. It is not always easy for humans to know what the Will of God is. Some of us think that the doing of God's Will means to sacrifice all things that pleasure them. This is most definitely not the case. The doing of God's Will has been badly misunderstood in the past. It is true that there is sacrifice involved. To bring these ideas from the spirit mind to the conscious mind you only need a reminder or a clue to open the gates of understanding. The sign may be a phrase you read, a song you hear, images that come to mind. There are so many messages that you will receive once you are tuned into the frequency of the UNIVERSE. These messages can come to you at any time, and only when you pay attention to these message will you find their meaning. The possibilities are endless.

More value needs to be placed in the cultivation and training of true character building. Sadly, fewer and fewer humans pay attention to the small voice of God within them. Some people believe that going to their places of worship, pay their penance and dues and think that this is enough and all is fine in their world. Some people go to work every day without ever taking the time to think if they are truly living their purpose. They don't search within themselves, to seek the Glory of God and the meaning and purpose of life. It is so much easier to have the better educated do their thinking for them. Some people choose to stay within the confines of the Status Quo. Some will never really understand that you have a choice and it is up to you to make the changes for your selves as well as everyone else. Just think what that means to finally understand that you are the creator of you destiny and when you work with the universal energy what you will create is going to be amazing. Always keep your heart open to the Light and the intelligently coordinated co-creative power that lives within you, and works tirelessly to bring you into alignment with your life's plan. This is your individual map, which will afford you the greatest personality development and Soul growth.

Remain as much as possible in this positive consciousness and receptive present now moment. This is the greatest tool for remaining connected to your Divine inner Spirit. A conscious, elevated faith and wisdom-seeking attitude is required to transcend the fearful animal-ego-mind. With the free-will decision to consecrate the higher reasoning mind can then be synchronized with the highest and most loving Will.

COSMIC INTELLIGENCE

Every planetary system has a governing body. Just like every country has a governing body. There is also a universal governing body and a cosmic governing body. We are in a multidimensional time matrix system. This time matrix is made up of our solar system and many other solar systems. Each system exists in a dimension zone. Our Earth has been in the dimension 1-3 zone. Our sun and other planets in our solar system are in dimension 4-6 zone. There are other higher systems in the 7-9 and 9-12 dimension zones. We live in a swirling sea of magnetic forces, smaller fields contained within even greater fields, expanding throughout infinity. As our understanding increases, a new picture of the Universe emerges, one of vast cosmic interdependence and connectedness.

Just like there are trillions of cells in a human body there are trillions of planets in this system created by the Supreme GOD Source. The planetary universal system works the same as the body layers system in each person. Each plant holds a certain vibration which directly affects each and every one of us. The Sun represent Individuation, Purpose, and Will. The Moon energy gives us Awareness, Consciousness, and feelings. Mercury is the sign of Mentality, and thinking. Venus is the sign of Love, Beauty, and Pleasure. Mars aspects are of will, desire, Jupiter is about enthusiasm and expansion. Saturn is about obligation, Uranus is about self, independence, freedom. Neptune is about vision, and Pluto is about obsession, and power. We know that every planet rules a sign of the zodiac. If you don't know much about your sign now will be a good time to start looking. What sign you were born into and why? There is meaning in everything.

From the moment of creation and within each incarnation your Soul aligns itself with either positive or negative energies depending on your Soul's choice. Every action your Soul ever took while it has been incarnated in the physical world generated certain energies. During every subsequent incarnation you have to deal with those energies also known as Karma.

SOURCE has created a system within itself that allows everything within itself to flow the same way all the cells inside the human system flow. Source observes and monitors everything within itself and lets its creation manifest. Its Divine intelligence has a system of seeding each cosmic and universal time matrix. A governing body overlooks each dimension time matrix. These are the GOD seed (beings). They reside in the higher dimension and overlook the well being of the time matrix system. Our God Seed Monad is huge. From its source energies it creates 12 over Souls. Each over soul creates 12 Souls. These souls reside in dimension 4-6. The Soul create 12 incarnates. These incarnates reside in dimensions 1-3. Where do we fit in all this? We are these incarnates. There are usually 2 incarnates sent to each time cycle one male and one female. These are our Soul mates. For all incarnates to experience life on dimension 1-3 (Earth) the human body uniform has to be worn, so all beings have a similar body structure. One of the conditions in this dimension is free will and choice. At the beginning of time we were created from one source of energy and that energy was split into smaller and smaller units until it came down to two Souls. These Souls would journey to Earth to learn and experience duality and the lesson of life. They chose to reincarnate over many lifetimes with the same intention to one day reunite.

Before we entered this dimension we had full knowledge of our Soul, Over Soul and God Seed layers. And knew why we chose to experience this dimension. Upon entering this dimension field (the matrix of this system) our memories are blanked out. We come into this matrix with no idea of who we are or the existence of our Soul.

The free will system does not allow outside assistance without our permission. We are not able to connect to our Soul layer for assistance as we are not made aware of its existence.

The ancestral belief systems created on this planet worship an outside God Source when we are actually residing inside the God Source. Just like our cells inside us, we are like a cell inside God's body. The part of our cell that is at its Divine level and purest with the highest connection to the GOD Source energy is our God Seed Monad. The only way for us to directly connect to the GOD source is through our God Seed Monad. The God Source does not want to be worshipped. We are its children. Source wants us to connect and be ONE with it. The ONENESS connection is only possible by going within our heart and through all our higher layers. The journey starts by expanding our beliefs and developing our Self by practice knowing that this life is temporary and has a purpose. What is it that we came here to accomplish? Learn about yourself, begin with a desire to know who you are and why are here. There are many tools available for each Soul looking for this light. Begin your journey into a realm that you would never knew existing before. Believe me it surely is amazing. I wish each and every person takes the time to fully discover their purpose. Your purpose in life is to live life on purpose.

There is a lot going on this planet that is not for our highest good. Most of what is being taught and practiced is not from the God seed levels. Become aware of the energies you are receiving from others especially if they are not opened to the higher dimensions. The safest energy zone is from the 12th dimension and above. A lot of energy on the planet is transmitted from Dimension 1 -4. Be cautious with negative energies as they can alter the progress to the higher layers. Psychic energy is mostly 4th dimensional (astral). Many entities reside in the astral realm. The 4th Dimension is the realm of purification. Shift your frequencies to 5th dimension and higher. It is through intention and practice of some techniques that will shield you from the lower entities and keep you away from the astral debris.

Prior to now this information was not available in the 1-3 dimension zones. There are billions of incarnates trapped in this zone. They all came into this zone over thousands of years and have been trapped in this system. The knowledge of our Soul, Monad and God seed layers is the key to discovering our journey back home. Take time each day to build your pillar of light. Know that when we accept what is in every moment and let go of our outdated beliefs we move in the right direction. Everything that happens to make us upset or angry is already in the past and cannot be changed. Keep in mind that you are true Divinity in action, tap into the High Self, the "I AM" presence, and see yourself for who you really are on a much, higher level of being. Each one of us is a perfect expression of the Creator's love incarnate, in the flesh. We are walking, talking miracles of love.

The realization that I Am a part of God needs to dawn upon you, and become totally clear in your mind. It is then when you will hand the decisions to be made over to that aspect of you, and trust that God will give you the proper and right prompts on how to deal with things. Faith is faith in word only. Our faith is imperfect when we impose own will, wants, needs and desires upon our Creator. Source desires for you to realize that Source knows all your wants, needs and desires, and your intent as well. Remember when in a situation which provoked you, you lost your cool and you afterwards ended up ashamed of yourself and full of remorse? Well, consider these tests in self-discipline on the way to self-mastery. You need to learn that nothing can vex you, because within you lives one who has the situation well in hand, never mind how dark and perplexing life may seem at that moment the world may seem to you through whatever situation you land yourself in. It is in the trust in God where true peace and freedom reign. It is in remaining composed in any situation. Remember at all times that you are creating these experiences so you do not become unglued by things that upset you. Become the master of your emotions. Yes, I know that this is not easy. There are different ways and means if temporary relief is needed, like certain herbs and homeopathic remedies that you can use when the going is a little tough at times. Try to rise above situations and see matters from a higher perspective. Concern yourself more with matters of eternal life, so there will be a balance in all things, and you will be more in harmony with yourself, as your Soul becomes free in the Oneness. Trust will often be discussed and frequently be interwoven throughout your lessons. Your trust will be tested through much practice, until you trust completely, and allow spirits advice to be followed, rather than you exercising your own will in your faith-walk. Your trust will one day reach a level which will signal to God that you are ready to become connected. This is the moment that you both are working towards, the culmination of oneness. Start to develop a habit of stillness where you express your gratitude for life and your desire to be an instrument of the Divine Will, be open to this Divine Will and develop a God-like character. Stop and look out at the world and see where you can be of service to someone. Doing one small act of kindness to another that would be out of your pattern of daily routine brings the entire world a degree closer to perfection. Doing this day in and day out as a new habit starts a chain reaction that changes the world no matter how insignificant it seems to you. Your choice to allow the Divine Will to function through you means you are a participant in God purpose for your life and not just a bystander. Experience is essential to maturity, and you simply cannot skip it. Either you are mature, or you are not. Unfortunately, some people do not seek life experiences that will contribute to their personal maturity; and so it does not matter how old they are, they will never mature. Maturity, then, is a process in which several factors must coincide. Some of these, however, are most essential in anyone reaching maturity. The first essential ingredient for maturity in life is experiences. As well, there are experiences that are altogether pointless. Bona fide experiences are the ones that are the result of seeking superior realization of values and understanding of higher meanings. People searching for values and meanings are not just seeking knowledge. They are seeking wisdom. Bona fide experiences can be both intense events and cumulative achievements that produce an experiential balance in facing life and its situations. Maturity in life is the fruit of meaningful personality unification. Either the individual is conscious of it, or he or she is not. The personality unification that produces ethical maturity is the one that, together with achievement of bona fide values and meanings, brings a balance to the physical, emotional and intellectual factors resident in a particular individual. This starts its realization when a person sincerely decides to do the will of God in his or her life. When you allow the Spiritual path to be part of your everyday life you have reach Spiritual maturity which cannot be reached without the conscience of the individual, and of both the Spirit Within and the Spiritual self, the Soul. The Spiritual dominance happens when the Soul, as the receptacle of all Spiritual growth, produced by the conjoint action of Spirit Within and the individual self, and by means of the human will, finally governs all actions of a person with a purpose and meaning. Spiritual dominance is a constant awareness of the Spiritual value of life in all its aspects. Your personal maturity is a multi-faceted process that culminates in Spiritual maturity. Seek out the experiences whose meanings will remain with you for all eternity. Among those, undoubtedly, are the ones motivated by love, truth and beauty. Spiritual maturity is not gained automatically; it is personal, and it depends of each decision you make, reaffirming this a priority in all you do. Aim for the best, and the very best will come ever closer to you.

The idea that it is impossible to make contact with the presence of God inhabiting each one of you, is widespread among you. One technique is to formulate a question in your mind for the Father and then search for an answer. You can search in books, on the radio, on television, or the internet, and you will always receive an answer. Better still, you can try writing the answer yourself. This works, because your mind is continuously looking for a way to more successfully influence you and communicate with you in a more effective manner. The ideas regarding what you want to know are immediately placed in your mind, even before the question is verbally expressed, because your inner spirit knows the desires of your mind and your heart.

Ascension is the complete permanent union of the raised and purified outer self with the "I AM" Presence this true identity that is the unique individualization of almighty God for each person. This knowledge is believed to have previously been taught for millions of years, who is the Source of all Love, Light, and Love in existence, and that all forms of existence and consciousness come from this energy. All Life is One and that there is One Substance, One Energy, One Power, One Intelligence as the Source of all consciousness and creation. This Universal Order of Divine Self-Expression is the means whereby God steps down this presence and essence of His Universal Being / Consciousness in order that all Life in time and space might give and receive Unconditional Divine Love. Your placement on this Ladder of Life in the Spirit Matter Universes is determined by your level of Spiritual Attainment.

Each person is an incarnation of an individualized presence of the most high living God as part of our very nature and being. God as life and love manifests in the created Universe through individual Divine identities. As embodied individuals, we are the outer expression of that God self in form. It is our unique and immortal true identity.

Ascended Master Saint Germaine, was quoted as saying: "When one individualizes within the Absolute, All-Pervading Life, he chooses of his own free will to become an intensified individual focus of Self-Conscious Intelligence. He/she is the conscious director of his/hers future activities. Thus, having once made this choice, he/she is the only one who can fulfill that destiny, which is not inflexible circumstance but a definitely designed Plan of Perfection. When you, the Mighty I AM Presence, Will itself to come forth into an individualized focus of conscious dominion and use the creative word, "I AM," your first individual activity is the formation of a flame. Then you, the individualized focus of the Mighty I AM presence, begin your dynamic expression of life. This activity is termed self-consciousness, meaning the Individual who is conscious of its Source and perfection of life, expressing through himself/herself. Whenever you declare "I Am" whatever you say follows. I Am invites that which you have declared. "As we will it so shall it be"

Remember what ever follows "I Am" will come looking for you. As we affirm and decree we invoke the Universes language and it brings to you that which you have declared. Affirmations invoke and send forth the Light of God to bless life, to bring forth the perfect Divine solution for every situation, and to fulfill the Divine plan. It is believed to be a way of externalizing more Divine Light, Divine Love, and Divine Life into the lower planes of creation through the dynamic force of sound vibration as creative energy.

Only the Self-conscious individual has ALL the attributes and creative power of the mighty I AM presence. Only then will you know who and what it is, and express the fullness of the creative power of God whenever you declare it by the use of the Words, "I AM." The outer human part of this energy is what is called the personality. It is the vehicle through which perfection should be expressed into the outer substance of the Universe. "Within the 'Pure God-Flame' is a Breath that pulsates constantly. This is a Rhythmic Outpouring of Divine Love, Its three attributes being 'Love, Wisdom, and Power in action. These pour out constantly, into the infinite sea of pure electronic light. This Light is the universal substance or Spirit, out of which all forms are composed. It is intelligent, because it obeys the laws through the command of the individual who says, or is conscious of, 'I AM.' These two words are the acknowledgment and release of the power to create and bring forth into outer existence, whatever quality follows that acknowledgment. For intelligence to act there must be intelligence to be acted upon, and the universal substance, being like a photographic film, takes the record of whatever quality the individual imposes upon it through their thoughts, feelings, and spoken word. The Words 'I AM' whether thought, felt, or spoken, release the power of creation instantly. Make no mistake about this. Intelligence is Omnipresent, and it is within the electronic light.

The nature of the Universal Mind is Omniscience (all knowing), Omnipotence (all powerful), Omnificence (all creative) and Omnipresence (always present). Know that this is your true nature. You have access to all knowledge, known and unknown and you have access to an infinite power for which nothing is impossible. You have access to the limitless creativity of the One Creator. All these attributes are present within you at all times in their potential form. There is a single intelligent consciousness that pervade the entire Universe. As it is present everywhere at the same time goes to reason that it must be present in you, that it is you. Your mind is part of the one Universal Mind. This is not simply an idea passed down to us through the ages. It is exact scientific truth. Know it believe it and apply it and you will see your life transform in miraculous ways.

Albert Einstein told us that "Everything is energy, that a human being is a part of the whole called by us the Universe. The universal mind goes by many names. In the scientific world it is known as the Unified Field, but in Spiritual philosophy we refer to it as The All or the Universal Consciousness and in religion we call upon it as God, Source or Creator, or Heavenly Father. The name is only important in as much as it resonates with you.

Each and every one of us is a manifestation of this single Universal Consciousness. We are all connected, not only to each other but to all of nature and to everything in the Universe. This is the Law of One. What you do to others you do to yourself. The separation we see is only an illusion of the personality ego.

The Ascension is believed to be the returning to complete "Oneness with God" raising the outer atomic structure of the physical, emotional, and mental bodies into the electronic structure of the" I AM" Consciousness, becoming an Ascended Master, eventually a Cosmic Being, and beyond. The Ascension into immortality through reunion with the God Self requires you to gain mastery over the matter planes. This means you learn to consciously use all of your creative power of though, feelings, and spoken words to create greater joy, perfection and love into the world. The use of negative thoughts, feelings or words can create limitations or chaos in one own experiences or in the world with a lack of this awareness. If you continue to dwell on the negative experiences than it will continue to present negative experience with in your life, things will multiply if you dwell on them long enough. So why not create positives thoughts. When you will make the effort to prove this to yourself or within your own atomic flesh body, you will then proceed to Master Oneself. When this has been achieved the Universe is willing to co-create with you to accomplish whatsoever one wills through Love.

FULFILLMENT OF THE DIVINE PLAN

We are children of God, Spiritual brothers and sisters, working, whether you know it or not, to help the planet ascend into a new golden age. This will not happen overnight, but the energies are building. What appear to be personal or global problems are really wake up calls and opportunities to heal and release old thoughts and behaviors in favor of better, higher ones. As most of you probably know already, you are experiencing a shift in universal energies, across the whole of the Universe. This is the START of a new phase of higher energies building upon the earth. The energies have already been building in readiness for this cosmic grace. As the earth approaches the changeover point, many Souls are awakening to the light. They are sensing that they are being guided to do something more with their lives, and being guided to help others and the world in some way. Awakening can be an act of Divine grace like a visit by an angel, or it may come in the form of a deep problem, which requires the individual to face things, make shifts and changes, and seek higher help and guidance, leading to a new path of joy, urging you to seek the path of light, in all areas of your life, with love and patience. Hold the intention that ALL aspects of your life become harmonized with you, and the planet's highest good. In truth, any parts of your life which are at a lower vibrational level, not in keeping with who you really are, will become increasingly uncomfortable during the coming years, necessitating appropriate changes. Focus on creating the highest appropriate harmony in every area, and the appropriate changes will happen more gracefully.

Call upon the angels for guidance. They are with you to help make positive shifts in your life, helping guide you regarding the changes you need to make, and when to make them, and how to make them in the highest, easiest and most appropriate ways. Then you can relax knowing that your life is being guided for highest good. Calling upon our Divine help in this way will help your life to grow and improve your life more smoothly and easily, rather than ignoring potential problem areas until they become crisis. Positive and pro-active prayers and actions smooth the way. Consider how making changes in these areas can contribute to developing more of the real you, your path of light, and helping you to contribute more to others and the world, for the highest good of all.

This Prayer is your connection to Source. It is a direct connection with the Father, the first Source and Center of all creation, and there is no better way to open up the layers of the mind for Spiritual input than to make that highest connection with deity. To communicate with God is growth; therefore prayer is an effective way to open the layers of the mind for Spiritual discernment and Soul expansion.

God grant me the serenity to accept the things I cannot change; courage to change the things I can; and wisdom to know the difference. Living one day at a time; Enjoying one moment at a time; Accepting hardships as the pathway to peace; understanding this world as it is, not as I would have it; Trusting that God will make all things right if I surrender to His Will; That I may be reasonably happy in this life and supremely happy with Him Forever in the next. Amen

Celebrate the positive transitions that will occur in your life. Welcome positive change. You are all constantly releasing lower energies, thoughts and situations, and developing higher and better ones. By doing so, you are also helping to raise the consciousness and energy of the planet. It is like climbing a ladder, to go higher (towards Heaven) you must let go of the lower rung, and go up to each next rung in turn. This applies to people individually and collectively, as a planet. Whatever rung of the ladder you are on, make today the day to advance up, climb to the top and be grateful for the time spent on the lower rungs, always reaching up.

This world is destined to again have a Golden Age, a "Heaven on Earth", that will be permanent, unlike previous Golden Ages millions of years ago. In the not so far distant future, will come forth a similar recognition of the Real Inner Self, and people will express in high attainment. The Divine Plan for the future is a condition of intense activity in the greatest peace, beauty, success, prosperity, Spiritual illumination. We as Light Workers are to carry the Christ Light and are here to be the Guide for the rest of the Earth receiving guidance from within, for this form of Spiritual communication is something most everyone experiences to greater or lesser degrees, yet all will receive some form of Divine guidance whether they are aware of its source or not. We students on the path can learn how to become more aware of this Divine input by practicing a few techniques to allow your conscious mind to notice the difference between your own thoughts and the leadings of your Spirit, Guides, or Guardians. Most of you will be surprised at how much information is directed toward you for the growth of your Soul or for the benefit of others, and when you learn to recognize it, you can benefit even more because you are less likely to dismiss its gentle prompting.

Whenever you wish to receive Divine guidance, you need to prepare your mind for Spiritual input. The animal mind, with its electrochemical operating system, is not optimally 'tuned' for Spiritual input because its normal state of awareness works in layers. The first layer of consciousness is primarily concerned with the interpretation of events that are stimulated by the sensory organs: vision, hearing, smell, taste, and touch. This first layer of consciousness is the primary interface of awareness through which all input, sensory, subconscious, or super-conscious must pass before you may process it in the brain and make decisions. The second layer, the sub-consciousness, seeds the first layer and influences conscious decision making through the circuits of the Mind Spirits: intuition, understanding, courage, knowledge, counsel, worship, and wisdom. These are like radio stations from the Mother Spirit that broadcast their influence to the subconscious mind and which will find its place in the first layer as it seeps in. This second layer of consciousness is vibrational, which requires that the first layer interpret those vibrations, and turn them in. This is also true for the third layer. The third layer is the Super-consciousness. This is the Soul mind and this is where Spirit operates coordinating all Spiritual input. This layer is the farthest removed from the conscious mind and of the highest vibration and so it is the most difficult to be interpreted by the first layer, the conscious mind. Like the second layer, it also seeps in yet only when the first layer is conditioned to receive its gentle voice. Those who live life on the surface and are Spiritually unaware have yet to condition their minds for Spiritual input, because they have nearly filled the conscious mind with nonsense.

In order to open the pores of the first layer to receive the higher, finer vibrations of the third layer, you have to consciously elevate your mood and thoughts (raise your vibration) to receive Spiritual input. The steps necessary to receive and to become aware of Divine guidance through the understanding and conditioning of the first layer of consciousness. This then transmutes the higher vibrational frequencies of the second and third layers. By your understanding of these processes, you can then begin to tune into the awareness of these higher forms of Divine communication. The first step is to reduce or clear out input from the senses and make room in the pores of the first layer. This can be done through stillness or bringing your awareness to a clear open channel. Monitoring what comes into the mind and choosing healthy stimuli is essential to achieving the ability to be at peace at any given moment. Being at peace is therefore the precondition for Divine reception.

The second step is to elevate your thoughts and feelings to attempt to match the higher frequencies of the third layer of input.

This can be done by having thoughts of higher vibration like: love, compassion, gratitude, forgiveness, joy and other thoughts that make you feel good. This conditions the mind and opens the pores of the first layer. Have you noticed that when you are feeling good that good thoughts come into the mind? Having negative thoughts (thick and low in vibration) restricts the pores in the first layer and so nothing positive can come in when these lower vibrational forms pervade the first layer. The third step is awareness. Having conditioned your mind for third layer input, you can place your attention on the thoughts that come into your mind which are not generated by your own mind. These are the thoughts that seep in and allow you to process and make decisions that are in alignment with the God's Will. It is your conscious decision (free will) whether or not to act on these inputs that constitute alignment with the Will of God. The fourth step is discernment, which you must exercise because of the fine line that exists between your own positive thoughts and those of Divine origin. This is a process that you learn through experience and practicing these methods of positive conditioning. The more you keep your thoughts elevated throughout your day, the more Divine input you will allow into the first layer, therefore you must stay positive and aware. Maintaining a nearly unbroken line of communication with Spirit in both asking and receiving is the best way to interpret and receive guidance. Now is the opportunity many of us came to take advantage of on Earth during this lifetime. We need to open our hearts to feel and know this, and allow our SELF to follow our heart's feelings. Once you raise our frequencies, the higher frequencies stay with you (even after letting go of our body). Our consciousness level is raised.

UNDERSTANDING CODES

Our physical reality is a consciousness program created by digital codes. Numbers, numeric codes, define our existence. Human DNA, our genetic memory is encoded to be triggered by digital codes at specific times and frequencies. Those codes awaken the mind to the change and evolution of consciousness. 11:11 is one of the codes for DNA activation. It can be a key to unlocking the subconscious mind, our genetic encoded memories, that we are spirits having a physical experience not physical beings embarking on a Spiritual experience. Every number sequence has a different meaning and those may different slightly for us in our personal lives. The number 11:11 is the most well-known of the codes. Many people who have notice this number have made wishes when they see this number but may not really understand the meaning behind it. 11:11 is the Universe's way of getting our attention and urging us to open our heart, our Soul and our inner intuition. It is serving as a wakeup call to us so that opportunities are not missed in this lifetime. I began seeing these number several years ago and at first thought it was a random experience. At first I just would smile and felt that something was happening but I was unaware of what that was at the time but I knew it was something special. I just kept my mind open and hoped I would find out what the numbers meant. Being guided by Spirit I keep searching and looking for the reason why I was receiving these codes. The codes happen gradually at first then they became more frequent. I realized that if I was experiencing this there must be others going through this also. Often times when things happen in our lives we may not realize that here is always someone going through the same things we are. Things that don't seem "Normal" are over looked and never discussed. We don't want to let others know that we have just had an experience that they just might not understand. We keep this to ourselves and wait until we feel free to talk about it. Seeing this number sequence means the Universe is trying to have us open our eyes and begin paying more attention to the synchronicities around us. It is also a sign for those who are aware that they are experiencing accelerated Soul growth which means that they will soon be finding themselves living a live that they had only previously thought about. Your inner world begins to change and we may find people and events coming unexpectedly into our lives all at the right time.

Millions of Souls around the world are now seeing these amazing signs. It's spreading, and becoming far more common; it's become a major phenomenon. Someone or something is causing all these folks to look at clocks, number plates, phone numbers or any source of numbers even when they make no effort themselves to look for these things. You can't stop it, because YOU aren't doing it. These 11:11 Wake-Up Calls on your digital clocks, mobile phones, license plates and microwaves are the "trademark" prompts of a group of just 1,111 fun-loving Spirit Guardians, or Angels, and the 11:11 prompt is their way of using our innate ability for pattern recognition to let us know that they are here. Once they have your attention, they will use other digits, like 12:34, or 2:22 to remind you of their presence. Invisible to our eyes, they are very real. How often have you noticed the numbers 11:11, 12:12, 10:10, 22:22, 12:34, 2:22, 3:33, 4:44 or 5:55 popping up all over the place? These number sequences are not necessarily only time prompts. To your mind, is this a coincidence, or are they too frequent to be random? The question everyone is asking is "What does 11:11 mean?" and "Is there a reason for this?" And there certainly is.

They can also be number sequences, like 333, 1111, or any sequence of numbers brought to your awareness. Numerology is the study of numbers and relation to certain aptitude and character tendencies as an integral part of the cosmic plan. Every letter and number has a value that provides a related cosmic vibration. There are 11 numbers used in constructing a numerology chart. 33 Represent Christ Consciousness, universal nurturing, social consciousness'. The 33 is the most influential of all numbers. It is the Master Teacher. The 33 combines the 11 and the 22 and brings their potential to another level. When expressed to the fullest, the 33 lacks all personal ambition, and instead focuses its considerable abilities toward the Spiritual uplifting of mankind. What makes the 33 especially impressive, is the high level of sincere devotion. This is shown in its determination to seek understanding and wisdom before preaching to others. The 33 in full force is extremely rare. 33 is a very significant number in Freemasonry. It represent the highest known degree among the Freemasons.

In numerology the number 22 is often called the Master Builder or Spiritual Master in Form. This master number includes all the attributes of the number 2, twice over and also those of the 4. People who are 22's are said to find themselves feeling as if they live in two worlds, one which is overwhelmed by the mundane and the other by the fantastic. 22 is a higher octave number of 4 and it contains the secrets to many esoteric questions. 22 carries with it psychic gifts such as heightened sensitivity, intuition, and psychic awareness. 22 Represent practical idealism, practical genius, and co-creators of the future, power on all levels, universality, and service to mankind. The number 11 carries a vibration frequency of balance. It represent the male and female equality. It contains both the sun and moon energy simultaneously but holds both in perspective separateness or perfect balance. The number eleven is thought of as a "master" number in numerology because it is a double digit of the same number. When this occurs the vibrational frequency of the prime number doubles in power. Meaning, the attributes of the Number One are doubled. Therefore, the very basic and primary understanding of the Number One is that of new beginnings and purity. When we see this digit doubled as with the 11, 22, 33 then these attributes double in strength. 11 represents Master Teacher, illumination, enlightenment, inspirational, idealism, intuitive, psychic abilities, channeling, poetry, art/artistic, symbols, expression, dreamer, revolution, alternate consciousness, mysticism, catalyst, prophet, celebrity, highly energized, radical, sensitive, visionary, enthusiastic, creative/creativity.

Our Earthly 1,111 Spirit Guardians, have been assisting people of all walks of life for many centuries. Some folks also notice lights going out or on when they pass by, such as street lights, or may also hear the door bell ring, yet there is no one in sight. It's all due to our fun loving midway friends. They will use almost any electrically controlled device to get your attention. A new age of Spiritual Uplift has begun on our planet. There are now literally billions of Celestial beings here, all of whom have been especially trained to assist with changing the course of this planet. Many more of these delightful Spirit Guardians are now ready to assist whoever will ask for their help. We are told that over 75 million folks are being given these 11:11 prompts, and a glance around the web will tell you something big is happening. Welcome to the Gateway, it's the doorway to your evolving self, your place within the current ascension of the planet. There is nothing to be afraid of, they are here to illuminate all of us. Here is an explanation for the number prompts you may have noticed.

111 * Monitor your thoughts carefully, and be sure to only think about what you want, not what you don't want. This sequence is a sign that there is a gate of opportunity opening up, and your thoughts are manifesting into form at record speeds. The 111 is like the bright light of a flash bulb. It means the Universe has just taken a snapshot of your thoughts and is manifesting them into form. The Angels will help you with this if you have difficulty controlling or monitoring your thoughts. 111 is a manifestation number. It means you are in a moment where you can create for your life. Be sure your thoughts are very positive.

222 * Your newly planted ideas are beginning to grow into reality. Keep watering and nurturing them, and soon they will push through

the soil so you can see evidence of your manifestation. In other words, don't quit five minutes before the miracle. Your manifestation is soon going to be evident to you, so keep up the good work! Keep holding positive thoughts, keep affirming, and continue visualizing.

333 * The Ascended Masters are near you, desiring you to know that you have their help, love, and companionship. Call upon the Ascended Masters often, especially when you see the number 3 patterns around you. 333 is the Christ Consciousness number, and not anything to fear. It is a sign that you are being blessed and the high Holy Beings are directly overseeing your life or something in your life at this time.

444 * There are Angels surrounding you now, reassuring you of their love and help. Don't worry because the Angels' help is nearby. 444 is an Angelic realm number for prosperity and abundance.

555 * Buckle your seatbelts. A major life change is upon you. This change should not be viewed as being "positive" or "negative," since all change is but a natural part of life's flow. Perhaps this change is an answer to your prayers, so continue seeing and feeling yourself being at peace. 555 is the number of creating positive change and forward movement.

666 * Indicates that your thoughts are out of balance right now, focused too much on the material world. This number sequence asks you to balance your thoughts between heaven and earth. The Angels ask you to focus on spirit and service, and know your material and emotional needs will automatically be met as a result.

777 * the Angels applaud you so congratulations, you're on a roll! Keep up the good work and know your wish is coming true. This is an extremely positive sign and means you should also expect more miracles to occur. 777 is a very high Spiritual number that signifies

teaching or learning a more spiritually conscious way of thinking and being.

888 * A phase of your life is about to end, and this is a sign to give you forewarning to prepare. This number sequence may mean you are winding up an emotional career, or relationship phase. It also means there is light at the end of the tunnel. In other words, don't procrastinate making your move or enjoying fruits of your labor.

999 * Completion. This is the end of a big phase in your personal or global life. Also, it is a message to Light Workers involved in Earth healing and means, "Get to work because Mother Earth needs you right now."

000* a reminder you are one with God, and to feel the presence of your Creator's love within you. Also, it is a sign that a situation has gone full circle.

The Angels say that our Universe vibrates to what in its simplest forms here on Earth are math and geometry. It is much more than that really but that is what our human minds see it as. This is also what music, astrology, numerology, and sacred geometry is about as well. The numbers you keep seeing are codes that signals your ancient DNA, your cellular memory and your higher consciousness to awaken. To awaken to a phase, a more Spiritual space in your heart and mind and within your life.

10:10 is the Alpha-Omega number. The number of beginnings and endings, it is full of promise, and of opening to the "Compassionate Heart."

12:12 is the number when the Higher Realms wants to download into your consciousness new ways of being a human being and experiencing life on Earth. It is like the switch, turned on for you to step into your Divine Path to be of service for humanity and every living thing on the planet. When I see these numbers, it reminds me to take a moment, breathe in deeply and say "I am ready to receive".

As we begin to recognize this phenomenon we begin to see change coming into our experience. The numbers along with other number sequences mean Pay attention and wake up. You will experience a sudden awakening after which reality is never the same. You are going to create clarity, healing and balance for yourself and others. Do not expect others in your life to be on the same journey with you. It is yours alone as it is for many Souls. You will have to seek new friends of like mind who are also being triggered by the digits. Once you open the Digital doorway there is no going back. Your Soul will automatically and quickly move you from level to level of experience until you get it. Your consciousness is expanding and therefore you will manifest faster and greater comprehension, becoming more aware of the meaning of synchronicities that will become more and more frequent. They are created by your Soul to help you remember that you are a Soul spark in physical form that is about to end and evolve back to a higher consciousness. Once this begins you may feel this sense of urgency or other related emotions. You need to relax and allow spirit to guide you. This signals a change in the patterns of your life. This is part of the Ascension process and reconnection back to Source. This is why you have chosen at this time to be here. Even if you are not aware yet you will be. Just Believe and you will receive, this is the Law of Attraction.

We may not realize how blessed we are to adorn a human body and mind? Some are not aware of their unlimited power? You are a Soul and not the body and the Soul is linked directly to the Supreme Energy. A direct gateway exists between you and an unlimited reservoir of universal energy. Our minds can be preoccupied by mundane desires and struggles of earthly life to even try to open up that gateway to Heaven.

Being human is the highest form of evolution and is blessed with a direct link to the intelligent cosmic life force that governs it. Humans in fact control their own destiny & future through actions (mental & physical). Every action has a reaction and this is how the entire cosmos is linked into each other. Ancient Masters used the power of meditation to decipher the secrets of the Universe and tap into the vast reservoir of universal energy, making them highly charged super Beings. What did they do to become so powerful? They attracted 'ENERGY' through concentration and established a perfect harmony with the Universe. They recognized the link between planets, asterisms, constellations, sounds mantras, nature's elements, and intelligent life, both human and cosmic intelligence (Divine).

The Soul is you and you are energy. You are a Soul having a human experience. The Soul lives in the heart of each of us. Each individual is a formation of different magnitudes of energy depending on our level of evolution. The higher your energy level, the more powerful and radiant is the person and their destiny. Understand this, if this energy is not balanced and channeled proportionately, extreme personalities are born who are as unbalanced as their destinies are. Now the question arises, whether we are capable of handling and channeling this extremely potent life force. The answer is a big NO is most cases therefore some are in need of assistance. There is a Galactic Federation of Light that oversees everything! Currently the mathematical templates of our energy bodies contain codes which distort the natural energy flows. Distorted frequencies have been contaminating our environment in ways not generally understood. This means that it is helpful to access frequencies which can protect against existing energetic distortions which would otherwise have serious consequences.

The secret to a perfect existence lies in harmony with the universal force. In other words, we need to distribute our energy equally through all aspects of our Being. We need to rise above our senses and look at life from a higher perspective. Since the measure of energy is constant, it is natural that the scale of life will tilt to an unbalanced position if the energy does not rest proportionately. When the pendulum swing how far does it go? It is evident in this world that people who desire money with a single mind, lose out on family bliss and actually feel that void at a later stage and vice versa. Whatever a Soul yearns for, it gets but mostly the desire is so concentrated on just one particular aspect. Too much of strength diverted to one particular item is not good as it dilutes a lot other aspects of life. This is the reason, it has been said to be very careful of what you desire and avoid obsession. Any desire is fulfilled if significant energy is directed in that direction. With an awareness to who you are and what makes you feel and think and be, you understand that with time you can change and you may never look at yourself the same way again.

As Earth frequencies raise the veils get thinner. Since there are many species of Beings on this planet in the human uniform, we may soon be able to identify ourselves as to who we are Angelic human or a species from another planetary system. There are Beings on this planet now able to raise their frequencies and connect to the 5th dimension Soul and higher Over Soul layers. This is the true journey of SELF EVOLUTION.

That is why self-healing courses includes detailed information about different kinds of energy currents and the nature our own multi-dimensional structure. It also includes information about the cosmos, which is a multi-dimensional system of holographic experiential domains interconnected by star-gates.

It is possible to access healing currents from the highest level, where our original encryption have been preserved uncorrupted, and access these currents to restore the original organic functioning of our DNA, and learn what else is encoded in the DNA template besides what contemporary science knows. Spiritual energy healing has absolutely nothing to do with either diagnosing or curing diseases, as defined by allopathic medicine, which does not recognize the existence of energy templates, multi-dimensional energy bodies, or even higher dimensions. Although some holistic systems work with the auras, chakras, and meridians, information about our multi-dimensional nature our true history is to journey to the higher realms. This information is the most valuable gift of all, because combining the positive currents with self-mastery empowers us to make enlightened choices every step along the way. This includes the ability to reclaim conscious control of our destiny!

This is the beginning of a Golden New Age, when techniques are out there to enable everyone to access the new frequencies themselves! Are you feeling sad, confused, experiencing unexplained body aches and pains, disorientation, loss of time, loss of memory, sudden career or relationship changes, you are experience some of the issues that others are dealing with during this shift. We may begin to feel more alienated than ever from the world, excessively lethargic, feeling lost, have heightened sensitivities to foods, or medicines, or supplements. You may have urges of unexplained emotion, unusual dreams, and lashing out, bouts of depression that is getting worse. Often you may feel like you are in several (or more than one) place(s) at once and are aware of alternate realities. If so, you are not alone. If so, you are most likely experiencing DNA shifts as we and all of creation is moving into a higher consciousness both physically and psychologically.

Nearly everyone is experiencing these symptoms to a degree. Very few it seems are gliding through Mother Earth's ascension into the fourth and fifth dimensions with ease and joy. Some people merely pass off these symptoms as physiological in nature, psychological, etc. This is not true. Everything is physically ascending. Therefore, maintaining an even keel, a balance within, working with ourselves and our issues and pain, removing yourself from stressful situations, graces our bodies, nurtures healing, bringing ourselves and others, healthy and smart, energy that can help ease us through this time of transition. As Things Get Lighter Some Things Get Darker. Learn to go with the flow and not against it. If you feel that you may be swimming upstream, you may need to change directions. You truly know when this is occurring, the first step is to recognize it and then have the courage to make the change.

As we move through these astounding planetary energies, gifting us with incredible opportunities for greater awareness and insight into who we are in all our Divinity, we have the chance to gladly and willingly love ourselves more fully than ever. The vibrational energy is rising on the earth; it is a natural evolution that occurs within all conscious structures be they planetary, human or other. Ascension is where we bring our spirit into our physical lives, so that on earth there is more of a connection with our physical bodies and our multi-dimensional selves. As we raise our energy vibration and ascend, so does the earth, it is also on its evolutionary journey.

There are many planets that are not visible to the human consciousness, that have been through the ascension process. This was achieved because of the HARMONY between the planet and the Beings that inhabited it. This connection has been lost on the earth, where there is a lot of abuse of the planet that we live on, rather than a connection with the various elements of the earth.

Imagine for a moment how another system of life might possibly run parallel to our own system of life and that all of time takes place at the same time, the past, present as well as the future. If we can tune into the idea of a so called past life, then we can also tune into future life, the Pleiadian Realm, Sirius star system and beyond. The idea here is for us now to begin to grasp the concept that time does not really exists. Neither does time run in a straight line. The time issue is much more complex than that, so much so that we are unaware of it. Pleiadian consciousness was integrated to seed the original humans. Some Souls who first incarnated had their first cycle on Pleiades and some decided to move to Earth during the fall. Some of them split and aligned with dark energies and some of them stayed loyal to the Divine Light. The Pleiadians were tasked to share their DNA (through the ether via light vibration) and to ground higher consciousness here. Many Pleiadians simply left their physical bodies here resulting in new Souls walking into an ongoing incarnation. Some decided to leave Earth and downloaded their unresolved karma to other Pleiadian Souls who decided to stay here. The Souls that took upon themselves other Soul unresolved karma may feel overwhelmed working through karma that is not even their own. The ones that stayed on the path of light are talented devoted teachers here on Earth. One of the main characteristics is that they are usually great visionaries and instigator of change. The Pleiadian Realm is not at the God level, yet it does exist in time beyond the human level. This realm is about 400 light years away from Earth. The Pleiadian Realm operates outside of our normal concept of linear time. It operates in another star system. The Pleiades are a cluster of beautiful, dazzling stars located in the constellation of Taurus. With a telescope, you can see about 100 stars. Without a telescope, you can see only six or seven stars. According to ancient legends, the stars are said to be sisters and the daughters of Atlas. The entire Pleiades cluster is actually the eye of the bull in the constellation of Taurus... Alcyone, Merope, Celeno, Taygeta, Sterope, Electra and Maia. They have been known for thousands of years, surrounded by fascinating legends and stories even to this day. In the clear and unpolluted night skies of antiquity the Pleiades star cluster was an object of wonder and interest. It was the subject of myth and legend in almost every culture on the planet. The rising of the Pleiades in spring in the northern hemisphere has from ancient times been the opening of the fishing and farming season and the autumnal setting marked the season's end. Life originated in the Pleiades realm long, long ago. They claim to have come to this world as Star seeds to bring Light and knowledge. Certain Pleiadians are highly evolved, more so than most of the human species. The Pleiadian Realm is the next step or level in our human evolution. It is for this reason that certain knowledge is being given to us by especially enlightened Pleiadian beings. There are those that want to help us toward our higher Spiritual destiny. This type of consciousness resides at a very high frequency that is lighter than what some know. The higher and lighter the frequency, the closer to the God source one becomes. The Pleiadians, highly evolved spirits from another dimension, have been preparing us, helping us to understand about this process for many years. We are all going through an accelerated transformation process. This can feel intense at times. We are waking up and humanity consciousness is expanding giving us a view of the bigger picture. You must prepare your mind to accept that life is an illusion, and at times may appear to be unpleasant. Pleiadians are connected with those who are called the Star seeds and Light workers. Light Workers and Star seeds are connected with Pleiadians, since they also hold the same fundamental and universal laws of peace, joy, and love. Star seeds are those who are currently living on Earth but know deep inside, a feeling that is unshakable, that their origins are not from this world. Often, Star seeds are commonly those who have a connection with the Pleiadians. Light Workers, are those on Earth that will tend to be Star seeds who have set out to accomplish the good work of the universal infinite intelligence and spread the knowledge and understanding of the positive powers humans and other races possess. Those who feel an inner connection with the Pleiadian blood lines, is because of the universal channeling between long lost brothers and sisters. Star seeds are constantly finding ways to be able to find the interconnections to their past and hope that one day they will have the opportunity to once again join their cosmic families! Light Workers are usually Star seeds because of the inherent need to find the positive powers of the Universe. Following the higher teachings of the powers that control good, Light Workers set out to teach others that there are different forces than those known to man, not all humans possess the sense of an ancient past and connection to the Pleiadians. So, those who consider themselves Star seeds will eventually gravitate towards the teaching of the Light Workers and seek the ways for the betterment of human life. Until we are once again in the presence of our original families, we will continue gazing into the Heavens and have the hope that perhaps one day, the Pleiadians, will travel the stars to find their long lost past here on Earth. My first experience happened in 1986 after watching the film "Out on a Limb". Being on the path and guided towards this information I found this movie very enlightening. I began to realize that I was being guided to something of importance. My guides were showing me where to look for the answers to the questions I had, so I trusted that there must be something to this and that my path of self-discovery would unfold. I realize that there were others going through the same experience as I was but now I knew. The validation at the time seemed positive but it was not always clear. I felt ok now what do I do with this information, and again I was directed to the answers. The Pleiadians have been here for years and have been bringing us information from other dimensions. It is said that the Pleiades transmit the light of God into our minds enabling God's light to descend on Earth. I know that many Pleiadian StarSouls are currently finding it desperately challenging here in this density but a resurgence of Pleiadian Souls are now gathering down through the densities toward the Earth, purposefully to reconnect with Pleiadian Souls embodied here. To many this may be your first experience with this kind of information. Many Souls are beginning to understand and accept that we are not alone in the Universe and that we are all waking up to this. Deep inside each Soul is a secret gift that you brought with you to Earth when you chose to incarnate. Your gifts will present themselves as you search deeper into your purpose for incarnating now. Remember to reach the best fruit you must go "Out on a Limb".

These Souls understand our fear of the unknown, and so they come to help in ways that are non-threatening. They are coming now, sometimes in physical form where they can blend in, but most often through human consciousness. Their intent is not to harm but to help us evolve and develop. Their message and action is not always one that you might comprehend at first. Thinking with a purely human mind, you might find it difficult or impossible for the human mind to grasp the scope of what is not familiar. Tuning into higher wisdom does not always mean greeting an alien or a spacecraft. The Pleiades are among the first stars mentioned in literature, appearing in Chinese annals of about 2350 BC. The earliest European references in a poem by Hesiod in about 1000 BC and in Homer's Odyssey and Iliad. The Bible contains three direct references to the Pleiades in Job 9:9 and 38:31, and Amos 5:8, and a single indirect reference in the New Testament. Revelation 1:16 describes a vision of the coming of the one – who holds, in his right hand, seven stars. So often, this is how wisdom and higher information is passed to us. Unless we open up to understand ascension the human race would get stuck and stay right where it's at. It is through our consciousness that the Higher Pleiadian forces of Light bring us information. This information is vital in our Spiritual development. Some have chosen as their work, a very noble and serious purpose. They strive to work through the layers of human consciousness to bring higher wisdom from the place they dwell at. They bring wisdom, as many have brought wisdom throughout the ages from higher realms. They are coming to us right here right now thru the words you are reading on these pages. This is their gift to us. The enlightened mind is the gift acquired when one transforms desire into Spiritual aspiration. In our early lives of expression, desire rules the thought life, coupled with the bold determination and strong will needed to acquire that which is desired. The Pleiades are the symbol of the Soul around which the wheel of life revolves. Their purpose is not to save your Soul, but to enlighten you more to the power and beauty of who you are, and to the Divine creation of which we all are a part. Our entire Solar system and our Milky Way has entered a highly charged position in space. This process is periods of intense light energies which began to come on board in the 90's and we will remain in this space for the next 2000 years. This is needed at this time as we begin to raise the frequency of this dimension. This carries the seeds toward enlightenment to everyone. The atomic structure within our cells are slowly returning themselves to match these raising frequencies. We are shifting from the third dimension to the fifth and for some higher dimensional in our Light Body. Everything is shifting to make this transitions possible for our whole galaxy. As the process of rebuilding our light bodies continues we will slowly begin to notice the effects. We become fully conscious or multidimensional. We experience life within this consciousness while still living in this third dimension and have a relationship with Beings, and energy in the higher realms. We learn to operate at the level of Christ consciousness state with our heart focuses on compassion and love. Eventually we will understand we are all one energy connected to our Source and here to live in this way.

Many of us have experienced a lack of love in our lives that should have felt nurturing on a deep Soul level. Instead, we have experienced harsh judging and accusations by others. We have experienced neglect and abandonment on many levels including past, parallel, and future lives. There are an abundance of people who cannot understand why things happen to them, why their lives have been filled with wrong choices, fear and manipulation. You are not a victim to of your circumstances. All of the experiences you have had up to this point was there to awaken you to who you are now. You can no longer look back and see things the same way. Growth comes through awareness.

There are deep holes inside of our hearts just begging to be filled with love. We sometimes search for a way to fill this hole through marriage, relationships with friends, volunteer work, careers, travel, spending binges, over-eating, and addictions of all sorts. While some of these are wonderful ways to experience love, they may not be what we're really requiring for healing. These all seem to fill this void for a little while but we always return to the deep hole or void in our hearts and discover the falseness of our recent little steps through life. We learn to see the truth behind the mask of our lives, that there has been no filling up of that space at all, which can plunge us deeper and deeper into despair and loneliness. Take a good look at what is happening during this ascension time and gain some clues that will assist you greatly along your path toward self-love. This ascension time of Mother Earth is filled with great gifts. These are planetary, stellar energies bombarding everything multi dimensionally including our three dimensional world called Earth providing us with newfound powers, gifts and talents we never knew we had. We are now experiencing the love of our brothers and sisters: the animal, plant and mineral kingdoms of our Earth Mother, the Archangels Michael, Gabriel, Ariel, and Raphael as well as many other Divine, loving forces of energy just waiting to assist us all in love unconditional. We are also learning how incredible the gifts of love Jesus the "Christed" One has to offer. His experience as Christ Consciousness on this Earth some 2000+ years ago has taught us to love ourselves. He once said that" We must love our neighbors as ourselves". When he said that he wanted us to understand how important it was/is to love ourselves fully for only then can we understand the depth of love for each other. In order to reach out to the world, we must first reach inside. Reach into our hearts and explore, examine and experience. Another gift from this ascension is the opportunity to let all our past life karma finally rest, be at peace, affording us the chance to be free. We must take responsibility for all our choices, good or bad. How reassuring this is to know that we have no need for the old patterns and belief systems we brought through to this lifetime. More people are open to other Spiritual options, realizing the great gifts of many of the world's religions. What matters is there is a grain of truth in all things and it is up to us to discover who we are and what we desire to experience in our life, opening up to your higher aspects and then do ourselves the honor to go out and live it fully. This will take practice so be patience, with you progress just don't give up. Imagine what a beautiful garden looks like, smells like, sounds like and feels like now create that same imagine in your mind and let that seep into your Soul. Because you are all of those senses, and more. As you look around are there any weeds in your garden or is it fertile and thriving. If you don't attend to the weeds they will take over and before you know it, it's not a beautiful garden, but a place that has been neglected.

Clearing the contaminated energies and shifting to the 5th dimension and higher layers is a process similar to our education system. It takes many years to go from grade 1 to graduating, as is the cleansing process can take many years. Many of us have been stuck in this dimension 1-3 system for thousands of years in spirit and physical form. We have accumulated a lot of negative blockages and dropped in density. Earth shifting to 5th dimension density makes our cleansing a lot easier and faster. The higher planetary frequencies allow us to tap into its system and clear our channels. This is the real healing everyone on this planet needs. The energies in density 1-4 are contaminated. By living in this system our energies are no longer at the level of its original blueprint level of purity. The fear based foundation of density 1-4 has also made our physical, emotional and mental body systems accumulate immense amount of negativity through our self serving and harmful thoughts, words and actions that have been created from life experiences throughout all timelines. These create energetic blockages in all our subtle layers and manifest karmic imprints. The heavier these blockages and karmic imprints are the more dense our system becomes. The healing process requires cleansing these energy blockages from all the lower density 1-3 layers (physical, emotional and mental). We are not able to shift to the higher dimension frequencies until they are cleared from our system. There is no quick fix we may have immense amounts of unresolved issues that we need to address in this lifetime. Once we clear these lower energies we can see why it was important that work with our guides to make these changes. It starts with our behavior attitudes and responsibilities towards ourselves and all beings. Knowledge of our whole being with all its layers, the universal system, the energetics of both our individual system and the universal system and the importance of increasing our DNA strands helps us understand why we have to heal ourselves.

As we journey to the higher dimensions we are also required to build the Kundalini and the Silver Cord bridges of inter-dimensional frequency that connects to the Soul Matrix. Further Kundalini development opens up to the Over Soul. This development opens up the Rainbow Bridge to the higher layers. The powerful healing transmutation violet rays originate from this layer. Connecting to the violet flame awakens your connection the Christ Consciousness (God Source) and transmutes negative thoughts into positive thoughts to free us of negative energies we are holding on to that are born from old karma or past negative influences. Feelings of guilt turn into acceptance, fear of fate become desired opportunities. The violet flame can be called upon through meditation. The Violet Flame is also known as the Seventh ray of the white light. White light is the space within the Universe where positive energies are stored. White light can be called upon for protection from negative energies or lower vibrations and can be called upon by healers, Empaths or anyone. White light cannot come to harm or be harmed in anyway. For this reason, negative energies can be sent to the white light for purification and transformation. You can request that the impurities you combed out of your auric field be sent to the white light for cleansing. The Violet Fire is a raising, transforming, purifying action of Divine Love from the Heart of God. It acts to transmute human creation that is not worthy of becoming Immortal. These high frequency teachings originate from ancient processes long before Atlantis, and Egyptian times that could not be brought on Earth until its frequency was high enough. The new higher Earth frequencies now allow for these processes to open our channels to the Higher Soul and Over Soul layers. We are receiving this information as we move through Ascension.

UNIVERSAL LAWS

There are seven Universal Laws or Principles by which everything in the Universe is governed. The Universe exists in perfect harmony by virtue of these Laws. Ancient mystical, esoteric and secret teachings dating back over 5,000 years from Ancient Egypt to Ancient Greece and to the Vedic tradition of Ancient India, all have as their common thread these seven Spiritual Laws of the Universe. Once you understand, apply and align yourself with these Universal Laws, you will experience transformation in every area of your life beyond that which you have ever dared to imagine. Law of Harmonics 1-3 Personality and Ego 4-6 Soul and future self-7-9 Over Soul level of Self- mastery.

The seven Universal Laws, the first three are immutable, eternal Laws, meaning they are absolute and can never be changed or transcended. They have always existed and will always exist. The other four laws are transitory, mutable Laws meaning that they can be transcended or at least have the ability to create your ideal reality. Your aim is to master each of the seven Universal Laws and only then learn to transcend the mutable ones.

1. The Law of Mentalism (Immutable): The first of the seven Universal Laws tells us that "The All is Mind - The Universe is Mental". That everything we see and experience in our physical world has its origin in the invisible, mental realm. It tells us that there is a single Universal Consciousness which we call the Universal Mind. From here all things manifest. All energy and matter at all levels is created by and

is subordinate to the Omnipresent Universal Mind. Your mind is part of the Universal Mind the only difference being one of degree. Your reality is a manifestation of your mind. This is true Mind Power.

2. The Law of Correspondence (Immutable): The second of the seven Universal Laws tells us "As Above, So Below; as Below, so Above". This means that there is harmony, agreement and correspondence between the physical, mental and Spiritual Realms. There is no separation since everything in the Universe, including you, originates from the One Source. The same pattern is expressed on all planes of existence from the smallest electron to the largest star and vice versa. All is One. Remember that ultimately nothing is separate in the Universe. All is interconnected through fields of energy. These various vibrations will be influencing every human in different blended measures (and other frequencies too). The Ancient Greek Temple of Apollo at Delphi was referring to this great Law of Correspondence in the inscription "Know thyself and thou shalt know all the mysteries of the Gods and the Universe".

3. The Law of Vibration (Immutable): The third of the seven Universal Laws tells us that nothing rests; everything moves; everything vibrates. The third and last of the immutable Universal Laws, tells us that the whole Universe is but a vibration. Science has confirmed that everything in the Universe, including you, is pure energy vibrating at different frequencies, that like energy attracts like energy, upon which the Law of Attraction is based, it's the foundation in this Law. Everything that we experience with our five physical senses is conveyed through vibrations. The same applies to the mental realm. Your thoughts are vibrations. All your emotions are vibrations where unconditional love in the sense of love for another is the highest and most subtle of the emotional vibrations and hate is the densest and basest. You

can learn to control your mental vibrations at will. This is true thought power.

4. The Law of Polarity (Mutable): The fourth of the seven Universal Laws tells us that everything is dual, everything has poles; everything has its pair of opposites; opposites are identical in nature, but different in degree. It is also the first of the mutable Universal Laws. It means that there are two sides to everything. Things that appear as opposites are in fact only two extremes of the same thing. For instance, heat and cold may appear to be opposites at first glance, but in truth they are simply varying degrees of the same thing. The same applies to love and hate, peace and war, positive and negative, good and evil, yes and no, light and darkness, energy and matter. You can transform your thoughts from hate to love, from fear to courage by consciously raising your vibrations.

    Rising above the Law of Polarity: This Principle of Duality may appear to be very real in your life but it operates only in the physical and mental realms, not in the Spiritual Realm where all is one. God is Above the Opposites. By always placing the all-powerful, all-knowing Great Spirit of which you are a part behind your every thought, statement and action, and by always focusing on the good, even when things appear to be going bad, then in time you will rise above the Law of Polarity.

5. The Law of Rhythm (Mutable): The fifth of the seven Universal Laws tells us that everything flows, out and in; everything has its tides; all things rise and fall; the pendulum-swing manifests in everything; the measure of the swing to the right is the measure of the swing to the left; rhythm compensates. It is the second of the mutable Universal Laws and means that the pendulum swings in everything. This principle can be seen in operation in the waves of the ocean, in the rise and fall of the greatest empires, in business cycles, in

the swaying of your thoughts from being positive to negative and in your personal successes and failures. In accordance with this Law, when anything reaches a point of culmination then the backward swing begins almost unnoticeably until such time that any forward movement has been totally reversed, then the forward movement begins again and the process is repeated. Rising Above the Law of Rhythm: Is to transcend the swing of the pendulum, you must become aware of the subtle start of the backward movement in any of your endeavors whether it be to improve your health, your finances, your relationships or any goal you may set in motion. When you feel the Law start to draw you back do not become fearful or discouraged. Instead, knowing that you are one with the Omnipotent Universal Mind for which nothing is impossible, keep your thoughts focused on your outcome and fight to remain positive no matter how far back this Law pulls you. Even if your efforts meet with failure, find comfort that by virtue of this very same Law, the upward motion must start again. In time, your perseverance will be rewarded as the backward movements become less negative relative to your previous backward swings and you raise yourself higher.

6. The Law of Cause and Effect (Mutable): The sixth of the seven Universal Laws tells us that every cause has its effect; every effect has its cause. In accordance with this Law, every effect you see in your outside or physical world has a very specific cause which has its origin in your inner or mental world. This is the essence of thought power. Every one of your thoughts, words or actions sets a specific effect in motion which will come to materialize over time. To become the master of your destiny, you must master your mind for everything in your reality is a mental creation. Know that there is nothing like chance or luck. They are simply terms used by humanity in ignorance of this Law.

Your Intentions are Instantly Created: The Law of Cause and Effect applies on all three planes of existence the Spiritual,

111

the mental and the physical. The difference is that on the Spiritual plane cause and effect are instantaneous such that they appear inseparable, whereas on the other planes our concept of time and space creates a time lag between the cause and the eventual effect. Know that when you focus on your chosen goals with intention using creative visualization that which you want to create in the physical world is automatically manifested in the Spiritual world, and with perseverance, practice and continued concentrated thought it will also come to materialize in the physical world. That what you think about comes about. Again think positive!!

7. The Law of Gender: The last of the seven Universal Laws tells us that Gender is in everything; everything has its masculine and feminine principles. This mutable Universal Law is evident throughout creation in the so-called opposite sexes found not only in human beings but also in plants, minerals, electrons and magnetic poles to name a few. Everything and everyone contains both masculine and feminine elements. Among the outward expressions of feminine qualities are love, patience, intuition and gentleness and of masculine qualities are energy, self reliance, logic and intellect. Know that within every woman lay all the latent qualities of a man and within every man those of a woman. When you know this you will know what it means to be complete. When you know this, you then possess the Magic Key and the doors open. "Mind is the Master-power that molds and makes, and we are Mind, and ever more you take the Tool of Thought, and shaping what you will, brings forth a thousand joys, or a thousand ills. He thinks in secret and it comes to pass; Environment is but his looking-glass." *James Allen*

The Law of Attraction as Part of the Equation: You will notice that the Law of Attraction is not specifically mentioned as one of the seven Universal Laws. This is not to diminish its importance but rather to highlight it because the Law of Attraction is the basic Law of the Universe which runs through all the seven Universal Laws. It holds everything together. It is through the knowledge of the Law of Attraction that one can rise above the mutable Laws of Polarity and Rhythm and gain a better understanding of each of the seven Universal Laws.

In accordance with the Law of Attraction, you attract into your life those things, circumstances and conditions that correspond with the nature of your dominant, habitual thoughts and beliefs, both conscious and subconscious. Every area of your life, including your health, your finances and all of your relationships, are influenced by this great Universal Law that "like attracts like". This is the basic Law of the Universe.

WHAT FREQUENCY ARE YOU ON

Everything, including yourself, your thoughts and anything else you may or may not want to experience, is pure energy vibrating at different frequencies. The basic premise of the Law of Attraction is that like energy attracts like energy. You attract to yourself that which you are in vibrational harmony with, not that which you long for or even deserve. Your dominant frequency is determined by your dominant mental attitude, which itself is determined by your habitual thoughts and beliefs. Simply put, a positive mental attitude attracts positive experiences and circumstances while a negative mental attitude attracts those conditions that we deem negative or unwanted. To consciously attract anything you want to experience into your life, you must need it, not simply desire, that which you want. To need something is to have a purpose for it and when something has a big enough purpose; it becomes a necessity rather than a luxury. You are able to attract anything you need to yourself because you are already connected to everything, seen and unseen. Nothing and no one is separate from you. The sense of separation we experience in the physical world is created by the way our five senses interpret this infinite sea of vibrating energy. You are one with the One Universal Mind from which all things become manifest. The creative power of your thoughts is limitless within in the realm of that which is possible. Unbeknown to most people their life is being run in strict accordance with a set of deeply ingrained subconscious programs that they did not consciously choose in the first place. To make matters worse, it is argued that most of these programs were locked in place by the age of around 10. This is because a child's ability to reason is limited compared to that of an adult. Children can absorb new information with great superiority, it also means that a child's subconscious mind is more easily programmed if left open to unchecked negative messages. By the time a child reaches their teenage years its reasoning abilities have significantly developed and so they are able to consciously choose what messages to accept. Anything that happened in your childhood is engrained with in your subconscious and may need to be healed. The way to consciously override these negative programs is by learning to access your all knowing higher self. To consciously attract that which you choose into your life you must learn to bring the energy of your thoughts and hence your actions into vibration harmony with the essence of your choice, be it perfect health, success, abundance, true love or anything else. Creative visualization is the basic technique by which you can positively and effectively reprogram your subconscious mind and so begin to attract to yourself those things and circumstances that you consciously choose. Life is so much more about the process of growth, and taking the much needed steps forward, at times falling backwards, always getting back up and leaning from the lessons. The most direct path forward that reconnect to your higher purpose and into the true light is the process of healing, releasing and relearning. This healing often make you peel back the layers until your authentic self is revealed. In this center you know and experience your value, your light, and infinite LOVE. Some experience require you heal your inner child, that part of you that may not have received the love or light you needed then. This can create feelings of worthlessness, insecurity, feeling unloved and lost. These feelings remain hidden only to be exposed in your later years. These past pains must be addressed and healed. Listen you made it this far don't let the past hold on to you any longer. It is time to let it go. You hold the key to a better future all you have to do is step through the door.

Thought power is the key to creating your reality. Everything you perceive in the physical world has its origin in the invisible inner world of your thoughts and beliefs. To become Master of your destiny you must learn to control the nature of your thoughts that are negative. By doing this you will be able to attract into your life that which you intend to have and experience as you come to know the truth that your thoughts create your reality. James Allen stated that" circumstances do not make a man, they reveal him" Your thoughts are alive. Each time you entertain a specific thought, you emit a very specific, corresponding frequency or energy vibration. If we obsess over negative or unwanted thoughts we give power to them, like the saying goes what we resist persist, simple try to replace them when they arise. Replace the negative with a positive thought until it holds no power. We live it, learn from it, be it, love it then we Master it. Make a vision board, see where you are on the board and place ideas on it that you wish to attract to yourself, then allow the energies to bring to you that which you have envisioned. Watch you life change for the better, Remember "As we will it so shall it Be". And so it is.

Know that by taking responsibility for your life, you also grant yourself the power to change it. The bottom line is that you attract to yourself that which you think about (a lot). There is no judgment call involved about whether a particular thought is "good" or "bad" or whether its corresponding circumstance is "deserved" or "undeserved". The Law of Attraction is neutral. It does not judge, punish or reward. It simply serves to bring like energy together. You submit your criteria via your habitual thoughts and beliefs and it brings you your perfect vibratory match, every time.

You do not have to learn to work with or apply the Law of Attraction. Being a Universal Law, it is already working perfectly in your life, whether or not you understand or accept it, and it never ceases to operate. Your primary goal is to adjust your mental attitude by changing your predominant thoughts and beliefs while creating a need or purpose for that which you want to create in your life. To become the master of your life, you must master your mind, not the Law of Attraction. It is already a master unto itself. The Law of Attraction is a major stepping stone in that direction but do not be misled into believing that it is the only one.

To experience profound transformation in any area of your life, you must first become conscious of the truth that the circumstances of your outside world correspond precisely with the nature of your inner world and are attracted to you all you need to do is work on yourself. Another aspect of your consciousness is your higher consciousness. It is also known as the super-conscious mind, your higher self. It is the least understood and least accessed aspect of consciousness because it does not belong to the physical or mental realm. Its domain is the Spiritual realm. It is the" you" that is All-Knowing and All-Powerful and is the same in kind as the One Universal Mind. It is the "You" that is beyond not only the physical world but also the emotions of your mental world. Your higher self does not distinguish between good or bad, wrong or right, happy or sad not because it is unable to but because it has no need to. It is you that knows only balance. It is you that is only true Love. It is the eternal observer. It is absolute stillness. We are made in the likeness of our Mother/Father God/Goddess.

Your higher consciousness knows that the physical, outside world you experience as your reality "is an illusion", as Einstein told us. It knows that your circumstances, whether wanted or unwanted, are simply a reflection of your inner world which itself is a product of your thoughts. It knows that your reality is the mirror that allows your consciousness to experience itself. In this knowledge, your higher consciousness is always still and at peace. It observes your success and your failure, your joy and your pain, your light and your dark and is not disturbed by anything. Ultimately, it knows that it is all a day dream. The Universal Laws of Mentalism and Vibration tell us that all is mind and that the entire Universe is vibrating energy. There is no separation in mind there is no dividing line. This also means that higher consciousness is not something you need to acquire or look for outside of yourself. You already possess it. All you need to do is become consciously aware of it and learn to access it. Tap into this energy every day and let it guide you on your journey. Repeat to yourself through the day I Am a Soul on a journey back to itself.

Most people are unaware of their higher consciousness. Most people operate in a sleepy-like state even at the conscious level, unwittingly allowing all the messages with which they are bombarded to be passed down to their subconscious mind for programming. This ultimately leaves their lives in full control of their subconscious, which in this state, is doing little more than running a bunch of programmers' that itself has no idea whether or not they are beneficial. If we are not consciously directing our existence, then it places us in a position no superior to that of plants. Before attempting to consciously root out and replace the negative programs embedded in your subconscious mind, your first step is to change how you think. Decide now to place your conscious mind on guard at the door of your subconscious mind. Decide now to allow only empowering, positive, nurturing messages to pass through that door. Decide now to hand over the direction of your conscious mind to your Higher Self and in so doing become the silent observer of your life. This is the step to start reprogramming your mind: Learn to be the unshakable witness to your old patterns and behaviors, knowing that they are simply illusions; the programs of a previously misguided subconscious mind. This is your time to let your higher self-take the wheel. Know that through meditation, creative visualization and the repetition of positive affirmations, these old patterns will in time be replaced by new empowering behaviors and beliefs which although just as much an illusion, will ensure your success rather than your failure. By allowing your Higher Self to lead you, you open yourself up to a world of miracles in which you can consciously create your reality.

Consciousness forms the foundation of the power of your mind. The subconscious mind cannot reason, the conscious mind is reason, and higher consciousness need not reason. In other words, where your conscious mind is the commander and your subconscious mind the subject, your higher consciousness is your kingdom. It is in reference to your higher self that Jesus Christ said "the Kingdom of Heaven is within". When you learn to consciously program your subconscious mind under the protection of your conscious mind and the direction of your higher self, you will see miraculous transformation in all areas of your life.

The cosmos loves testing us often time placing us in challenging alignments, apparently trying to throw us off-target or discover who amongst us has super-human abilities to suffer setbacks with poise and then get off the mat again to gain victories over stagnation and fear. We have all been tested at one time or another, we are not victims we become victorious!!

THE HIGHER ASPECTS OF THE HUMAN SYSTEM

We exist in Dimensions 1-3 these levels of Earth from its core to the surface. The fourth dimension is the realm of the collective thought that bridges the physical and the unseen world, and the firth thru the ninth dimension is celestial. Our collective goal is to shift our frequencies within the next few years (2008 to 2018) and beyond into the higher dimensions. Many of us have been set on this path years ago as the first wave of light and energy. The rising frequencies of Planet Earth now makes it easier through the high frequency processes, for us to clear the pathways that have been blocked in our grids and open us up to the higher layers. An opportunity we have waited for a long, long time. Insights into ones character and lifestyle and emotional makeup are all determined according to your astrological alignment. We are all born with a certain destiny in this life. There is a life purpose for every Soul that comes into existence. Fate occurs when events happen as intended.

Each Soul is born of unique features. As a Soul travels through many life cycles it picks up different attributes from the places in which it has existed before. The Soul is that culmination of values and experiences that have to do with the identity of the individual that survives the life in the flesh. It goes on to a higher level of perfection through the process of Ascension. Ascension is what we all strive for as we incarnate into human form. The values and experiences that were born from the Spirit and which found a channel of expression in the individual through the discovery of truth, beauty, goodness survives and becomes the true essence and identity and personality of the ascending Soul or the "Real You". Throughout our lives the Spirit has prepared your mind for these survival experiences and begins the process of harvesting those experiences in preparation for the next phase of your ascension. There is a balance between what Spirit can inspire the individual to accomplish and what the free will of the individual will allow. If the student is willing to embrace the values of truth, beauty and goodness then Spirit has a wider channel in which to work. As we open to this energy we see that life takes on a whole new meaning. It is often a long and sometimes a difficult process for Divinity to communicate with the nature of the human. Some are just starting out on the journey from imperfection to perfection. The Spirit has to compete with the distractions of life and find a way to spiritualize the mind. Through this process of Spiritualization, the mind, and Spirit plants seeds along the path that will hopefully sprout and grow into an awareness of Divinity at work in the life of the individual seeking Ascension. Once the connection is made, the channel of Divine expression opens up and the Soul really progresses and flourishes and begins to seek perfection. Once this desire begins the Soul or the individualized part seeks union with the whole. It is upon realization of this desire for God-likeness that the individual is born of the Spirit. The partnership of God and man/woman has then been consummated and the eternal adventure begins. We then feel very blessed knowing that we are awake and indeed able to actively live in this state of awareness. You become aware of the Divine relationship in which you have entered. Within your essence you find your other half and merge into the oneness vibration of union with your Twin Flame. Your life mission will naturally connect to that of your Twin Flame as you shine together and the light of unconditional love and union. Remember the promise you have made throughout many lifetimes to Shine the light of Divine Oneness and do it with each other. There can be no fear in the partnership of the Twin Flames as the energy of love is the only thing that is there. As the Twin Flames unite it will send a ripple out to the Universe of unconditional love which increases the love vibration and your role is to feel your amazingness. All of our relationships have brought you to the here and now and you are ready to receive and ready to give equally. You know the way of Divine partnership. It is to love without expectation with a complete acceptance and open arms. Your then become divinely designed to accomplish that which you were created to BE.

And so it was morning as God stood before his 12 children and into each of them he planted the seed of human life. One by One each child stepped forward to receive his appointed gift.

To you Aries I give the first seed that you might have honor of planting it. That for every seed you plant one million more will multiply in your hand. You will not have time to see the seed grow, for everything you plant creates more that must be planted. You will be the first to penetrate the soil of people's minds with my Idea. But it is not your job to nourish the idea nor to question it. Your life is action, and the only action I ascribe to you is to begin making others aware of my creation. For your good work I give you the virtue of **Self-Esteem.** Quietly Aries stepped back to his place.

To you Taurus I give the power to build the seed into substance. Your job is a great one requiring patience, for you must finish all that has been started, or the seeds will be wasted to the wind. You are not to question nor change your mind in the middle, nor to depend on others for what I ask you to do. For this I give you the gift of **Strength,** Use it wisely. And Taurus stepped back into place.

To you Gemini I give the questions without the answers, so that you may bring to all an understanding of what people see around them. You will never know why people speak or listen but in your quest for the answer you will find the gift of **Knowledge.** And Gemini stepped back into place.

To you Cancer I ascribe the task of teaching people about emotion. My idea is for you to cause them laughter and tears so that all they see and think develops fullness from inside. For this I give you the gift of **Family** that your fullness may multiply. And Cancer stepped back into place

To you Leo I give the job of displaying my creation in all its brilliance to the world. But you must be careful of pride and always remember that it is my creation, not yours. For if you forget this people will scorn you. There is much joy in the job I give you if you but do it well. For this you are the have the gift of **Honor.** And Leo stepped back into place.

To you Virgo I ask for an examination of all that humankind had done with my creation. You are to scrutinize their ways sharply and remind them of their errors, so that through them my creation may be perfected. For this I give you the gift of **Purity of Thought**. And Virgo stepped back into place.

To you Libra I give the mission of service, that humans will be mindful of their duties to others. That they may learn cooperation, as well as the ability to reflect on the other side of their actions. I will put you everywhere there is discord and for your efforts I will give you the gift of **Love**. And Libra stepped back in to place.

To you Scorpio I give a very difficult task. You will have the ability to know the minds of the other people, but I do not permit you to speak about what you learn. Many times you will be pained by what you see and in your pain you will turn away from me and forget that it is not I but will come to know them as animals and will wrestle so much with the animal instincts in yourself that you will lose your way but when you finally come back to me, Scorpio, I have for you the supreme gift of **Purpose**. And Scorpio stepped back into place.

To you Sagittarius I ask that you make people laugh, for amidst them misunderstand my idea they become bitter. Through laughter you are to give people hope, and through hope turn their eyes back to me. You will touch many lives if but a moment, and you will know restlessness in every life you touch. To you Sagittarius I give the gift of **Infinite abundance** that you may spread wide enough to reach every corner of darkness and bring it light. And Sagittarius stepped back into place.

To you Capricorn I ask the toil of your brow, that you might teach people to work. Your task is not an easy one, for you will feel all of humankind's labors on your shoulders, but the yoke of your burdens contains **Responsibility** of your Brothers and sisters which I put into your hands. And Capricorn stepped back into place

To you Aquarius I give the concept of the future that people might see other possibilities. But for this gift you may have to endure loneliness. For turning people's eyes to new possibilities I give the gift of **Freedom** that in your liberty you may continue to serve humankind wherever they need you. And Aquarius stopped back into place.

To you Pisces I give the last difficulty task of all, I ask you to collect all the worlds' sorrows and return them to Me. Your tears are to be ultimately My tears. The sorrow you will absorb is the effect of people's misunderstanding of my idea, but you are to give them compassion that they may try again. For this the most difficult task of all, I give you the greatest gift of all. You will be one of my 12 children to understand me. This gift of **understanding** is for you Pisces; for when you try to spread it to humankind they will not listen And Pieces stepped back into place.

And the children left, each determined to do the job best that they might receive these gifts. But none fully understanding the task or gift, and when they returned puzzled God said: You each believe that the other gifts are better. Therefore, I will allow you to trade and for the moment each child was elated as they considered all the possibilities of this new mission. But God smiled as he said "You will return to me many times asking to be relieved of your mission and each time I will grant your wish. You will go through countless incarnations before you complete the original mission I have prescribed for you. I give you countless time in which to do it, but only when it is done can you be with ME.

As we evolve we know that we all have been given many gifts and there has also been many challenges we have to face. It is unfortunate that so many of us live our lives in fear and never give ourselves that chance to fully express ourselves or explore our gifts and untapped potential. It is the Spirit within that seeks this channel of expression, and for most it is suppressed by fear of judgment and disapproval by those who are not themselves conscious of their own true identity and who stay hidden behind the cloak of illusion set securely in the molds of their mortal conditioning. **He who knows others is learned, he who knows himself is wise– Lao-tse.** The quest for self knowledge and personal identity has been a pursuit for humans for millennium. Why do certain Beings commit their lives to spreading their wings and others clip their wings with despair. The answer is fear and judgment.

The expression of your true self is that ability to be without inhibition, without hiding who you really are to the world. Your inner desires become known to all and you release the tension of holding back the fears of disapproval, because you know deep down that this is your destiny to speak your peace and shed the cloak of unreality that you might have been living with most of your life. Finding that peace and freedom within is beyond all spoken words. This is a feeling that you have come full circle and a new beginning of a greater more complete personality that is progressing and moving inward and onward toward perfection in the Universe.

It is now the time for you to really live for your tomorrows are uncertain and you may not get a chance again in this life to do and to be as you would like. This life we have on the worlds of time and space is one of the most important developmental lives we will live, and for those who live life to the fullest, without fear, expressing who they really are, will find the most joy and the greatest satisfaction one can experience. Those who are living the life of their dreams are not dreaming, but are experiencing what is possible by releasing the fear and shedding the cloak of the illusion that was once their reality. There are no real limits to what can be accomplished by moving out of the cozy cocoon and into the brave new world of manifesting your deepest desires. It is true and available to all, if only you would believe. The law of Attraction states, we must ASK<BELIEVE<AND RECEIVE!!

Spirit is here to assist you in making your desires a reality, for the Universe was designed to respond to your co-creative powers. Spirit seeks expression in your life, and desires for you to live life in a way that is the most beneficial to your personality development, and so by living true to yourself, you are releasing the expression of Spirit and allowing the potentials of deity to move through you to create truth, beauty, and goodness in the Universe. Allow yourself to have this experience for those who let go and let God, will find they will never look back and will know for the first time what power truly lives within. This force of pure being and the Soul Essence within each one of us represents the unfolding energy of wholeness in human nature. Clearly Christ Energy is a Divine Energy that brings and blends together the essence of Soul and Spirit within all of us. As seekers of truth, we make a distinction between the Cosmic Christ and the manifestation of the force that descends and unfolds through the channel of consciousness in an Enlightened Being becoming an individualized expression of the Cosmic Christ. This represents an enlightened and self-realized expression of pure Being. This level of enlightenment can only manifest in a purified and well prepared vehicle, in which consciousness is awakened fully. By purified vehicle, I mean the purified physical, psychic and Spiritual bodies in which the energy and characteristics of the force of the Cosmic Christ become apparent to you. This force is an active and universal power house that functions through human vehicles forever. Therefore nothing gets lost, and the vehicle and characteristics of Master Jesus still continue functioning through all enlightened and realized human Beings. The same principle is applied to all Enlightened Beings. This needs to be awakened and activated by consciousness. The essence of the Cosmic Christ is innate to all sentient beings and part of our Spiritual blueprint. JESUS THE CHRIST represents a perfected vehicle that has existed, and still continues to exist eternally, since it represents one of the perfected Expressions of Primordial Wisdom. The process of manifesting Primordial Wisdom opening a channel and vehicle in which a high level of initiation will take place, and this is a process of awakening and of enlightenment. The energy of the Cosmic Christ exists everywhere and remains the same, for everyone, since they are made of the same pure essence of Primordial Wisdom and therefore are ALIVE and ACTIVE expressions of the same unique source.

The Model image within each one of us is hidden within consciousness. When consciousness awakens in a seeker, then the Presence of the Model image appears. It is through the purification of the psyche and the enfoldment of the inner process that the expression of this image becomes clearer and is revealed. The meaning of this model image should be understood intuitively by the genuine seeker because this symbolic expressions should clarify the understanding that it is not the ego personality and the intellect as such that choose this image discovering its corresponding to your creators vison of you.

We also realize that the world of the psyche belongs to the world of duality, since the mirror of the psyche transfers and projects, images, ideals, intuitions, which are reflections of the God vision. This unfolds the process of awakening and its vehicle, the Model image is the ground on which the awakening process takes place. It is the purified psyche the mirror of the Soul in which ideal images appear. Our ego consciousness experiences and now trusts the unfolding inner process of the Soul that Divine Grace reveals to us and in which the old self has to enter and die so that The Holy Spirit can descend to awake and manifest Christ Consciousness.

When this is truly understood and put into practice, you then will become an awaken one, meaning a pure container in which the Essence of the Cosmic Christ will fully manifest, just as it did with the Master, when the Spirit of Christ emerges completely in our level of consciousness, we will have realized that the Christ Essence and Spirit are the REAL part of who we are, the silent Witness the Un manifest "I" that belongs to the level of unity and wholeness. This level within us that has no reflection, because it is part of everything.

In terms of our physical universe, and the world in which we have our being, the Christ or Cosmic Consciousness represents the healing medium, the vehicle that sets in motion the Spiritual blueprint or Spiritual DNA in our own limited level of consciousness. We go from unconsciousness to self-consciousness and from self-consciousness to Cosmic Consciousness. These are evolutionary steps on the ladder of CONSCIOUSNESS. These steps unfold different stages and planes of existence that allow Consciousness to take form and express whatever it needs to commune and manifest.

The ego is formed so the UNCONSCIOUSNESS of BEING becomes CONSCIOUS of BEING. To begin with the ego needs to believe that it is a separated subject from the rest of creation, it is still far from understanding its own function and remains ignorant of its own Source. It feels as though it is separate from everything. We, as self-conscious seekers are living in a world of duality, a world created by our mental and emotional patterns, a world in which we feel alienated and divided between me and you, between good and evil. As a Spiritual seeker, the ego's level of self-consciousness unfolds an inner process of inquiry into the nature of being and gradually it discovers its own uncorrupted nature, which is unveiled with the appearance of the Seal of the "Anointed One" or Christ Consciousness.

This Divine Nature allows the "ego" the realization that it is nothing more than a projection and a shadow of Christ or Cosmic Consciousness functioning in duality, the ego self represents the stage when the Blueprint of Christ or Cosmic Consciousness is still in its unconscious and ignorant state. When initiation happens, the self-consciousness is baptized with Fire and Light and it becomes the ANOINTED One, the One who knows that all forms of creation are God's dreams, thoughts, ideas and children. When by the Grace of God, the process of awakening happens in a seeker, then self-consciousness turns gradually into Cosmic Consciousness and the seeker becomes an anointed relationship of the Divine Light. The seeker becomes an enlightened being working from within the inner spheres where the Spirit of Christ Consciousness dwells. Initiation reveals the actual Light that was for eons inactive and latent in our Spiritual blueprint and DNA. When the hour of our redemption happens, then, this Light unfolds the AWAKENED ONE in the flesh. And through the power of the HOLY SPIRIT, awakened seekers are transformed into Holy Grails, the purified vehicles for the Spirit to function properly as Christ Consciousness in the world of duality. This is a great mystery. It means the level of the "ego self" assumes a new relationship with the Source of Being which is the Center of the Absolute God, the Father of us all. CHRIST Energy unfolds the BODY OF LIGHT: The sanctified body working and witnessing in harmony with Christ or Cosmic Consciousness. We can see that it's impossible for us to jump suddenly from a world of duality into a world of Pure Being. We know that the Law of Duality governs our daily life, which is the law of observer/observed. By keeping ourselves in that state of separation and division, we persist unconsciously in keeping ourselves apart from our own Center of pure Being. So, if we focus solely on the external rather than going within ourselves to our Center of Pure Being, we will find it impossible to find that Center, since the presence of the unknown God is the same center as our Center of Pure Being. When you are in touch with your Center of pure Being, you learn to weave and surf via the subtle and sublime energies existing within that intimate center. By this Spiritual and subtle process, your ego is attracted to your Center of pure Being. Then, an indescribable level of consciousness opens up, harmonizing and blending your ego with your Center of pure Being to fulfill us, God devours us and feeds us at the same time. Your body is indeed your temple, so by blending your ego with your Center of pure Being, your temple becomes whole. As a result of these transformations, you are made a perfect witness to your own awakening since, from that moment, your consciousness enters a new dimension, your ego no longer living a separate existence. You are reborn, and your will effortlessly expresses God's will in the miracle of your ordinary, everyday life.

We are here, immersed in the heart of Omnipresence. We are the ones that change because only consciousness can move and change the energies in and around us. It is indeed consciousness that harmonizes blends and transforms our perceptions. We are made of pure energy. Different Spiritual energies pour into our psyche all the time, but some people remain unaware of them until a direct mystical experience brings you face to face with an aspect of the Unknown God. This aspect reveals and reflects in us our own Angelic nature. This shows us that unless we look into the mirror of our own purified heart, we will never be sensitive and change into our own Angelic essence. It is only after we cooperate in the purification process of our psyche that the muses pour upon us their gifts. With each Divine reflection emerging from within the darkness of our own unconsciousness a new level of consciousness appears in the light of our conscious mind. A new reflection manifests itself within our heart. This reflection emphasizes the fact that to understand something Spiritual, we must project or receive an image, even if this image reflects an abstract idea we must be moved and excited from within by what we see; so as to attract to ourselves and learn to blend with the Divine. Each image represents a level of consciousness. Allow yourselves to be magnetically pulled in by the Divine image that attracts our psyche any expression or wording that expresses our own understanding of this unknown presence within our own Center of being. There is a hidden path opening up from within and this path belongs to your inner and Divine Self. The seeker must desire with all its heart to succeed in the quest and persevere until the end of the process. This means until the end of our incarnation and when the time comes and we are ready to let the Divine Light appear in you, this energy will take the most appropriate Divine face for you, to attract and transform us with LOVE from within our being. To receive such Divine gift, we must first learn to let go and discard the old ego patterns, the old faces and models, so as to be able to be reborn anew.

As personalities, we do change and with those changes our traits change too. As we purify our psyche from the complicated stories and excuses that we make up, we enter slowly into a new-world, unveiling subtly a Divine face. This now projects an imprint into our own face like a hologram and in this way our level of consciousness is affected by these subtle energies. Our traits and attitudes soften and mature. They become more beautiful, and therefore more attractive and magnetic.

We also understand however, that there is an important Spiritual work going on within our psyche. These are subtle alchemical operations that must remain sealed in the darkness of an inner being for our own protection. If we are to be called, our first step on this path is to learn to OBSERVE ourselves. Generally, we find excuses to cover our own mistakes, faults, weaknesses. Only on that level of spirituality will you learn to let go of our egotistic patterns and experience what is meant to vanish completely into the Center of God's OMNIPOTENCE, and OMNIPRESENCE. We understand that one must desire to climb the ladder of Light within himself so as to reach higher levels of Consciousness. This is guided by the inspiration, impulses and gifts given to you through the HOLY SPIRIT. You must acquire the appropriate level of consciousness allowing you to receive the inspiration and guidance of the Divine wisdom, one must first free oneself of all the chains of the ego and abandon them one by one releasing them into the Source.

Spiritual psychology teach us to be vigilant, alert and conscious of our own mistakes, faults, and weaknesses. We all create around us a personal "STORY", meaning that we skillfully make up excuses for our own shortcomings, accusing others, or blaming instead of looking objectively into our own cynicism. We should understand that faults are in themselves distortions of qualities. The fact is that Spiritual awakening cannot happen unless we become conscious of our own patterns and have a strong need to change them. As we enter the Labyrinth of our journey there is only one way in and it is up to you whether you enter or not.

The role that our IMAGINATION plays in the creation of Spiritual and sacred Ideas is very important. We could say that the role or mission that our imagination takes for us is to make visible and understandable different manifestations of unknown, uncreated, un-manifested impulses we receive. These impulses will only occur when we are ready and well prepared. This process is indeed a lifelong Spiritual project that demands our entire dedication. This project comprises the purification of our astral and mental bodies and a simplification of the way we live. That is why a wise mystic knows that God is nearer to us than we are to ourselves and therefore, God is a better judge of our personal needs.

When we are touched by Grace, our ego unceasingly finds itself being purified of all past misconceptions and mistakes, and gradually learns to integrate with its lighter Divine counterpart which is the Soul. This delicate and refined blending of ego and Soul manifests in our everyday consciousness as an unclouded, bright and clear presence, guiding our every step from within. This presence within our being is the awareness of the I Am. The emergence of this I Am Presence within our consciousness makes us suddenly see life differently, so clearly that it looks as if we have instantaneously entered a new world. From the moment the I Am Presence directly animates our consciousness, our life is never the same, even though to others and the outside world, things seem unchanged. In reality, however, nothing remains the same, as if a Divine hand gently pushes us forward, accompanying and encouraging us silently from within to adopt the right and suitable path. When we learn to trust the I Am Presence absolutely and follow its directive to the point of letting God's hand lead us wherever He wants us to go, purification proceeds in earnest. From that moment on, we feel a sudden release of our burdens, duties, and obligations. We then become aware that we have become a rightful follower of God's infinite love and will.

The I Am Presence within us is Source in action in our world. Feelings of liberation and joy enter an awakened ego because, at last, it becomes aware of its real function, which is to become an empty receptacle ready to be filled with the Divine Presence. When the desires and needs of the ego are unconditionally and completely drawn to, and attuned to, the vibration of the Soul. Then, God's will becomes the ego's will, too, manifesting fulfillment and happiness into our lives and the lives of others. This transformation remains a delicate and mysterious process, as it is not of our doing, but the doing of the Soul and the Grace of God.

When God's reflection moves in our individual Soul, it enlivens our ego, too. Signs and evidence of this potent presence begin to appear in our everyday life, impacting our consciousness as events become deep and meaningful, and affect the core of our being. These everyday occurrences and incidences are initiated by the Divine hand of God and our receptiveness does the rest. However, we must experience for ourselves the incredible and moving events in profound silence, awe, humility, and amazement. From then on, we know that we ourselves have become the never-ending quest. Gradually we begin to understand that these miracles originate in ourselves, and are indeed projections of our own I Am Presence.

Real transformation sets in our being, shifting completely our sense of perception; our whole world is altered and yet nothing changes. The I Am Presence is responsible for these transformations, and we are changed forever. When the process of opening up to the energy of the Soul begins in us, our level of consciousness attunes itself completely with the I Am Presence and progressively masters the method of embodying the loving and exquisite energy of integration and oneness. It lets itself flow and breathe through us, bringing with it a new level of consciousness marked by a lack of personal judgment or reaction to anything of any kind. Therefore, the ego becomes the vessel of the Soul, allowing the I Am Presence to pour its qualities and powers into our consciousness. We then become free of our past shortcomings, and become self-reliant in carrying our Divine mission. When we learn to live in the present, we are awake, living and experiencing life through this transparent and magnetic presence. We are then guided and attracted to the right places at the right times, and we live each instant with new wonderment and awe.

With the simplification and clarification of our life, a new kind of reality appears before us, and a new order of existence unfolds its truth in our being. In a strange way, this new existence fills our whole consciousness with new kinds of vibrant perceptions and thus all phenomena and events in our life are suddenly perceived as being new and yet friendly, surprising and yet humbling, moving and loving, sad and joyous at the same time. We feel at home everywhere, and nothing seems foreign.

The I Am Presence in us is also the center of Cosmic Consciousness in which the whole cosmos and creation have their foundation. This follows since truth unfolds from within our being; from within the center of the I Am, we are in harmony with our own inner center, allowing the Divine Presence in us is also eternally awake. It is from this point of the I Am that our Soul merges with the Universal Soul.

The more we are allowed to integrate and unify with the Divine Source, the more Cosmic Consciousness manifests in our life. As the center core of who we really are is infinite, our ego becomes simply a tool, a limiting one at that, but still an important vessel, as it represents also the purified ego, the Grail which is our sacred communion with God. We certainly need the ego, for a consciousness without ego means simply a purified one in which the Soul and I Am Presence are completely living the ordinary and extraordinary life. Each one of us is unique, we all strive for happiness and contentment, but few realize that we have a choice between two paths, one leading to the empowerment of the ego, and the other to the empowerment of God's Presence in us. We must choose. This is law! Once the choice has been made, a set of energies unfold their powers and qualities, influencing our tendencies and reactions in life that automatically lead us to one path or the other. The Soul can guide the ego only when the ego has made its choice, and has an unquenchable thirst and desire to unify with it. The choice is yours. Esoteric teachings tell us that once on the path, there is no turning back. The wind blows where it wants, so why question the direction it chooses?

Consciousness has two functions. Firstly, it reflects our own understanding and interpretation of creation. This helps us to develop our inner potential, innate wisdom, and individuality. Secondly, it shows us that consciousness will always remain a mystery, and the realization of which is our real mission in life. Consciousness itself takes all kinds of forms in creation and yet we know that, as an inherent part of the Essence of the Unknown God Himself, consciousness can never be created but consciousness grows and transforms us, we are inhabited by consciousness. Our role in creation is to be a vessel, and to receive those mysterious energies that consciousness bestows upon us the gifts of mind and love. We are not the creators of these essences but the receivers of them, and our mission is to incarnate and manifest them in our lives. When we become the center of these mysteries, then, we are no longer just human. We become an awakened consciousness reflecting the whole of creation in ourselves, and when we experience that portion of consciousness, then we realize that consciousness, through us, is also the source of this creation. Then we live on both levels of consciousness at the same. Initiations opening in the seeker a genuine and true dimension of what a real quest and initiation is all about. As seekers, we unfold the quest in ourselves, since we are both the quest and the path. The goal of initiation is the direct awakening of our consciousness to a higher level. Initiation also reveals to us that while we are awakening a new level of consciousness in the world, we are also letting go of our previous one. When the student is ready, the Master appears, so, strange encounters and inexplicable events take place in our lives when we are open to receive initiation. It can happen suddenly in a most ordinary and natural way, and rupture our consciousness, helping our Soul to intervene and awaken us to our true Self.

Consciousness could be transformed by any event in our life, an initiator or catalyst is needed, an awakened, enlightened Soul who knows what kind of initiation each seeker needs, a Master in whom the seeker has complete trust. Some seekers need to be handled subtly, others more roughly, but what counts is the opening that initiation brings. Consciousness enhances and expands throughout our life. No two of us are the same; each of us experiences life differently, since experiences are the result of the various conditions and unique circumstances created just for us. First and foremost, we must learn to observe our own thoughts and emotions, so as to understand why we behave and react the way we do. This kind of inner work and self-analysis unfolds and develops our Spiritual intelligence, or intuition. We come to know ourselves; indeed, through these subtle operations and transformations, we gradually awaken in ourselves refined psychic and Spiritual faculties, our inner senses opening for us the inner gates of consciousness where pure knowledge and wisdom reside. The journey into the depths of self, begins with the adventure of consciousness; we do that to experience and understand that we, as consciousness, are mirrors reflecting the whole of creation.

We are not just mirrors; we must also discover that we are also centers of creation. The goal is to reach our own mystery, the core and heart center of our own Being and to unite with the presence of the unmanifest light within. This means that we must go beyond the mirror of reflections of consciousness, to a place where our ordinary level of consciousness is transformed into the light of the Soul itself. This is where the subtle impulses concerning the mysteries are revealed and known.

This mystery cannot be understood or explained; it can only be lived in a fully awakened consciousness in the present moment; in other words, when our self-consciousness is fully awaken and living in the now! This means that we have successfully united our self-conscious state with Soul consciousness or Cosmic Consciousness in ordinary, everyday circumstances that transforms how we experience life. Through the effects of Cosmic Consciousness, the permanent seed of our Soul awakens and unfolds its Spiritual qualities. Together, they both energize in us the presence of our Soul entity; they make known and clarify for us our inner archetypal models, our blueprints, the parts in us that can never be manifested independently, since they are Divine ideas and ideals that we must learn to integrate and manifest within ourselves here on our ordinary level of consciousness.

Unfolding Cosmic Consciousness

The Soul entity activates within our seed or blueprint, two complementary, co-existing energies, one active, positive, and masculine, and the other passive, nurturing, and feminine. These components of our Soul entity are complementary to each other and together form the seed. We must awaken these two sacred witnesses in ourselves, and incarnate their respective qualities in our individual consciousness so as to harmonize them in our own mind and heart. This is indeed the only way for us to reach enlightenment and finally be re-united with our Soul entity.

While these two elements of our Soul entity are asexual, they behave in relation to each other as two complements that can differentiate themselves like the Father-Mother archetypes from which they come, and they do that without abandoning their unity. Spiritual psychology has shown that we must come to know our inner nature, our feminine and masculine aspects within us so as to harmonize them and become whole again.

Consciousness in its purest and simplest form has to open itself to higher and deeper levels, reaching this level of consciousness means that we no longer have reflections on the mirror of our consciousness or shadows in our consciousness, but instead a fully awakened consciousness, filled with the bright light of the pure consciousness of the Soul entity.

All Spiritual hierarchies within us represent degrees of purified and Spiritual consciousness in potential, like seeds awaiting the right conditions to germinate and vitalize our ordinary consciousness. To reach this point, the two Divine witnesses have to guide our intuition before trusting us with important keys that are necessary tools to open and enliven one of the parallel Spiritual dimensions within our consciousness. By this process, our ordinary level of consciousness gradually begins to reflect the qualities belonging to that specific level in our ego. This delicate inner processes of transformation must manifest in our ordinary life before our consciousness is allowed to blend and merge completely with it. The awakening processes of consciousness become more subtle, refined and purer as it approaches the Center of Pure Being

The two Divine witnesses of the Soul entity transform the mystic from within, when the ego is attracted to their energies. Spiritual psychology has validated the importance played by the masculine (Father Archetype) and feminine (Mother archetype) energies within us. These two energies in our psyche are usually shadows awkwardly reflecting their real Spiritual counterparts. Because they are unconscious of their existence and are not yet in touch with their own higher Spiritual principles, most people usually mishandle and distort these archetypal qualities.

To get in touch with and harmonize with our ideal archetypes Father and Mother, we must first become conscious of how we distort the pure emanations of our two Divine archetypal witnesses. We do that by observing how our masculine and feminine energies act and react within ourselves, and by meditating and attuning to their archetypal ideals. Then we allow our intuition to guide and teach us how to open up to their Spiritual qualities. Intuition is a Divine gift granted to us by our two witnesses to help us restore our light of pure Cosmic Consciousness.

Unless we know who we are, how can we genuinely give ourselves to others? So, probably the most important journey we shall ever take is the one inward. The quest can be long, but help is at hand, and we are never left alone. Our two witnesses are our Divine guides and they accompany us on our sacred quest to the core of our Soul entity from where they came. Therefore, approach the quest without fear, look inward, and awaken your two witnesses within your Soul entity and allow them to carry you to fulfill your destiny. And from two, you will become three a trinity connection with Source. Your journey within starts with Soul desire and Spirits guidance to create with the help of Divine Intelligence an Embodied Master of Light. You will know you are ready once you feel you have released the hold of duality. You will be ready to embrace your new journey into a higher dimension.

Dreams are tools of transformation. Dreams stop being dreams and instead become Spiritual levels of consciousness. But, in the meantime, dreams open invisible doors to subtler levels of Spiritual growth, awakening in seekers of truth and wisdom, our permanent witness or Soul within our conscious selves. What is reflected in dreams are the thoughts and emotions of our good and bad intentions and experiences. It is in the mirror of our psyche that real purification and understanding take place, since we must become conscious of what appears on the surface of our psyche. The conscious impressions coming from a dream have an important role to play in the awakening process as a whole, and each dream, each symbol enriches this process, since Spiritual dream work takes into account the subtle purification process. Dreams about purification are given to those of us who want to awaken our permanent and Spiritual witnesses. To do that, we must unite them in our ordinary level of self-consciousness. We must become aware of our unconscious traits that need transformation. Without this, our ego cannot continue on this journey. If dreams appear confusing, it is because these types of dreams release the pressure and stressed energies blocked in our psyche. To release stress in dreams, the symbols are magnified so as to make an impact and emphasize certain aspects of a problem. Another reason for disturbing dreams is to help us become conscious of the nature of our stress or anxiety. We should use our intuition to look at the symbols in our dreams, trying to respect their meaning. Intuition assists us in reading what goes on in our psyche, since like a mirror, it reflects what goes on within us. This is how, we receive some practical solutions and interpretations. Intuitive ideas and feelings between our psyche and ego occurs only if our ego is open to change. If we are willing to work with the symbols, then a special flow of energy streams in, allowing us to understand what we must do to remove the problem, and transform what needs to change.

The quest to awaken our Spiritual awareness can begin only after a certain amount of purification and transformation of the psyche. Our consciousness, having taken the downward journey, is eventually drawn towards an ascending path. Then, what we receive becomes more subtle and enlightening since it comes without distortion directly from the Soul. When our ego or self-consciousness "awakens" to its true nature then dreams and the inner process take a new direction, and we see, understand and experience them in a totally different way since, from then on, our ego or self-consciousness realizes that it is just a vehicle for Cosmic Consciousness. We then perceive all kinds of dreams and astral projections differently, since the veil separating them from Cosmic Consciousness is no more. The mission of Cosmic Consciousness within us is to enlighten our ego. In other words, Cosmic Consciousness actively guides the process of awakening the ego to its true nature, and it directs the inner world of dreams and astral projections during sleep. Cosmic Consciousness takes over and creates whatever is necessary for our self-consciousness to understand and experience our ego. The ways that our Soul carries out its initiatory course of action to awaken our ego and open up the rainbow bridge to infinity is a source of great gratitude and awe. Dream work helps those who want to know themselves, since like a mirror, it not only projects who we are but also displays what we need to do. In other words, dreams are the best guides to reveal what you have on your conscience, what needs to be worked out in your life, and how to become a better and happier person.

TWIN FLAME CONNECTION

During the course of your life you may have had dreams, or visions of a mysterious person, one who you know you were going to meet. You may have gotten a feeling and the energy of this person feels familiar to you. You may have met in the past or someone you will meet in the future. You may sense that this person in somewhere out there just waiting for your paths to cross. There may be synchronicity surrounding your initial meeting with your Twin Flame. You may have a certain feeling or knowing that you may not be able to put into words. Your first meeting may seem unusual but the Twin Flame will come into your life in an unexpected way. Most Twin Flames are physically at a distance which prevents the Twin Flames from being together from the beginning of them meeting. There is a lot of energetic work that may need to be done before the physical meeting can happen. If the physical meeting occurs to soon the energy exchanged can be intense.

The connection that you have once you meet feels unreal. You feel comfortable with them and you feel you can truly be yourself around them. Conversations can last for long period of time all through time seems to stand still once you are connected. You can share you deepest feeling with this person and open to a level of understanding between you that brings a comfortable and intriguing sense of completeness. The love you feel is genuine and heartfelt and you feel magnetically drawn together. You share a vibration that feels as if you have known each other before. Intuitively you know that you will play an important role in each other's life. Twin Souls often times communicate thru telepathy. This form of communication occurs frequently since each twin can sometimes pick up on the others feelings or thoughts. Twin Flames often reflect each other's moods and can feel each other at a distance. When Twin Flames gaze into each other's eyes there can be a profound intensity. The eyes are the windows to your Soul, so making eye contact with your Twin Flame can feel unusual at times because it is as if you are staring into your own Soul.

The Twin Flame journey is that of unconditional love and it is always marked by a Spiritual awakening in order to allow your Soul to merge to its original source, so you can finally return home. The meeting of your Twin Flame brings awareness that you still may need to work out some lesson and healing. Each flame is still an individual aspect of your Soul meeting as an energetic mirror to your own Soul. The chemistry between the twins can be extremely powerful, moments of complete certainly that they are meant to be in each other's lives for a reason no matter what and that there is a higher purpose for their union with one another.

All emotions either negative or positive are exaggerated compared to other relationships. There is more emotional and energetic intensive feelings between Twin Flames because things are felt on the Soul level. Twin Flames are often empathic with one another and it can become an overwhelming emotional roller coaster at time when they are absorbing each other's emotions and feeling the intensity of their own. Reoccurring numbers sequences are common occurrences within the Twin Flame connections. When we see the 11:11 it means that our Twin Flame is ready to manifest itself physically in our lives. We may both be aware of the meeting of our energies that will soon take place, there is often the feeling that something is going to happen. Separation is a common theme in the Twin Flame relationship. There is usually a back and forth reunion that occurs often times due to distance or the inability to come together in the physical for reason. Emotional baggage may be the cause for the separation that each twin may be carrying. There is much healing work that may need to be done before the twins may have permanent reunion. We surrender to what is and let go of what was and have faith in what will be.

The relationship with your Twin Flame will change your life. Each one of you is transformed in many ways through the connection. It challenges each to grow and expand into the highest potential; to fulfill their mission and purpose on the planet and in each other's lives. At times the frequencies exchanged can be so intense that one of the twins may run from the relationship or there may be difficulty in being together for long periods of time. There are differences between you also since you are also a unique individuals. Twin Flames are connected at a Soul level and can feel each other beyond the physical often times feeling each other energetically. The relationship is so connected that each other may feel and know what's going on even if no words are spoken. Picking up on each other's thought and sometimes even finishing one another's sentences.

You may encounter many Soul mates throughout your life which may resemble the Twin Flame dynamic, yet there is only one Twin Flame. All relationships have the potential to be Twin Flames relationships but keep in mind that the experience and signs of a Twin Flame relationship are never one sided. If you feel that someone could be your Twin Flame but they don't feel the same way this could be simply a Soulmate relationship. These are important relationships also which may involve some karma or a lesson or the need to learn something about yourself. Soulmate relationships prepare us for the Twin Flames connection whether it is meant to occur in this lifetime. Remember you are always connected to one another on a Soul level no matter what the circumstance, understanding the timing may not be right until each individual has done the inner work of healing. If you are meant to reunite with your Twin Flame your Soul will allow that to happen. Once the Souls are ready to reunite there will be unconditional love and acceptance understanding that one partner may not be ready yet.

Once we surrender to God's will we surrender to the Universe knowing and trusting what is and that only love is real. You must go within. It is a time of having dreams and remembering, starting to recall a deeper nature within each other, becoming strong Spiritual Pillars for one another, and sounding the Souls cry to come forth. In this they find themselves once again after millions of years becoming one, reuniting for a grand purpose to assist humanity. A new way of Being unconditional love and light is the new order of things, the vibration in which we will exist. We are on the brink of a quantum leap in consciousness. This is a Spiritual evolution of consciousness that is awakening to our true purpose why you chose to incarnate during this lifetime. Many of us on this path are preparing for this in our own unique ways. This is an opportunity to awaken to your own original blueprint and to realize your potential as human beings and to take responsibly for our planet. The Twin Flames have a special contribution to make and they care coming together in numbers now to assist with the ascension joining together in harmony and love. This creates a vortex of energy that can be imagined as a light in the darkness of society consciousness.

As portals begin to open the masculine template will be uplifted to a higher octave of Love. The old repressed emotions are being brought to the surface for healing. The Twin Flame pair begin to unite and each one knows that there is still hope for their reunion. Uplifting energies bring a new plateau for those who have been taking action on their Spiritual path, confronting their inner shadows and healing their old wounds of abandonment. The fear that needs to be cleared is centered on the past. The masculine energy templates are being reworked with gentleness now as that had not been the case prior to now. This gives the male energy fuel for the journey for action and the ability to get things done. In the past the masculine energy has been misused and therefore is out of balance with the feminine energy. Remember without the yang there is no yin. The feminine energy must go within to understand her counterpart and look deeper into the aspects of the yang essence. Then she can appreciate and show love for the good traits of the masculine energy. We must let go out the past negatively and begin to see a new light dawning sending gratitude and sending love to the energies we embody. As Soul, we must release the old ingrained programming and clear energetically so we can uplift us all into unconditional love. The masculine/Feminine energy does not always have to be biological sex. Some females have masculine energy emphasis and some males have a feminine energy emphasis. We all have both polarities present but in difference degrees. Some twins are fairly balanced most express an emphasis toward one side or the other. One energy moving and the other receiving. If you are in a Twin Flame relationship you already know what energy exist between you both. The new cosmic energies are supporting a new high vibrational archetype to emerge and develop for the male energy. Many males are coming into their own light who are twins and Light Workers expressing and embodying the Divine masculine. This energy is an enlighten sense of power leading from the heart and taking action for the good of all, coming from love not from domination. Once the masculine and feminine energies align they find themselves on the same page coming together again to fulfil their mission, this is progress. The Twin Flames mission is of love and within your Soul you know that you will always be pulled back together for this reason. One of the reasons that the twin have not been able to be together up to this point is due to their karma from the past. That must be resolved and consciously addressed and be willing to let go. Karma will keep expressing itself over again in your lives circumstances and repeated until those issue are resolved. Twins flames will run and separate due to the past life karma of abandonment between the pair. Clearing karma is the most transformative method on the ascension path. This has the ability to change your outer reality for the better from the inside out. During the process you are reminded that this purging and releasing of the human trait of feeling the need to control things and worrying about the future is all do to the clearing process. You may find that things are off right now because you are releasing the old outdated energy stored within you to make way for the next phase of development, the reuniting. This change is already happening within the Twin Flame and Light Workers. The Universe is reshuffling the situation to make way for what we have been asking for. We have had Soul contracts that have ended making way for the new ones to take over, this is all according to our Creators plan. The two flames will always work together on the Soul level to come back to together to ultimately reunite harmoniously.

Imagine a white light above you and see the light. You will feel a deep strong reconnection and you feel ecstatic connection straight away via your Soul. There is no doubt whatsoever regarding the Soul connection. It can also be described as a powerful heart opening. You have an extremely strong passionate bonding felt as sensual energy, which once again is part of the Soul energy connection. You become speechless at times because of the level of the matched Soul frequency which is overwhelming through the heart center. Your heart beat increases due to this vibrational alignment as well. After the first recognition of each other there seems to be a magnetic pull towards each other and the Universe seems to orchestrate a flow of synchronistic sharing's that validate the connection as you feel closer and closer through the heart center. The Divine is orchestrating once again through synchronicities a Soul merging that is of the deepest passionate vibrational energy ever before felt. You literally do meld together as one. It makes no difference how far apart you are on the planet you feel each other. Through this Soul merge there seems to be what is called an activation. Then the True Twin Flame journey begins a journey of knowing the depth of the self, the Whole self. There seems to be a series of situations that cause deep questioning after this activation. It is all perfectly divinity orchestrated for you to know the whole of yourself beginning the journey into Christ Consciousness of balance within. The true Twin Flame reunion is of the Divine love heart vibration. The Divine requires this vibrational preparation to enable synchronicities to occur for the full physical reunion via the matched tonal harmonic alignment. You view all of life as an amazing magical journey of beauty through the eyes of this Divine Love. The heart has never been this open or felt such intent passion and Love. You feel as if you complete each other energetically and the whole becomes greater than the sum of the individual Soul. The two aspects create three a trinity and the third aspect is a very potent force of love and light at an extremely heightened and pure level. This helps the Twin Flames expand their own service work for humanity.

There are many stages that the Twin Flame energy process through. Recognition, Spiritual awakening, testing, crisis, runner dynamics, surrender, radiance, and harmonizing. In stage one both twins recognize one another at the Soul level and feel as if they have met before. Certain synchronic events surround the union. The heart charka opens and both should quickly merge into a third unified energy. Both twins experience an acceleration of Spiritual understanding. During this period the purpose is to activate the memory of each Soul life mission to help awaken each other to the higher levels of consciousness. The initial temporary Spiritual awakening (illumination) fades. The ego or little self begins to reemerge. One or both of the twins may attempt to fit the relationship into the old model of love, couple hood and relationship as it relates to their ego's desire and learned belief system. This can cause inner conflicts to arise. The twins may feel inspired yet still have doubts making one or both twins to begin to view their beloved critically or suspiciously. This purpose is to cause outdated mental concept about relationships to rise to the surface to be cleared. In the crisis stage the twin has realized they must reject their egoist beliefs about love relationships or reject their twin. Having to shed the ego or the identity based on beliefs and desires to embrace a higher expression of love can lead to stubbornness and anxiety. Fear can take hold triggering many habitual dysfunctional emotional patterns. In staying present with the patterned they can be witnessed and released, despite fears, both twins naturally come together in cycles of bonding, confession, forgiveness and lovemaking. These rituals cement higher levels of consciousness to the energy field of both twins. This purpose of crisis is to provide opportunities for the healing and maturing of the mental and emotional bodies.

The next phase is the runner dynamic where the human ego naturally fears annihilation in the face of the Divine unified consciousness encoded inside the Twin Flame union. The pain body rises up and old ego survival mechanism or the bottom of the barrel emotional and mental patterns like defiance, resistance, manipulation, anger, punishing, and judgment arise. One or both twins become emotional and mentally flooded with a deep pain from what feels like a Soul level of rejection and abandonment. The unbearable Soul level pain leads one or both twins to withdraw physically and block communication in fear. One or both twins may also unsuccessfully try to recreate the original unified harmony. The purpose is to propel both individuals towards Source for healing and to mature the Spiritual body. The temptation to engage in ego battle or withdraws is very seductive and difficult for many to resist which is why many twins never reach the next stage of surrender, radiance and Harmony. There is no room for judgment in the twin Soul pairings. Each Soul learns much from walking its own path and choosing through its own will. Your non-attached loving thought will be felt by your beloved Twin Flame in the subconscious keeping them strong. The direction and outcome of the relationship is surrendered to Source in full faith and trust that the union is under Divine protection. It is accepted that what is best and destined for final physical harmonizing will transpire in its own time but both twins must reach illumination in order to harmonize in the physical. The runner twin is allowed the space and freedom to choose to evolve at their own pace in their own way. At this stage the frequency of compassion returns and maintains itself. The surrendered twins hold a heart space for their beloved while fully exploring life on the way to becoming an illuminated human. The purpose is to help each Soul release the ego, and develop regular communication with Source and demonstrate their full trust that what is best and when the time is right all things will come to fusion. During the next phase of self-realization, illumination and radiance the ego dies and the God force energy emerges and takes over the body. This leads to a complete Spiritual awakening arriving at one's fully awakened Divinity. This is the stage of radiating Divine Love rather than seeking romantic love. At this point the surrendered twin's emotional, mental and Spiritual bodies are a full maturity. New creativity and healing abilities arise which are put in service to assist others. The purpose is to establish an outward flow of Divine love through one's body and works which vibrates at a level that uplifts humanity. The next stage is that of harmonizing. By this stage both twins have awakened. They come together in the physical to assimilate their newly evolved energies, flowing into the new dynamic of the unified potential. Both twins integrate fully into the third energy of unconditional love in a way that influences others toward their own heart openings. The purpose is to fulfill the intended mission of the Twin Flame Union. The Twin Flame relationship comes into your life to help mold you to embody the vibration of unconditional Love. If this resonates with you in some way you have probably found your Twin Flame. The love felt for a Twin Flame is so deep that you might have never known that you could love someone so much it is overwhelming. You feel a sense of completion, often something that cannot be described in words. You just feel like you've found something that was always missing but you might have not realized what. You can actually feel your Twin Flames touch from miles away and hear their voice even when they aren't talking. Your nature might change so much that you actually feel like a different person. There will be little things that will make you feel like it's just meant to be. The entire Universe will seem to be giving you signals and trying to bring the two of you together. Your love for your Twin Flame feels truly Divine and sacred and you have a deep knowing inside that the two of you will be together even after you have passed this life. There is no sense of time when you are together. It becomes non-existent. Life becomes meaningful and you get a very strong feeling that this is it. Your Twin Flame brings a new meaning and joy to your life. Almost like life is truly worth living for this relationship. Some people come into our lives through strange coincidences. Their presence seems mysterious but they are here for a reason. We don't always understand where they come from or why they manifest in our life. Usually they are compassionate individuals who we have attracts by something we have said or done. Sometimes their light is so bright and their words are so warm and kind that we feel we are experiencing Angels, in the form of a human being. When the Twin Flame relationship can hold the pure

Divine love at the core of their union is when the Twin Flame union will come together. This is a rare occasion in this dimension. Each half has to balance the Divine Feminine and the Divine Masculine energies within themselves to unite. Joining would be the purpose of serving humanity, the evolution of the Soul in each other. If the twins cannot steadily hold the energy of Divine love at the core of their relationship without the ego they will be separated. What if you have found your twin and they are not awake yet or as evolved as you are? You can't ever control another you can only control your own thoughts and feelings, when both twins are awake and whole they will come together to join in sharing their love with the world, bringing the vibration of Love and Light and sending out a signal of light and love to the world. The Twin Flame love shall heal the world. The process of this scared union reunites the inner masculine which is consciousness with the female energy which is feeling. This gives us the ability to co create together in the magical manifestation process of attracting our Soul mates into our lives. As you call forth your inner magic you receive that light which is you own power.

You have many Soul mates throughout your lifetime and as you go through your relationships you rise higher and higher up the ladder of love ending at the top of the ladder which is the union with your Twin Flame. Sometime the space that is between the rungs of the ladder can last many years. In finding your Twin Flame you will find yourself and in finding him/her you find your way back home. Sometimes the relationships can be so intense that the couples cannot stay together. If there is no love between it may intolerable to stay together as you once did. This means that everything from the past will need to be healed. This could be a false flame relationship where a false twin lacks their own inner connection with their Soul and higher purpose and will unplug from the relationship. All Soul mates and Twin Flame relationships are important relationships. This connection of the Soul or Twin Flames is about wholeness. It is a quest of the Soul to seek each Soul on its own Spiritual path, experiencing our divinity within. We are one!

The metaphysical definition of a Soul mate is someone you knew in a past life, and the following basic soul mate relationship traits have been consistently karmic. Most are predestined by your Soul, not your personality, before you were born. We all have many Soul mates but our personalities and emotional baggage will more often than not interfere with a compatible relationship. Not all Soul mate relationships are meant to be harmonious. Not all Soul mate relationships are meant to be long term.

Some people say that our Twin Flame or other half was created at the same time as us, and if we could just find each other, we'd live together forever in bliss and harmony. While the idea is certainly appealing, unfortunately, past life and life-between-life research has found no evidence to support it. A more reasonable Twin Flame definition could be a Soul mate with whom we're very compatible and with whom we share incredible chemistry. Alternatively, Twin Soul or Flame relationships are not always meant for love; Edgar Cayce, the famous sleeping prophet, defined Twin Souls as Souls who come together to achieve a joint task. The Twin Flame in the Spiritual heart does have a conscious intelligence, yet each Soul is sovereign and by Divine order. The highest level of evolution is related to the Spiritual heart, which is the fire in the Spiritual heart and the kundalini energies. As timelines have changed, it is the next evolutionary generation that will ascend us in forward motion into pure LOVE. When both Souls met, there is an exchange of energies that stimulate the quick movement of changes that make for humanities changes. It can be done by remote Spiritual connections, actual physical connections, or telepathic connection.

It is true that we all are destined to become ascended. Only the Soul timing will allow for further growth, which is always ascension by different pathways given upon Earth and the Soul's agreement. Each Soul's fire of the Spiritual heart will unite and complete the necessary evolution as designed by the lock and key of each DNA of each Soul as the connection is done. When the Ascension of both has taken place, each is the complete balance of all masculine and all feminine qualities within oneself. Then the threefold Flame of Life is completely unfolded, the individual becomes Master at Cosmic Levels of creation. This becomes the Cosmic Activity of the Power of the Three times Three. When both Souls have made the Ascension, then the individual works with systems of worlds instead of just in one world. This is the way the Godhead is ever expanding the Perfection of Itself throughout Infinity and keeping order throughout interstellar space.

You can create or influence your reality, but only within the confines of your destiny and karma. The bad news: Unfortunately, this means you can't avoid your (love) karma. The good news is most major relationships and events seem to be destined. You then have a choice or free will about how you perceive and respond to them. For example, if you're not destined to be involved right now, you have a choice of accepting it, concentrating on other areas of your life and preparing for a new relationship, or allowing it to cause you unhappiness. As another example, if you meet a wonderful person with whom you are destined to share a short-term, mutually compatible relationship rather than a life-long one, you have a choice of accepting this and enjoying it for what it's meant to be, or allowing the fated ending to cause you unhappiness. You can take the high road or the low road. Reacting out of love rather than fear will create a better life and karma for the future.

Much importance is placed on relationship permanence in our society. It is often said that a relationship failed if it didn't last a lifetime. The surprisingly common expectation of being compatible with the same person for years, while being the best you can be is ideal but outdated and usually unrealistic. Relationships in the past were more for economic and practical reasons. Couples were expected to stay together forever, no matter what. Times have changed. Fewer people are trying to fit the old relationship mold and are following their hearts and instincts about the kind of relationship and partner that is best for them. The Twin Flames are two halves of the same unity. We all have Twin Flames, which was created by God with the purpose that we would move away from the point of creation to grow and lean and evolve into our Divinity, returning to our original point of origin as perfected Beings of light. At the point of creation each single consciousness contains the seed of the Divine Feminine and the Divine masculine. The Alpha and the Omega, the yin and the yang, the opposites of one reality. On the decent into this dimension these two aspects of the one Divine and the Twin Flame was created. Twin Flames don't normally incarnate together except for a higher purpose. Both flames incarnate to lead separated lives always aware on some level that there is an aspect of themselves they have yet to discover. During this time many evolved Twin Flames are incarnated to assist in the raising of consciousness of humanity.

Just as the moon has phases and the Earth seasons, each of our lives follows individual cycles. In other words, it doesn't snow in the summer; and you can plant a garden in winter. Each relationship has definite time limits and will end or transform whether or not a couple stays together. It is possible to determine when you'll have a strong potential for meeting compatible people, break-ups or relationship transformations, and many other probabilities; life is full of preset circumstances destiny and events, and it is up to us how we deal with them. You can't control anyone's actions, but you have a choice of how you respond. Avoid being abusive, argumentative, closed-minded, critical, dishonest, domineering, evasive, impatient, indecisive, insecure, irresponsible, jealous, overly sensitive, pessimistic, resentful, secretive, selfish, self-centered, shallow, stubborn, vain, quick tempered. Choose the light over these darken states of being.

We are programmed to believe we need to find the one perfect person to meet all of our needs for the rest of our lives. This is impossible, but many still strive for it and then think they "failed" if their expectations aren't met. Distorted idealism and sky-high expectations set you up for disappointment. Stop looking for the Soul mate to fulfill your every need for the rest of your life and, instead, be open to Soul mates with whom you are compatible and share chemistry now. Do yourself a favor and forgive and release everyone who has ever hurt you. You'll remain trapped until you do. Forgiveness isn't about letting the person who hurt you off the hook. It's about releasing the anger and resentment or guilt that you harbor within, so you can get on with your life. This is an on-going process; every time you think of the person or experience, feel the forgiveness until you mean it. Also, try to think of them as your teachers instead of enemies and ask yourself what you needed to learn from the experience. We're all mirrors for each other, so you can't blame anyone.

There is one word that can free us from all the weight and pain of life. The word is Love. Good relationships are like no other feeling on Earth. Bad relationships feel like hell on Earth. Your energies are not in sync. If life is a school and we are here to learn, relationships are advanced classes. Relationships are magnifiers. It can show what is great about ourselves and what we, may not like about ourselves also. We are made to relate with each other. We are born to connect and love others. If you are so busy and want to try to find someone or you are holding on to the past hurt, the Universe will not put someone on your path just to turn them down or potential hurt that person. Releasing the animalistic urges, and transcending these energies will allow you to attract into you live those who are meant to be there. Use your intuition to attract the people you want in your life. What you are in mind of you attract either good or bad. Rid yourself of residue from the past or present relationships. If you don't learn your lessons the first time you will do the same thing and repeat the same lesson until you do. Do your best to graduate from the lesson and move to the next level. Put out your best energy. Get things in order and be content with yourself. To attract love begins with self love. Acknowledge your own completeness before you will attract the same energy into your life when the time is right. When you are open having cleared your emotional blockages, stop making excuses and move relationships higher up your priority list, you will be surprised who shows up. Once your energy is a clear signal you can use your intuition to tune into what others are sending you to evaluate potential people and avoid those who are less likely to work out. A Soul mate is anyone who helps you grow. It can be anyone not necessary a romantic partner. The energy of Love is powerful and healing on the spirit plane as well as here. If you want to experience something new you must try something new. How we see is a metaphor of how we think, perceive and put our world together. Our eyes process images and our brains process this information. What would the world be like if we are aware of our power of perception? Perception is your reality. When we truly see and take an interactive role in this process we can create a world that makes sense. We must create a stronger relationship with ourselves and take responsibility for our perception and enjoy the experiences of being fully present. When we use our senses we open a portal to discover that we might be missing out on the mysteries that surround us. Our sense of smell, touch, sight, hearing, taste as well as our other senses brings us into our present moment. Our senses give us the ability to be grounded in our bodies, having our feet stable and firm beneath us, living in the moment with a view of the future. Being who you are and being real is the key to gaining respect, demand the best of yourself is the key to quality and lifelong achievement. Be deliberate and unafraid are the keys to being different, unshakeable and unstoppable under less than perfect condition. Use this power and passion and boldness to attract the right kinds of people into your life. You must understand that being patient with the process and determined to finish well is possible to create a better future for yourself and for others.

EE Cummings said" To be nobody but yourself in a world which is doing its best to make you everybody else means to fight the hardest battle you can and never stop." If you allow other people to tell you who you are people will underestimate your worth and value and overestimate what you can actually do, neither is healthy or acceptable.

We are all created to receive love and then to give it away. Source is with us to give us that love and then lift and liberate us. Grace knows that our Creator loves each one of us, trying to be anything other than that is a waste of time. We may over work ourselves to gain approval but we must ask whose approval we are really searching for. Embrace your uniqueness everyday without apology. Everything comes from Source, never doubt the power that you hold inside. Connect to that and see where life's paths take you. Excel at being who you are, where you are, with what you have, while you can. Excellence makes people nervous especially people who settle for second rate reality. Striving to be something you're not is a chance to be disappointed. Be your best not someone else. To be the best and live up to your full potential we pull out all the stops, think outside the box, stop trying to make life work and start trying to appreciate and enjoy life. You are an original not a carbon copy of anyone else. Forget about what others think you are and become who you really are. You are a child of the Creator and you have been given a great inheritance it is up to you to go and claim it. Put one foot in front of the other and walk your path because this is your journey only you can decide which way leads home. As the Twin Flames becomes more in balanced and their service here on the planet becomes more in their awareness they spiritually grow at a faster rate than when they were apart. Each often possessing a gift the other does not have. They are sensitive to each other energy flow and stresses. Being separated and apart is like functioning at a reduced level. Together they become balance and more of who they are just by being in each other's energy. Energetically connect to the 3rd dimension the flames of the Alpha and the Omega are ignited, until this reunion the flames are dormant. When the ignition occurs a coil of golden light will move up the spine and open the gateway into oneness. As they shared once before their Christ light connects now forming a union of the two flames becoming one. This is the journey home as a two parts of the one whole reunited in service. You are an incredible and manifest Soul created to love and lift others. Shift your consciousness and move beyond all the issues of the past by being authentic and honest and be the best version of yourself you have yet to experience. Your Souls are calling for that reunion to occur and when the time comes you need to be ready.

SOUL AGREEMENTS

Soul Agreements are pre-incarnation contracts between two or more individuals. The theory behind a Soul agreement involves life scenarios conceived prior to birth. Souls choose relationships and family ties based on the lessons they wish to learn in the human form. Among some Spiritual groups a Soul's growth can advance more quickly through human incarnations than in Spirit form. When making these agreements prior to birth it give Souls a game plan to use to advance their Spiritual growth objectives when choosing future incarnations. Soul agreements are not intended to be too restrictive or set-in-stone based on the belief that free will is attached to human life but Soul agreements have built-in out clauses. Soul mates are those Souls that you have chosen to share life experiences with. This can be friend, family, or lovers. A walk-in is a person whose Soul exchanges places with a Soul that originally incarnated a body at the time of birth. These are stories told by walk-ins about their transition into a personality that has already been established. Walk-in Souls do not steal or kidnap another person's body. A walk-in happens when two Souls agree to swap places, making a Soul contract. The original Soul makes the decision that it wants out of a life and contracts with another Soul to continue the life stream. The walk-in will reside in his body and continue living out the personality that has already been established. Reasons why a Soul decides to depart from the physical and return to Spirit can vary. When the Soul has met or surpassed the re-negotiate their Soul contracts one or more times during a lifetime and continue living in the body. But, in some cases, the Soul wants out entirely and will offer the body along with its formed personality for another Soul to walk into. Other times a Soul will choose to opt-out because it feels the challenge of being human is too difficult and wishes to be released from the physical and reflect on its choices, and re-evaluate their life plan while residing in the Spiritual Realm. Soul agreements are often re-negotiated behind the scenes throughout a lifetime to adjust to situations that disrupts the original ideological scenarios. Unlike the more rigid karmic connections people who are connected through Soul agreements choose to hang out together for a variety of different reasons. Some find it to be really cool if next time around these Souls will meet up and could arrange to be siblings, business partners, lovers, friends or whatever. Soul agreements are also sometimes based on tough love. For example, a Soul may want to experience rejection, abandonment, or some other difficult emotions in the human life classroom. Another Soul agrees to take on the role of nemesis. Try looking into the eyes of an enemy; you may be surprised to see a friendly-Soul looking lovingly back at you.

When a Soul decides to vacate the physical form another Soul may opt-in and take up residence in the body. Both Souls have to be in agreement for a swap to happen. The exchange or transfer of Souls will usually happen during a trauma in a personality's lifetime such as an auto accident, major surgery, suicide attempt, and episode of depression or some other suffering. Sometimes a Soul will exit the body at the end stages of life allowing another Soul the opportunity to experience being in a coma or other pre-death experiences. This could account for some terminal patients not recognizing family members sitting vigil at their death beds. Sometimes a Soul will rent out its body to another Soul for a short period of time, allowing itself a respite from human life. Transient Souls will walk-in to a human body similar to professional house-sitters. The transient walk-in will play house with your family, friends, neighbors, etc. until the original Soul returns. Sometimes a Soul will agree to walk-in and reside in the body alongside the original Soul as partners. This is much like opening up your home to a guest, having a roommate, or employing a live-in housekeeper. The guest walk-in will agree to co-inhabit the body for different reasons. A walk-in may come in as an observer, merely wanting to shadow your life. This may happen when the original Soul is considering exiting the body permanently but hasn't made its final decision. Or, a guest walk-in will arrive to help out or support the original Soul while he/she is recuperating from a trauma or facing a difficult challenge. Many different scenarios can be played out when two Souls choose to co-inhabit one body/personality.

Walk-in Souls often struggle to identify with the personality that they are taking over. This is because they usually come in when the personality is emotionally damaged or the body has been harmed in some way. Walk-in Souls also have the responsibility to learn how to live among other Souls who are the original Soul's life mate's friends, family members, neighbors, co-workers, etc. If you are feeling estranged from your own being, or are having difficulty relating to the people in your life, in theory, you could possibly be a walk-in. When you reach a certain level of consciousness or a higher frequency in a lifetime you Soul will split into in order to come back down into a physical body. Being of a lower frequency or vibration and having to regain your consciousness could be a challenge that may take several lifetimes to overcome in order to reach the stage that you once were at. When the energies begin to align you exist in harmony and balance. When you are imbalanced there are flare ups or conflicts and issues that need to be dealt with. Life can be such an illusion at times so it is important to strengthen your connecting and begin to open up to the miracles life has offer us. This is the path back to oneness both with yourself and for your higher self. This is unconditional love and alchemical experience of embracing your shadows and facing your heart so you can release and heal.

This is a journey back to yourself as an infinite being of light for all other beings that come after you. This is the key, you are here for a reason and you have everything it takes to be happy and reunite with you Soul purpose for being here NOW! The more you understand that you are not the karma and or negative experience of the past you are now free to truly be yourself. You carry a deep Soul memory of this oneness that you may have lost vision of in the past. You need to stop playing the hiding game of who you are. Not shining you light or tapping into your gifts will no longer be possible once you realize that you have gained strength, confidence and wisdom. There is a wave of energy right now supporting you on your journey.

If you have ever met someone an had an overwhelming sense of joy or that something felt familiar you may have connected with the spirt of someone is you past life. Meeting someone from your past life especially a Soulmate usually means you have an important mission to complete with them during your time here on Earth. You can feel like you can just be yourself around them without judgement. They embrace you unconditionally and you feel as if you know their Soul to the core. It may have felt that something powerful has happened to you upon meeting them. Your paths have crossed again and you may even share memories of your past life together. You just intuitively know and remember things that have been carried over into this life. You may unleash parts of your Soul to this person and feel like for the first time you are heard. They can make you feel that baring your Soul without judgement is ok so you do and for the first time feel understood. You may feel like you lose the thought of time and sometimes forget the reality around you. Before you know it hours have passed and you feel in tune with this meeting and lost track of time, space, and reality. Even if you are not in the same place you may still feel the connection. This is destiny letting you know that you were meant to meet again. If you have felt misunderstood or alone before in your life meeting up with them makes you feel connected and you can form an unbreakable bond that feel more powerful than anything else felt before. Being with this person is effortless. You may have the ability to communicate telepathically receiving message before they were sent by the other person just know that you should either call them or that you are to meet again. Your hearts and Soul have become intertwined due to the cosmic relationship. You have traveled to many places together before and will continue to do so again and again. Even if you are not with each other you still carry a deep Spiritual connection. Your connection with them goes much deeper than just the surface. You share the same views spiritually, emotionally, and mentally. You two balance each other and feel totally comfortable expressing yourself in all aspects and Realms. You feel the unbreakable bond. You may have never had this type of connection before but you feel in awe within their presents and moved just by the thought that you have finally connected. Your Soul mate makes you a better person, but not everyone possess the power to bring that change in you. If you have met your Soul mate they should lift you up never drag you down. Feeling more alive and vibrant just by being with them fills the empty spaces with light. You become lighter in spirit. This feel as if you have finally awoken from a very deep sleep.

SPIRITUAL PATH/ SIGNS OF THE AWAKENING

The deepest Spiritual wisdom of all is contained within you. Whether you know it or not you are part not a part of an amazing story. Spirit speaks to me, I speak to you then we all are connected. Stillness gains access to your inners world. A place beyond thought, words, or language and it has the power to reawaken every aspect of your life. Life is not perfection, unblemished success, constant happiness, predictable, ultimately controllable or fully knowledgeable. It is beautiful. It is waves of light and waves of darkness, highs and lows, positive and negative, ebbs and flows, creation and destruction all at the same time. As without so within, success comes from within not from being without, hope and faith. We experience ups and downs, positive, negative, proud, ashamed, strong, weak, brave and scared moments, everyone experiences this. Socrates said "Know thyself". "Knowing yourself is the beginning to All wisdom"- Aristotle. Life is a journey to find you. The human condition gives us the abilities that can bless us and stress us, predict the future, love romantically, demonstrate compassion, feel guilt, and take responsibility. "It is better to conquer yourself than to win thousands of battles" (Buddha).

Human beings are tied to the earth, but not wholly of the earth. The time we spend in our physical bodies will not last and should thus be cherished. For one day, when our evolution is complete, we will return to the source of life to become Beings of light once more. What counts in a human career is not how one starts it, but how one will finish it. The one who really sees this truth, realizes their own nature as the Soul or Pure Being.

We are basically asleep and unaware, lifetime and lifetime trapped in the illusions and going through the motions of being human. We may have a very difficult situation or personal calamity happen that will often propels us to find some real answers. The process begins when we have our eyes opened giving us the understanding that we need to explore and find out more about ourselves. We start to release and let go of the old way we were and welcome the newer version of yourself. We start to feel excited about this new journey and often times become our own healers and teachers. This is the very heart of transition, the walk through the fires of transformation. This is where our whole duality based world as we know it begins to shatter and fall apart; where our familiar and comfortable reality system begins to change. It's when, the rug is pulled out from under our feet, our safety net disappears and we no longer know who we are anymore. It's where we're challenged and stripped to the very core; where our old self dies in order to give birth to our New Divine Self. Integration happens when we unite with our true higher self, or Spirit using, meditations, affirmations, invocations, magic rituals or sacred ceremony and just by simply allowing and being.

You begin to live like you never lived before, with total compassion and understanding, without karma, drama, rules, agenda or illusion. This is where all the old energy mind games, all the striving, struggling, controlling and manipulating end and a new energy begins. A life where everything is in perfect Divine flow, where everything we could need or want appears at precisely the right time, right place, in the NOW.

So how can we navigate our way through the ascension process? By staying out of fear and into balance with ourselves and our outer world. Letting go of resistance and going with the flow. Taking ourselves off autopilot in our daily busyness and finding out what we are really passionate about, what our purpose in this world is and bringing more of that into our lives. We are all going through a major period of purging, letting go of people, places, things and situations that no longer resonate with our energy vibration. This is all part of the ascension process of creating Heaven on Earth. There is a time to be born, a time to die, a time to sow and a time to reap, a time peace and a time for Love. This is the purpose under Heaven, for everyone to listen to your hearts calling and embrace ascension.

We need to take total responsibility for ALL that we create, we create with our thoughts. If we don't like what we are seeing in our world we need our thoughts to be more loving toward ourselves and others, shifting our awareness to bring about the peace in our lives and world that we pray for. At time you may experience many changes in yourself. We all experience different symptoms as we process through our ascension. You may experience not feeling well due to the physical changes that are going on in you. You may start waking up around 3 or 4 in the morning. Extreme fatigue for no reason. You may need to rest more. You may experience ringing in the ears as your ears are trying to adjust to the new frequencies that have awaken within you. As your body start to let go of the toxins you may experience flu like symptoms. Hot flushes and sweats can be cause by energy coming in. As your charkas begin to open you may experience that your heart is fluttering. You may have a sense of disconnectedness, or be over emotionality as emotions are coming to the surface to be released and healed. Your vibration is increasing and you are not resonating with your old life and may feel the desire to get away from it. You develop a sense of knowing something important is happening, but you don't know what it is.

Spiritual Ascension is bringing our Soul into Physical form through our heart. As you start to awaken we go through a process often called the Dark Night of the Soul. The promise of Ascension is the hidden heritage and legacy of the human condition, the fulfillment of humanity's evolutionary blueprint. Ascension is not some lofty Spiritual concept design by the mind, it is a literal, tangible scientific process of the evolution of consciousness and biology within the laws of energy mechanics that apply to a multidimensional reality system. You can go about your human lives, with your consciousness confined to the limitations presently imposed by your physical body, or you can learn the mechanics by which those limitations can be released, and begin to experience the reality of freedom that is the comprehension of yourself as a Soul.

Your sleep patterns change and you feel restless but seem to have more energy. Get used to it your body will adjust in time. Shivers, crawling sensations, tingles on your scalp or feeling pressure on the crown like someone is pushing down, your may experience flashes of great inspiration or creativity or thought. You may also feel vibrations around your head or ears. Don't worry this is the opening of the Crown Chakra and Divine energy is flowing in. Embrace this! Sudden waves of emotion or feelings of sadness, feeling lonely or happy or angry for no apparent reason. This is the release of blocked emotions and can come from the heart chakra. Try not to be too hard on yourself. Just acknowledge the feelings as they arise and let them go with love and kindness. Old issues may keep coming back and at time you feel very lost. You're never lost. This is often considered the Dark Night of the Soul. The term "dark night of the Soul" is used in Christianity for a Spiritual crisis in a journey towards union with God, like that described by Saint John of the Cross. Saint John of the Cross' poem narrates the journey of the Soul from its bodily home to its union with God. The journey is called "The Dark Night", because darkness represents the hardships and difficulties the Soul meets in detachment from the world and reaching the light of the union with the Creator. This experience can be seen as the painful experience that people endure as they seek to grow in Spiritual maturity and union with God. While this crisis is usually temporary in nature, it may last for extended periods.

The Dark Night of the Soul is a lonely painful process in which consciousness is clouded by uncertainty to unravel the entanglements of ego within the self. As the pain and suffering within self and the world are faced and embraced, eventually the heart-beat of love is freed to express its many rhythms of service to others, God, and self, one and the same. We can only enter the dark corridors of this purification of consciousness if we accept the courage that comes from our Spirit. Courage sustains our mind and body on our journey through the deepest agony, suffering and pain. By entering and accepting the intense pain and emptiness that accompany this state, liberation, enlightenment replace the ego's distorted clouded perceptions with clear flowing light. The deepest understanding of our true self begins to unfold and awareness surfaces that we are in tune to service and compassion to ourselves and to others. In this liberation of consciousness, we become free to know the unity of the One, the Divine. This state opens us to understanding the interconnectedness to everyone and everything as we lucidly begin to witness the timeless flow of Divine Consciousness in the eternal now moment. Through realization and acceptance, Divine Consciousness may begin again to fully resonate in the empty spaces and places within the self. The dark night of the Soul is an avenue for reintegration first through disintegration. Through a painful de-conditioning, we begin to understand that reconnection to our true self is not a singular process but a reconnection to everyone including our self and God. We begin to recognize that the feeling of abandonment by God, common to the experience of the dark night, is really abandoning the false sense of self and others we have developed. A realization unfolds that service to Self, others and God are all the same.

Whether or not you view ascension and multidimensional evolution as a reality while you are alive on Earth, you will be directly faced with that reality once your consciousness has passed out of physical life and into the multidimensional framework. At the death of your physical body you will discover that your consciousness lives on and your evolution continues. An "awakening" is a moment of clarity in which a new insight or understanding is gained. With this new awareness the experience of life is seen differently, and new possibilities are opened. Changes in patterns of thought, emotions, and behavior occur. An awakening allows the possibility of growth to new levels of psychological and Spiritual maturity. This de-conditioning is not easy and is a lonely and desolate place of suffering. You may feel that you are caught between two worlds, the perceived painful world where you and other people helplessly suffer, and the enlightened world where unlimited higher consciousness and Divine Love reigns. The ego cannot understand that you need to let go of certain things and let the Universe guide you were you need to be. The process is painfully stressful to the body and agonizing to the mind as the ego interferes and keeps you perceiving a hopeless never-ending battle between these worlds. Your ego is in the process of being shattered as you begin to recognize that your ego's many strategies are from the ways of the world, not the love of God. All the noises, illusions, preconceptions, conditionings, socializations, false images of self and others are being called by the higher consciousness. The ego is being dissolved and disintegrated during this most painful emptying process. Out of this lonely internal battle deep within, begins to flow the wisdom of living purely, free of the previous ego's distortion that everything you do must be rewarded. Through this state of real being, you more fully realize that you can be in the world, not of the world. You may be in the suffering, but not of the suffering.

There are many reasons that a dark night of the Soul experience presents itself. Each of the reasons is ultimately a matter between your Spirit and what you came into this existence to learn. The dark night may occur to salvage the remainder of your life when living has become full of disharmonious habits and you are no longer living consciously. The dark night may be an offering by your spirit to meet the challenge of purification and regeneration of your being before the end of your life. Whatever the reason, a person must gather every ounce of their conscious energy to accept this deeply painful transmuting of ego energy back to meaning, purpose and service as they are one and the same. Some of us may have to endure several periods of the dark night of the Soul throughout life. Others may be guided by their Spirit to stay in this state for intense work the remainder of their life before they die. Many reject the gift of the dark night repeatedly throughout their life as they follow their ego's perception that Spirituality should bring instant gratification and should feel good. True transformation is a painful process and takes time. It is difficult to know that your heart is not beating freely if the weight of the ego upon it is all you've ever known. We each have the heart that beats freely in the infinite space and is connected and alive in the world. This is the liberation, the enlightened, that comes through enduring the painful transformation of the dark night. The enlightenment frees the mind to really see with illuminated perception. As the mind is free from the entrapments and cages of the ego, it frees the body as well from "dis ease" and sickness that was previously being passed onto it by the ego-influenced mind. Intellectually, you may have the insight that the ego never was your true Self, but this provides no emotional relief from the feelings of emptiness during the process.

You cannot learn to love God with ego. Your ego has nothing to do with learning to love yourself or others. Higher consciousness is entered freely for its own sake. The fundamental lesson that loving the Divine, Self and Others unconditionally, are one and the same. To enter higher mystical consciousness we experience directly all the pain and suffering within and without. This consciousness reflects and reminds us of the poverty of Spirit that remains collectively among all human beings. Love is the eye in which we see God. Love itself is understanding God through the dark night. The dark night of the Soul is offered as a gift of illumination to every One of us. The full spectrum of higher consciousness is available in both our personal and collective evolution. As one of us participates, it may be shared in consciousness for all the same.

Once you face these old issues that arise deal with them so they can be healed. This is necessary and deeply cleansing. Your physical body can change as well. Your eating habits become healthier. Your whole body and mind are changing too. This will settle down as you deal with the old issues. Your vibration will rise as you surrender with Unconditional love. Your senses increase in their sensitivity. Your 6th sense opens up and you become much more aware of subtle energies. You may begin to see sparkles of light or shadows of energy or movement from the corner of your eye. These are signs of Spirit or your guides. Never fear. Remember that you are always in charge and you can set down rules. Always practice discernment when you are dealing with Spirit. You will begin to see the world with new eyes. You feel loving and at one with everything. Keep in this flow. Free your mind of clutter and be in the flow of positive energy. Be in perfect harmony and allow the manifestation to this positive state of being. Be compassionate and loving as best you can and don't be hard on yourself when you have a bad day, be gentle with yourself as your awareness expands. You will desire more and more to break free from the restrictive patterns and old habits that no longer serve you anymore. Have the courage to do it and clear out the old to make room for the new. You may begin to notice more and more signs that speak directly to you on a very profound level. Things will have great meaning to you as your awareness blossoms. Synchronicity flows faster during this stage. These wonderful events flow when you are on the right path. Allow your heart to lead the way and you shall find your mission in this life. Meeting people that are like minded is part of the process. There are no coincidences so try to feel the messages you receive and trust your intuition or inner wisdom. All that is, is, All that was, was, and All that will be, Will be.

Your life is a sacred journey, and it is about change, growth, discovery, movement, transformation, continuously expanding your vision of what is possible, stretching your Soul and learning to see clearly and deeply, listening to your intuition, taking courageous challenges at every step along the way. You are on the path exactly where you are meant to be right now. And from here you can only go forward, shaping your life story into a magnificent tale of triumph, of healing, of courage, of beauty, of wisdom, of power, of dignity and of Love.

It is so very important that you grow your own belief system as spirituality is a totally personal matter, and is never to be forced upon others. We all have in our minds a Spark of the Creator God. This is the light which works to uplift your thoughts to a higher level. It is your mind, first of all, which can be brought under your control. It is very important that you question that which benefits you. Look at things that you want to manifest with soft eyes and it will naturally flow towards you. Everything will fall into place. You need to find your flow of energy that is with your Soul. Don't think about it or feel it just know that this is possible. Hell on Earth is living a life the way you've always lived it but Heaven on Earth is breaking free of those long standing patterns that we created. Fate, destiny and the power of the spirit allows you to create your own destiny. It is important to let creativity have a say in your mind. You are far more creative than you think yourselves to be, but you allow mundane thoughts to interfere, so you lose the thread of your thoughts. The easiest way to learn to control your thoughts is to confide in yourself who can teach you, how to control your thoughts and at the same time give life with you insight as to how to live the better way with the least amount of stress. I am telling you, that this is the greatest favor you can do yourself to reap the most Spiritual growth in the process. Think what a great partnership could be if you involved your Creator more consciously. Our Creator put inside each one of us what the secret is. You create your own reality. Christopher Robin put it like this "Promise you will always remember you are braver than you believe and stronger than you seem, and smarter than you think"

THE WHEEL OF LIFE

As the wheel goes around so does life. This wheel seems to be an image about the emotions of change. At the top of the wheel is happiness, things that are normal and well. The wheel turns with a clockwise movement. Change begins, as the turn occurs you are no longer in the same position you where because you may seem upside down and feel like you are falling through space with distress. This can often be described as a feeling of loss. As the movement continues to the bottom of the wheel you may feel like life has pulled you down. In this place you feel like your suffering. Once the wheel starts to turn again you begin to feel the rise to the top, and hope that once again you will reach the place of happiness. The lessons you obtain during the turning and how you process through these experiences give you back the momentum to continue. Understanding that we are always in one of these position on the wheel we remember that happiness is where we want to be. When in the place we are succeeding we are comfortable and we are not falling apart. There could be a variety of events have signaled this change which usually means that you need to let go of what is not working and open yourself up to a new path. Again the wheel will turn, you job is to try to turn the wheel as quickly as possible. Your positive thoughts and actions will make that happen. As you follow the wheel into suffering you begin the phase of transition, you are either allowing the suffering to occur or you want to have the experience. You must go through the experience fully and then implement your plans for another ride around the wheel. We must go through it with even if it is unpleasant. It is out of this suffering experience that hope then arises. Hope comes when our plan is working and process can be seen and felt. Our goal comes into view and we have a vision of a return to happiness. Just not like things were before because we now have regained balanced. Happiness is found in a new state of equilibrium. We may now be in the place for a while but if we look ahead we may sense the winds of change once more. The wheel always turns. Our happiness, is not a permanent state. More change is coming and the journey around the wheel into loss, suffering and hope begins again. Whenever change enters our lives we experience the emotions of change causing us anxiety, worry, feeling sad, or angry, irritated and frustrated. Grieving needs to be done. Eventually, hope brings a renewed energy, optimism, and enthusiasm and happiness brings a sense of satisfaction and peace. The wheel of life teaches us that we cannot get happy and stay happy. Change always comes. Change brings growth. The emotions of change are expected and normal. They cannot be avoided. Accepting that you as well as others are always in the process of change. Where you are on this wheel called Life is determined by your attitudes and thoughts.

When life throws you a curve, you can't wait for the turmoil to be over with. You just want to pick yourself up and move on but that is not always the case. You may try to create a plan to gain control but you must take a look at what is really going on to understand that to get through anything you must go through it. We may try to resist the emotions that rise to the surface and dismiss them but until you face those shadows about yourself you cannot move forward into the light. Looking back on my seasons of experiences I realize that every storm came and went and that there were hidden messages within each experience. The seeds of hope were hidden but began to grow in my consciousness. Darkness is a part of this process, often times stopping you in your track and it may feel like life has changed for you. Know that 'This too Shall Pass' and you have to trust that the process will become lighter. Try to focus on the things that bring joy, purpose and love into your experience. If you need to reach out to someone for support please do it there are Souls that are just waiting for you to ask for help. Being vulnerable is part of this process. This is your moment when you rise out of the past in enter a new phase of your journey. Like a "Phoenix rising from the ashes"

Opening up to the new energy that you are receiving you begin to start see the beauty that surrounds you. Things start to shift when you decide to find direction in each moment-to moment experience. Each moment there is clarity, a "yes" that shows you the next step. The best you could do is ride the waves. After a while the storms pass and you realize that you had gone into the darkness and found your way out. The human spirit is resilient and wants to find its way home to wholeness. We experience responsibility for life choices which allows consciousness to grow. When we suffer in this sense we are opening ourselves to experience the fullness of life's diversity as a natural process of growth. These life experiences must occur for Spiritual maturity to develop. The philosopher Alan Watts speaks to this point when he says, "Because human consciousness must involve both pleasure and pain, to strive for pleasure to the exclusion of pain is, in effect, to strive for the loss of consciousness." Life's goal is to increase consciousness; so, the temptation to avoid life's legitimate pain must be resisted. "Pain is weakness leaving the body"

Aspects of yourself will no longer exist as we spiritually evolve. When we release what is no longer serves our highest good we create space for something better. This can be a painful and powerful process but it is temporary. Don't hold onto the old way of being just because it seems familiar there is no growth there. Invite the new energy because that which you resist will still persist. Just trust the process. Align yourself with the natural flow of energy. Positive thoughts create positive paths. Each new path will require a new version of you. Envision yourself in the future and then go and create that. Whatever the path you find yourself on now own where you are and begin to take the necessary steps needed to get back up. Take as long as you need to heal that which is no longer a part of your life. Regain your strength and align to the new path which will present itself to you. You have a choice which path is right for your understanding that they will always be another path for you to adventure down. Life can be an adventure of wonder and awe once you tap into the universal energy flow. The process of Ascension is simply going "up", going up the dimensional scale by raising your frequency rhythm of your body. It's a concept because that is what the concept of Spiritual Evolution really is about. As you do this you start to connect with your God/Source. Remember you are an infinite power! Align with the flow of light and love by remaining peaceful. In this peaceful state of Being you become in touch with your own power and become a reality shifter. By connecting to your Divine source and energy you have taken the steps towards self-mastery. You become aware of the conscious and unconscious belief system operating in you. Immerse yourself in this frequency and begin to manifest your desires. Use the Law of Attraction.

Shifting out of the 3rd dimension into the 5th is like a massive upgrade to your entire operating system. This is upgrading a human consciousness to a galactic consciousness. When you are ready to move beyond the 3rd dimension you enter the 4th dimension first before you can enter the 5th. The 4th dimension is a filter to purify you. This realm is of the heart energy which fills you with love and oneness and light. In the 5th dimension the energy is lighter in frequency, contains pure light and love and cosmic consciousness. This is a true multidimensional reality.

Body aches and pains, especially in the neck, shoulder and back are often experienced. This is the result of intense changes at your DNA level as the "Christ seed" awakens within. This too shall pass. Feelings of deep inner sadness for no apparent reason are common, you are releasing your past (this lifetime and others) and this causes the feeling of sadness. This is similar to the experience of moving from a house where you lived in for many, many years into a new house. As much as you want to move into the new house, there is a sadness of leaving behind the memories, energy and experiences of the old house. This too shall pass. Crying for no apparent reason. It's good and healthy to let the tears flow. It helps to release the old energy within. Sudden change in job or career. A very common symptom. As you change, things around you will change as well.

You're in transition and you may make several job changes before you settle into one that fits your passion. Withdrawal from family relationships. You are connected to your biological family via old karma. When you get off the karmic cycle, the bonds of the old relationships are released. It will appear as though you are drifting away from your family and friends. After a period of time, you may develop a new relationship with them if it is appropriate. However, the relationship will be based in the new energy without the karmic attachments. Unusual sleep patterns. It's likely that you'll awaken many nights between 2:00 and 4:00 AM. There's a lot of work going on within you, and it often causes you to wake up for a breather. At times you'll feel ungrounded. You'll be challenged with the feeling like you can't put two feet on the ground, or that you're walking between two worlds. As your consciousness transitions into the new energy, you body sometimes lags behind. Spend more time in nature to help ground the new energy within. You'll find yourself talking to your Self more often. You'll suddenly realize you've been chattering away with yourself. There is a new level of communication taking place within your Being, and you're experiencing the tip of the iceberg with the self talk. The conversations will increase, and they will become more fluid, more coherent and more insightful. You're not going crazy, you're just moving into the new energy. Feelings of loneliness, even when in the company of others. You may feel alone and removed from others. You may feel the desire to stay away from groups and crowds. As much as the feelings of loneliness cause you anxiety, it is difficult to relate to others at this time. The feelings of loneliness are also associated with the fact that your Guides have departed. They have been with you on all of your journeys in all of your lifetimes. It was time for them to back away so you could fill your space with your own Divinity. The void within will be filled with the love and energy of your own Christ consciousness. You may feel totally disimpassioned, with little or no desire to do anything. That's OK, and it's just part of the process. Take this time to "do no-thing." Don't fight yourself on this, because this too shall pass. It's similar to rebooting a computer. You need to shut down for a brief period of time in order to load the sophisticated new software, or in this case, the new Christ-seed energy. You may experience a deep and overwhelming desire to leave the planet and return to home. This is perhaps the most difficult and challenging of any of the conditions, but this is not a suicidal feeling. It is not based in anger or frustration. You don't want to make a big deal of it or cause drama for yourself or others. There is a quiet part of you that wants to go home. The root cause for this is quite simple. You have completed your karmic cycles. You have completed your contract for this lifetime. You are ready to begin a new lifetime while still in this physical body. During this transition process, you have an inner remembrance of what it is like to be on the other side. Are you ready to enlist for another tour of duty here on Earth? Are you ready to take on the challenges of moving into the New Energy? Yes, indeed you could go home right now. But you've come this far, and after many, many lifetimes it would be a shame to leave before the end of the show. Besides, Spirit needs you here to help others transition into the new energy. They will need a human guide, just like you and me, who has taken the journey from the old energy into the new. The path you're walking right now provides the experiences to enable you to become a Teacher of the New Divine Human. As lonely and dark as your journey can be at times, remember that you are never alone.

This is why it is important to clean all negative energy before you can shift. Thoughts equal manifestation, so thoughts that are negative like fear cannot co exist where peace and love and happiness exist. If you live in fear you will create a living hell. There is a window of opportunity now to make your thoughts your reality. We have incarnated here to make a difference. Remaining in trust and love and surrender to your highest self you begin to naturally ascend and open up to experiencing the 5th dimension consciousness. This is a Spiritual adventure of an amazing journey guiding humanity into the Age of Aquarius as a unified consciousness.

The 4th and 5th dimensions are liking receiving a major upgrade in your DNA. During the upgrade from 3rd to 4th you begin to experience a deep feeling of inner peace. In the 4th and 5th dimension you will not live in fear as we experience in the 3rd dimension reality. The energy is lighter as you ascend. When you integrate into the higher energies certain issues may come up for you from your subconscious mind to be processed and released. Just let them rise for healing and then release, letting them go. Once you begin to understand the process of letting go you will feel lighter accepting you are a Spiritual Being who is limitless, powerful and deeply connect to Source of all that is.

We have all traveled here at this time to do the work of learning the lesson that you as a Soul came to learn. If you carry issues from one lifetime onto another life time those issues may need to be healed by reviewing them and re-experience them. These issues can take you deep in the core of your being when you merge and melt into it and then transform them. This is Alchemy. Here the Universe turns the dense heavy energy into an Enlighted experience of life that feels like liquid light. You will know that you are communicating with the 5th dimensional Beings who are tuned into you be deep interconnected feelings in your head and chest. You mind begins to quiet down and you will know that you are ready to receive downloads from them. It becomes easier to understand the messages from the 5th dimension Begins but you have to learn how to integrate what they are saying and learn how to apply this information into your life. Your accepting that you are speaking with these higher dimensional Beings depends on your beliefs and your ability to open your mind and transcend the layer of the limited thoughts that restrict your consciousness from expressing itself. You are an eternal Being and you are here to full fill your Soul's mission.

Intuition is the process of reaching accurate conclusion based on inadequate information. It can transcend time and space and can tell you what the right or wrong answer is at a split second you need to make it. It is the golden pillar that lies at the core of our Soul. It is hidden; it must be discovered and actively used for it to make a difference in our lives. This occurs when we dip into that universal energy and receive a message pointing us in the right direction or warning us of danger. When the Universe gives us a message, your responsibility is to be aware of it and listen to what is says and then follow through. If you feel like a fish swimming upstream against the current of Universal energy, check to see if your desires are attuned with the Universal energy. If not stay away from that path unless you chose to venture down it. Following your intuition points us in the right direction to take advantage of the powerful current. You must believe it is possible to hear the whispers of your inners voice. When the Universal is calling you, answer the call. Challenge yourself to think outside the box and understand that there really is no box it only your beliefs that thinks there is. Amazing synchronicities will be of an everyday occurrences. The Universe will be sending you messages constancy giving you signs along the way. The energies will guide you to a miraculous journey through a magical world and anything is possible. Sometimes the answers come before the situation occurs or even at the same time.

There are many lessons we have to face to grow, life is a school and were all here to learn important lessons before we can graduate to a higher level. You have immense power which gives us access to all the power and goodness and love of the entire Universe. There are negative energies that like to trick you as well. The key to using your intuition is to be aware of that power, respect it and learn to use it with good intentions for yourself and others. With some preparation, intention and desire to align with the goodness, love and wisdom of the Universe, your inner wisdom can guide you and give you the abundant loving and joyous life you desire.

We have the power to tap into our inner wisdom which is the ultimate guide that shows us how to experience more love and happiness, health and success. We all have our energy blueprint that identifies us as who we are in this lifetime. How we live our lives, the choices we make and how we act and react shape that energy. Intuition gives us the ability to sense the unseen energy. It works by putting us in touch with the life force that unites us all. Intuition works by tapping into the energy of the Universe. Everything, everyone, plant, stone, body of water, star, even the air we breathe has a power and energy contained within it. We are all connected at the deepest level because we are all part of the same stuff. This energetic life force is in everything it's all part of the same energy. This is quantum physics. Every atom and molecule in the Universe is connected. The human body and psyche can sense the powerful forces of energy that compose the Universe because the same energy flows through us; it is part of our connection to the world and beyond. This energy runs through our bodies via our medians or charkas. This energy is hardwired into the nervous system. More and more people are coming to believe in and use this natural six sense. We can recognize the value of intuition and how it puts us in touch with forces beyond what we can perceive with our conscious minds. Intuition also allows us the ability to tune into the little energy signals we get from the Universe. When your 3rd eye is fully open you will start to see through this dimension into the 4th and 5th. This means you will begin to see light portals or layers of energy. As the star gates open those that are aware will receive more energy in their bodies, allowing us to upgrade our light bodies.

When it comes to making choices in our lives, it's important to know what to look for. The Universe signals us with what we often times call coincidence. The Universe steps in to take care of us and show us whether or not we are in tune. Life is like a treasure hunt and the Universe is always supplying us with clues on how to find our treasures. These clues come in the form of coincidences. The meaningful coincidences in our lives and experiences are the Universes way of trying to show us what is coming. It is just about us noticing and interpreting what the Universe has to say. A chance event can lead us onto a path of Divine intervention. It also teaches us lessons to "Be Aware" of something even though it looks like it is meant to be. Coincidence can confirm that we are going in the right direction. These coincidences can also tell us our plans are not in sync with the Universe, we need to pay attention to those promptings also. When we recognize a coincidence sometimes we get the feeling of wow or awe. It may take you awhile to recognize a coincidence by making the connection between the signal and what the Universe is trying to tell us. The more you practice and tune into the messages from the Universe the more frequently they will appear in your life. The main purpose in developing your intuion is to put you in touch with the Universal consciousness which is everywhere and that is composed of goodness, love and wisdom. It helps us make better choices here on earth by tapping into a level of awareness and information. Intuition is like a receiver that can be tuned to different frequencies. We must work with the highest level of Universal consciousness and oneness for guidance. It is connecting to something much greater than the Universal energy source where all the wisdom guidance and abundance comes from. To gain the best guidance you need to go to the most powerful level and highest plane of goodness, love and wisdom. It has been said that coincidences are God's way of remaining anonymous. We often have serendipity occurring in our lives as a way to show us we are on the right path. As you trust your intuitive knowing you'll find these synchronicities occurring more often. How does your intuition speak to you? Do you receive information in words, feelings, and a body sensation? Do you just know? Ask your intuition questions and pay attention to the answers and act on the information you receive. The feeling of enthusiasm is one of the ways your intuition speaks to you. What makes you excited, happy, delighted? What do you look forward to each day? Do more of it! The root of the word enthusiasm literally means "God Within." Just think, when you feel enthusiastic about your dreams it means that God is speaking through you and saying "yes" to your goals! Maybe you're beginning to feel as Mother Theresa once did when she said, "I know God will not give me anything I can't handle. I just wish that He didn't trust me so much." The Universe has a perfect plan for your growth and unfolding as a human being. As you learn to be guided by your intuition you're beginning to act on this wisdom from the Universe. The Law of Attraction is a well-known Divine principle that all things come from the energy of thought, which is the energy of intuition. Everything in our world began with a thought. We can step out of our confinement into a world of everyday reality and tap into the Universal life force. Learn to use you intuition or internal guide to direct your thoughts and actions, then we become partners in our destiny at the deepest level.

The journey is not easy when you are climbing mountains. Do you have the strength to climb that mountain? The road less taken is always an uphill climb. The climb is worth the effort.

Intuition with intention can harness the highest power of the Universe to help you in every step of your journey through life. When we recognize our own sixth sense we tap into our unique energy signature. Thoughts can either help or hinder the development of intuition. Thoughts are a powerful force in the Universe. Thoughts create reality. With our intuition it's the subconscious mind that is active and the conscious mind that creates the block. Our thoughts can hold us back from using our sixth sense. This sixth sense can guide you and give you warnings and connect you to the vast wisdom of the Universe. Becoming aware of your thoughts is essential to develop your intuition and also maintain your psychological and emotional health. Focus your power of thoughts on the best outcome no matter what the situation. Your intuition is the search engine that connects us to the Universe. Our job is to simply choose what we want to create and then pay attention as the Universe delivers our desires. Distinguish between intuition and your thoughts, emotions, desires and wishful thinking. When you receive an intuitive feeling it's a feeling of knowing and being at one with the Universe. You're balanced and peaceful. Being right and not fooling yourself. Use both logic and common sense to the choice we make, in the beginning when you first start tapping into your intuition you will probably make mistakes. Use these mistake as stepping stone to what you really desire to create learning what to trust and what not to trust. When you use your intuition you are opening up to the energies that can be positive, neutral or even negative. We create an open channel between ourselves and the Universal energy we have to protect ourselves from any negative energy that might want to interfere. Using your intuition to help guide you in life and reach a higher level of responsibility because we are reaching beyond our own desires and wishes and asking guidance from a higher place. This puts us in alignment with the Universal plan. To use your intuition to guide you in life requires courage to have the guts to see beyond your own desires and take action based on a bigger plan. Confidence to believe in yourself knowing you can carry out what the Universe guides you to do, commitment to develop your intuition and join together your inner wisdom to create your destiny, and to be patient with yourself as you learn. Conquer your thoughts, your fears and your doubts and the doubts of others. You must triumph over any desire to hold on to what isn't in alignment with your inner voice. The intuitive mind is a sacred gift. William James said "The greatest discovery of my generation is that human beings, by changing the inner attitudes of their minds, can change the outer aspects of their lives". It's easier to create a life you love when you give yourself affirmative messages. Begin everyday declaring to the Universe how grateful you are, how blessed you feel, and how excited you are to be given the opportunity to start a new day. This is the gift, truly living in the present moment.

Intention is where thought and intuition join hands with the Universal energy. It puts the power of both conscious and subconscious mind behind our pure desire and links it to the World and Universe outside ourselves. When we will things into our lives our intent must be strong and direct. You have to know you deserve it. When you send a thought out into the ethers you must have confidence, any doubt can stop the creative flow, just let it happen. We are each given a path that we are supposed to walk on. When we put all of our power together we find our journey on Earth to be more fulfilling and our lesson more rewarding. We align with what the Universe wants for us and to our deepest desires which leads us to learn and grow and love. You learn how to draw more of what you want into your life and banish what you don't want.

The Universe works by specific laws. Before you activate the Law of Attraction take time to consult your inner wisdom. It will always have your best interest at heart and it will keep you aligned with what the Universe wishes to offer you for the highest good. Accessing this wisdom is actively using your inner wisdom to create a better, happier and healthy life. Be mindful and pay attention to every moment and every action you engage in. Information comes to your from your highest self which is not of this world but of all dimensions. Your purpose is to open the connection to Spirit. As you become aware, you will be placed in a location in which you can serve. You are there for a reason, you want to experience whatever is happing in in your life right now. That is growth as long as you keep moving forward knowing that things that you thought were impossible before can manifest and change at any given moment.

As your mind begins to adjust to the higher vibrations you will hear your guidance from your guides, Angles, Spirit guides and other dimensional Beings. These guides were assigned to you before you chose to incarnate. They have been guiding you all along. Embrace this and be grateful that these beings have been helping you feel safe and loved. These being appears in your 3rd eye in your mind's eye. Visualize the bright light above your head, this is the area of your pineal gland. Once activated this gland begins to release DMT, allowing you the ability to see into other dimensions and connect to your guides. Ask for guidance and open your mind to this dimension. This is a higher dimension then you may have been used to so try to stay grounded. Remember nothing is being done to you it is done for you. You are evolving into the version that you were created to be. This is a journey home back to Source and your essence is inside the partial we call GOD> everyone here has a Divine purpose and it's up to you to be willing to step into that light. The Universe will meet you where you are today and lead you where you need to be tomorrow. Being on a Spiritual path does not prevent you from facing times of darkness but it teaches you how to use the dark as a tool for growth. You may have been given a mountain to show others it can be moved. God will not allow any person to keep you from your destiny. It's what we do for Christ in the here and now that will make a difference in the future. This is the return to innocence. Where there is will, you will be shown the way!

ARE YOU AN EMPATH?

Do you often feel the pain of others, does reading between the lines come easily to you, and do you search for answers often wondering WHY to life's circumstance. Do you prefer solitude over social gatherings? Is care giving a natural response you give to anyone hurting? Do you cry easily or feel physically ill while watching movies with violence or tragedy. Do you consider yourself to be in harmony with nature, Earth, water and sky? Are you a good listener, compassionate to the needs of others? Empaths process enormous amounts of empathy, which gives us the ability to read and understand people and be in tune with or resonate with others, voluntarily or involuntary of one's empathy capacity. Empath's have the ability to scan another's psyche for thoughts and feelings or for past or present and future life occurrences. Empaths sense deep emotions- feeling another's true emotions to a point where empathy can relate to that person by sensing true feelings that run deeper than those portrayed on the surface. Often people put on a show to express themselves. This is a learned trait of hiding authentic expression in an increasingly demanding society. An Empath can sense the truth behind the cover and will act compassionately to help that person express his/her self, thus making them feel at ease and not so desperately alone. Empaths experience empathy towards family, children and friends, close associates, complete strangers, pets, plants and in animated objects.

Empathy is not held by time or space. This allows the empath to feel emotions of people and things at a distance. Some are empathic towards many different things. Empaths are highly sensitive. This is a term commonly used in describing one's abilities to another's emotions and feelings. Empaths have a deep sense of knowing that accompanies empathy and are often compassionately considerate and understanding of others. There are also varying levels of strength in empaths which may be related to the individualist awareness of self. Generally those who are empathic grow up with these tendencies and do not learn about them until later in life. Empathy is genetic inherent in our DNA and can be passed from generation to generation once you awaken those energies within yourself. It is studied both by traditional science and alternative healing practitioners. Empaths often possess the ability to sense others on many levels. From their position in observing what another is saying, feeling and thinking they come to understand another. Empaths can become very proficient at reading another person's body language or study intently the eye movement. While this in itself is not empathy it is a side shot that comes from being observant of others. In a sense empaths have a complete communication package. Everything has energetic patterns that originate from the speaker, they have a specific meaning particular to the speaker, and behind that expression is a power or force field better known as energy. It is the person's feelings (energy) that are picked up by empaths whether the words are spoken thought or just felt without verbal or bodily expressions. Empaths are often very affectionate in personality and expression, great listeners. They will find themselves helping others and often putting their own needs aside to do so. In the same breathe they can be much the opposite. Empaths are often quiet and can take a while to handle a compliment for they're more inclined to point out another's positive attributes. They are highly expressive in all areas of emotional connection and talk openly and at times quite frank in respect to themselves. They may have few problems talking about their feelings. They are most often passionate towards nature and respect its bountiful beauty. Empaths are usually drawn to nature as a form of release. It is a place where they can recapture their senses and gain a sense of peace in the hectic lives they may live. The time to get away from it all and unwind with nature becomes essential to the empath. Some are very good at blocking out others and that's not always a bad thing at least for the learning empath struggling with a barrage of emotions from others as well as their own feelings. They have a tendency to openly feel what is outside of themselves more so than what is inside of them. This can cause the empath to ignore their own needs. Any area filled with disharmony creates an uncomfortable feeling in an empath. If they find themselves in the middle of confrontation they will endeavor to settle the situation as quickly as possible if not avoid it all together. Empaths are sensitive to violence emotional dramas, depicting shocking scenes of physical or emotional pain inflicted on adults, children or animals which can bring an Empath to tears. At times they may feel physically ill because they have taken on someone's negative energy. They struggle to comprehend any such cruelty and will have difficulty in expressing themselves in the face of another's ignorance, closed mindedness and obvious lack of compassion. They cannot justify the suffering they feel or see. People of all walks of life are attracted to the warmth and genuine compassion of empaths. Regardless of whether others are aware of one being empathic, people are drawn to them as a metal object is to a magnet. They are like beacons of light. Even strangers find it easy to talk to empaths pouring out their heart and soul without intending to do so consciously. It is as though on a sub-conscious level that the person knows instantly that empaths would listen with compassionate understanding. There are the listeners of life. As far an empaths are concerned where a problem is so, too is the solution. They often will search until they find one, if only for peace of mind. They are attuned to vibration frequencies. They are vulnerable to taking on emotional junk belonging to others which can cause them to feel anxious, fatigued or overwhelmed or hurt. As an empath you are part of a much larger group of sensitive people who are asking the same things! Some empaths want to turn their sensitivity off. There is no special on or off 'switch.' You can only cope with it by moving away from energy, remaining neutral and grounded while experiencing energy, or by moving toward, embracing, or otherwise amplifying the energy. Each of these choices can be done either in balance or out of balance. An example of moving toward energy in an out of balance way would be if we know we are being drained by another's energy but we encourage the person to continue. An example of moving away from the energy in a balanced manner would be to take yourself out of the situation or to simply share with the person that their energetic state is causing you to be drained. It is most important that empaths remember to shield themselves whenever they feel like they are assuming others energy. Surround yourself in white light sending the intention out to the Universe. This shield can steer you away from those lower energies if they become uncomfortable.

When you experience negative energy, the heart chakra often will automatically close to limit the energy input and feeling of pain. The body will do this to protect you. The closing of the chakras can result in feelings of tension, restriction, and your heart chakra being pulled on. It can feel like an enormous weight is sitting on your heart. After time, however, too much closing of the heart chakra can result in suffering and illness. You can learn to exert conscious control over your chakras and learn to keep them flowing. You may feel that something is wrong with, you but there is absolutely nothing wrong with you. On the contrary, you have a great gift that all the great Spiritual Masters have learned to work with and accept. Jesus, Buddha, and all the great Spiritual Masters were Empaths.

Emotional empathy is one of the most common because you can feel and process the emotions of others. Sometimes knowing other times unknowingly. If you feel drained in the presents of certain people who may be struggling or feeling low, this would be a sign that their emotions have leaked into you aura and you may need to do remove the lower energy from you. This can be done by showering, meditation, any form of clearing. By releasing any and all thoughts from your Being, situations and energies that are no longer of service to your highest good. Ask that all of the energies that are less then love be transmitted for the highest good of all.

Medical Empathy is a known ability where you may just feel an awareness on or around the physical body when you are treating others. You can see blockages in the person's energy field signaling you that there is some work that need to be done to help move the energy for them. If you feel that you are a medical empath you may need to strength you energy field before taking this on. Those that practice Reiki need to shield themselves before giving any type of healing.

The next type is a place empath which means that you may be unsettled in certain locations. You may be able to feel the emotions left there by other Souls. Often it will feel like a desire to leave or you may experience the chills which indicates you are aware of the old energy or emotions. It can feel unsettling to some and so you may not want to stay there too long. Environmental empathy speak of those Souls who are gifted to feel a connection with nature, and trees, and landscapes and want to keep them as natural as possible. Empaths can use their helping power to send love to the earth.

Intellectual empathy is a gift that allows you to tap into the thoughts or perspectives of those around you. If you have people around you who are upset or are operating on a lower frequency, protecting you mental body is a must. In order to be a healer, you must deeply understand the suffering of others. As Spiritual warriors, empaths are greatly in touch with the shadow. Your ability to simply perceive the darkness/shadow of others is often mistaken for a feeling that it is you yourself that is wounded. It's not you. It's simply the energy you perceive that is wounded. You have a choice with what you are to do with this gift or sometimes preserved as a curse. You can run away from it by ignoring it, suppressing it, or you can embrace it to help others. The choice is yours. The sooner you learn to accept your sensitivity without judgment, the sooner you'll be on your way to fulfilling your destiny to help others.

We experience a variety of emotions, anything from happiness to sadness to extreme joy and depression. Each one of these emotions creates a different feeling within your body. Our body will release different chemicals when we experience various situation that make us happy and each chemical works to create a different environment within the body. The brain release serotonin, dopamine, or oxytocin, when you are feeling good and happy. If your body is stressed it will release cortisol and you have an entirely different feeling associated more like the feeling of your body in survival mode. Negative thinking all of the time can creates more stress therefore releasing more cortisol throughout your body.

By dealing with, and accepting, the shadows you begin to heal yourself. There are many ways to do this. You will want to find a sustained method of personal ritual to help heal wounds and make you strong enough to have enough Light to overcome the darkness. Getting your body worked on professionally by a healer, be it, Reiki, massage therapy, etc. are all helpful during these stress filled times. Listen to the tone in which you speak, if your tone is off adjust it by changing the way you speak. Begin to use words that express Love, and kindness, and appreciation. You will begin to see things that represent this lighter tone. You will have more experiences that incorporate these vibrations into existence that are beautiful and amazing and precious. The connection between your mood and body is a very powerful and although it may not be seen visually the effect your mind can have on your physical body are profound. We can have overall positive attitude and deal directly with the internal challenges and in turn create a healthy lifestyle or we can stay in a negative self-destructive state having negative thoughts and not dealing with our issues.

Our emotions and experiences are essential energy and they can be stored in the cellular memory of your body. If any emotional memory or pain has not been healed it can leave a scar if not released. If you still have memory of that pain it means that you are holding energy in that area of the body. When you have pain, tightness or injuries in certain areas it is often item related to an emotional feeling within yourself. When you deal with the emotion that is causing that pain in your body and address the unconscious thought patterns you will being to lighten up and the pain will begin to leave the body. If you are not feeling well your body is asking you to observe and try to find peace once again with yourself. Remember you do have the power to get through anything that life throws at you. Instead of labeling the experience as negative or positive try to see things from a higher perspective. Ask yourself how can this help me to see or learn something. Can I use this to shift my perception? Whatever it may be instead of simply reacting slow things down and observe. You will find you have the tools to process emotions and illness quickly when you see them for what they are.

Refusing to see other side of a questions and being stubborn and inflexibly you may develop a pain in your neck. If your shoulders feel sore you may be burden by you attitude. The spine responses to the support you get of life. Issues in your upper back may be due to a lack of emotional support, feeling unloved or you hold back love, this will signal a pain or stiffness in your spine. The lower back you may have an issued where you have a fear based on money. The elbows represent changing direction and accepting new experiences. Pain in your hips may show you the fear of going forward in major decision, nothing is moving forward. The knee means you are stubborn and may display and inability to bend or won't give in. This is case by ego and pride. Weakness means you may need some mental rest. The movement of the body is a reflective to your inner work. The Angles will send you signs encouraging you to look for the reason of your bodies discomfort and also send you message as to how to heal these issues also.

Even if you are not aware of it, you are experiencing others' energy in your body. You may perceive other people's thoughts, and can feel others intentions tugging on our own hearts. The only way to tell what is coming from others (either on the Earth plane or from other Spiritual dimensions) is to have a quiet mind. The ego must be sublimated. The only way you can do that is through being grounded. By tuning in to the sensations in your body and you must have released the energy that has been stored up in your cells through the years. Abuse, trauma, and nasty energy does get stored in your aura and body. Aim to be clear and clean in order to accurately perceive other people's energy. Bipolar disorder, anxiety disorders, depression, chronic fatigue, lupus, and fibromyalgia are some of the most commonly diagnosed mental illnesses in empaths. These symptoms may have their origins in a lack of balance in energy input/output. Interestingly, these often have nothing to do with the mind, and everything to do with the body and its sensitive nervous system. Many empaths are diagnosed with these conditions because they have relatively open heart chakras and nervous systems that allow them to perceive massive amounts of subtle energy in our environment. Using social anxiety as one example; this condition results from being in environments where other people are nervous. The body cannot process the energy fast enough and we fidget, our hearts race, and our thoughts may follow. With all energy-based syndromes, there simply may be too much energy input for the body to handle, and over time, the nervous system attempts to protect us by gradually shutting down, which results in chronic deprivation of energy and illness, work to re-train the nervous system to learn that it is more beneficial to be open, not closed.

As we know, we live and develop self-consciousness with the help of our five physical senses. In turn self-consciousness gradually develops an ego. From childhood the ego is the part in us that learns and separates itself from others. It teaches us to discriminate between this and that, putting limits around oneself and others, develops traits of character, expresses the impulses coming from the Soul in creative and unique ways. However as part of our human inheritance there exist in us two more subtle senses. In some people these two senses are awakening and in a process of development. We shall call them the intuitive and Spiritual sixth and seventh senses. Their role is to let our level of consciousness be influenced by the impulses coming from the Soul and Spirit levels in us.

Trying to activate these two Spiritual senses in us depends entirely on our level of purification and of mastering the functions and impulses coming from the ego. This means that we must first learn to master and transmute our animalistic instincts and stop over rationalizing with our intelligence so that these two Spiritual senses unfold their Spiritual attributes and qualities in us. This sense is based on the innate knowledge that belongs to the Spirit in which dwells the sublime knowledge of the creation of the Universe and of its Source. It also includes the knowledge and processes of the mystery of incarnation and of reintegration into the Absolute Uncreated Light. We understand that for us, this knowledge is still incomprehensible, since, to be able to enter in its dimension, we must have first perfected the seventh sense and its corresponding level of consciousness in our being.

The sixth and seventh senses function properly only when the Intelligence of the Heart is open in our psyche and is in harmony with the two Divine Witnesses (Soul/Spirit). It is the awakened functions of the Soul within us. These qualities which evolve gradually through intuition, and reveal the Soul's Divine gifts are of an awe-inspiring quality. The seventh sense is of a much higher Spiritual nature and is not based on ordinary human understanding and logic but rather the awakening and merging of Soul spirit which are for the time being still dormant in most people. The mission of these Spiritual functions cannot be revealed since they belong to the Spiritual part in each one of us. The sixth sense allows the Soul's impulses to filter into the consciousness of us. As for the seventh sense it performs perfectly well when the Spirit and the Soul blend and harmonize within the transfigured self-consciousness.

The sixth sense is the Spiritual faculty that gives us a sudden "hunch", an inspiration, an intuition and our creative and artistic faculties. It makes us care, nurture and sympathize with people. The language of the Soul is a Spiritual faculty that can be developed only through the Intelligence of the Heart. The seventh sense is something different. It activates, awakens and harmonizes all our subtle bodies through the action of the HOLY SPIRIT. It means that the Soul and Spirit have finally united and reintegrated their Pure Essence. This means that there are three major processes in the complete transformation in us. PURIFICATION of the old process that involves and uses our sixth sense of intuition. The second phase involves the process of RESURRECTION, having purified the mental and emotional bodies, ascends together with the regenerated conscious self. Together they blend with the Soul's complementary partner: the Spiritual Witness. The third phase brings about REINTEGRATION of the whole essence of being meaning that the three aspects have reintegrated back into the Source. Before all these stages can unfold their Spiritual procedures in us, the sixth sense of the Soul must integrate and function properly in our ego. The ego must have reached a very high level of purification. We are here to learn and develop our Being and to become the best version of ourselves. This is what we call Ascension. Moving to a higher level of awareness or consciousness. Being aware of you higher purpose and how you are part of the process aligning yourself with the Divine. The most important thing to remember is how determined are we to follow through with it.

So the most important question that we should ask ourselves is this: are we ready to open up the energy and impulses coming from our inner vision. If the answer is yes, then we have nothing to fear, since all these inner phases and planes of discovery will open up their secrets to us in their own time. This being said, this sublime transmutation of our lower energies into their Spiritual counterparts can only happen through the development of our sixth and seventh senses. Knowledge received through the seventh sense makes us participate instantly and fully with what is being received. In other words, the knowledge and the one receiving the knowledge unite, and become one and the same thing. When do we become aware of Divine Love and Knowledge? This occurs when the ego, the Soul and Spirit unite in the acceptance of the enlightening Wisdom. This happens only if we choose to do so. It is therefore up to us to act now. Our sixth sense takes us behind the veils of the illusions helping us unfold within the subtle planes of intuition bringing about change and transformation. The path entirely depends on our ego wanting to recognize its true essence it is most crucial and important to allow the process of our sixth sense to unveil for us whatever the Soul wants us to become. This is our destiny. Through the channel of our sixth sense of intuition our Spiritual development unfolds more subtle qualities in our ego. This process is based on the purification and transmutation of the lower energies of our Soul Personality to their higher counterparts, so that the pure knowledge and Divine Love can flow freely and filter its intense and radiant Light through our transformed ego. It is recommended that you become the observer of your own actions and reactions. This is your personal connection with your Inner Self; that sacred space within, you. It is in that silent place that you will appear whenever you are attuned to your Soul.

The manner in which one enters these very subtle levels of intuition cannot be explained or shown, since these refined senses are in themselves levels of consciousness and inner paths of knowledge and enlightenment. The only way to describe and comprehend this is through the development of your own personal and individual intuitive faculties. As you get in touch with yourself and learn to unfold your personal goals you begin to experience that expression in your Soul. It is our Soul that selects it so as to attract us towards itself. The Soul selects the Divine connection according to our karmic needs and attunements. The thing we call our intuition is your Soul, learn to trust what it is telling you. The wiser I get the more I understand that it is okay to live a life others don't understand!

At the beginning of this Spiritual process, the Soul needs to take a certain appearance so as to attract our ego, and harmonize it to a specific Spiritual level. And since the ego and the five physical senses belong to the same physical world in which we live, they must first be magnetically attracted to something more ethereal and Spiritual than themselves in order to be purified. The path must be attractive to our ego, and should move us to the core of our Being, so that it reverberates and energizes in all our subtle bodies. First, the Soul attracts and operates within our etheric, astral and mental bodies purifying and refining the limiting characteristics of the ego. It also takes the personal boundaries and limitations of each person into account. People often have difficulty accepting that they have been blessed with psychic abilities because without a frame of reference it is almost impossible to identify an extrasensory experience and to distinguish psychic sights, sounds, and sensations from the projects of the unconscious mind. To some extent, every human being on the planet is clairvoyant, clairaudient, and clairsentient, although most people discover that they are naturally adept at one more than the others. When you trust in and take steps to tune into your innate clairvoyance, clairaudience, and clairsentience, you will enter a new realm of being in which the Universe, your higher self, and your Spirit guides lovingly conduct you toward a more aware existence. Clairvoyance, or clear seeing, is the ability to see with the mind's eye. An individual who has tuned into their clairvoyant abilities may be able to see in their mind's eye events in a remote location; to witness incidents that have yet to occur; or to perceive shapes, colors, and other images that are physically invisible. Clairaudience, which means clear listening, is the ability to hear sounds not physically audible. A person with the gift of clairaudience perceives psychic information as auditory resonance and may hear Angelic voices, music, or other sounds. A clairsentient, or clear feeling, individual is able to sense physical, emotional, and Spiritual energy in the form of seemingly unearthly scents, touches, and movements. Each of these psychic abilities can manifest themselves within us voluntarily or involuntarily. It is natural for us to have these abilities; you just need to practice. Developing your psychic talents is a matter of releasing your fear of seeing, hearing, or feeling unexplained stimulus. Before you attempt to consciously tap into your gifts, ground yourself to anchor your mind in the present to disconnect from any involuntary psychic experiences you may be having. Concentrate on your intuitive responses to the world around you and notice any sights, sounds, or feelings that enter your mind. If you trust your perceptions, you'll discover that each psychic impression you receive will be in some way relevant to your experience even when that relevance may not be immediately recognizable. Perceiving the Infinite and using your psychic gift experiences are a natural part of our everyday lives.

Unless we open up and become interested in each others' way of being, and search for common understanding of the essence of reality, life will remain a mystery to us. If we want to connect with each other, we must go beyond our limited perception of reality and search for common ground. So the first step in opening up and understanding our differences is to be aware of the limitations imposed by our ego. It is our egos that separate my reality from your reality. Fortunately, there are ways of interacting and respecting each others' different ways of "being in the world." The point is that this can potentially steer you in a new direction, show how to proceed in your quest, and inspire those who are in harmony with the essence of these messages coming from the Source of Being. The messages are intended to harmonize you with seed ideas, signs and symbols scattered here and there in the messages. These are the keys that will open up for you the abstract world of hidden and dormant knowledge that is inherent in your center of pure consciousness. These seed ideas will resonate within you, become clearer, and fall into place in your psyche because, through their essence and symbols, you will be prepared to intuitively pass through the gateway to your own inner Universe. Subsequently, your own Center of Pure Being and the center of the Universe will gradually blend and harmonize, and consciousness will have recognized its own reflection in the mirror of consciousness.

The average person who is not a seeker identifies perfectly with ones ego, and is not worried about the ego or how others perceive truth and reality. The seeker, on the other hand, knows that ego is the problem that it must be under the control of the Soul that it needs to loosen and open up, that it must be transformed so that the Soul can express the Divine qualities within the human psyche. The goal of the Spiritual process is simply to make the ego realize that it has no independent existence, that it is merely a reflection of the Divine Essence that is at the source of consciousness. Since consciousness needs a vehicle to become aware of itself, it can only do so by expressing itself in the world of duality. Cosmic Consciousness expanding and then enters vehicles that become individual, limited reflections of it. Apart from the self-consciousness of the ego, which makes one aware that "I am me," there are two more important levels of consciousness. The second awakening of consciousness still functions in the ego and the world of duality and dualism and it says,

"I AM conscious of being a direct individual expression of the Soul or God."

This is the key that will unleash the gates of your true Being. You will pass through various inner processes that will, throughout your life, reflect different levels of consciousness, until that moment when you become aware that you have an inner "model" that follows each of your steps, a Spiritual mapping showing you how to proceed in your quest. It is a thread that you must follow to reach an inner purified plane that leads to pure consciousness, in which the astral and mental bodies will be ready to be reshaped in the Divine image. In this image, your self-conscious will blend with the essence of your Soul, encompassing within it its Divine ethereal features. This mold will chisel your Divine Face within all of your subtle bodies, and in time, you will become conscious and know it well.

When you, the seeker, attune and connect with your Divine Face and express it here on the physical plane, you will still have to "live" in duality. This means, that your Divine Face manifests and is attuned to everything you do through your human faculties. All your experiences and the work you do bear the imprint of the essence of your Soul and are therefore reflected in whatever you do, say or think on this plane of existence. You were given a name at birth and are on a journey of self-discover, knowing that you must share whatever you have learned on your journey. As you discovered your Divine essence imprinted in your consciousness you uncover the truth, I am simply energy coming from the un- manifested Presence of Being. As individuals, we become conscious of its existence only when certain impulses and experiences have been aroused and stimulated in the subconscious and subjective parts of our psyche. This means that our quest to understand our own mystery, the mystery of the meaning of life itself, begins just then and can never really exist before that crucial moment. I encourage you to begin in earnest your search for the beloved Presence within you that is your Divine Essence. This presence will gradually reflect itself back to you through dreams, insights and intuitions, slowly revealing the image of your pure Being in which you will have to enter so as to take a new shape and receive the new features (qualities) of your Divine Essence.

The wisdom of an enlightened being comes directly from the source of Wisdom and the way to open up to its influence comes by following a special path, a path that unfolds from within. As you being to vibrate and are in resonance with Source the seeker has to recognize and follow the inner Path that unfolds the initiatory process of reaching the enlightenment. The seeker must take into account the karmic links that have been forged in the past and discover the special requirements that must still develop and experience. Gradually, by attuning and merging with the essence of source the seeker's level of consciousness unites with the center of wisdom. This explains how consciousness appears within oneself. It appears, when the inherent qualities of Source manifest and enlighten the consciousness of a seeker. Everyone is gifted with the ability to reach this level of development, but most people never open these passage ways.

Romans 8:29 says, "From the very beginning God decided that those who came to him. . . should become like his Son." God wants you to learn to think like Jesus, to talk like Jesus, to act like Jesus. Those character traits are summarized in Galatians 5:22-23: "The fruit of the Spirit is love, joy, peace, patience, kindness, goodness, faithfulness, gentleness, and self-control." How does God develop those qualities in you? He does it by putting you in the exact opposite situations. For instance, God teaches you to love by putting unlovely people around you. He teaches you to be joyful by allowing hardship in your life. He teaches you patience by letting you sit in traffic. Fruit doesn't grow without fertilizer, and God uses hardships to fertilize the seeds he plants in your Soul so the fruit of the Spirit will grow.

If God is going to make you like Jesus Christ, that means he's going to take you through the same kinds of experiences that Jesus Christ went through. Were there times when Jesus was lonely? Yes. Were there times when he was tempted? Yes. Were there times when He could have become discouraged? Yes. Do you think you should be exempt from those? Of course not! They are all part of character development. Remember, this life is a test. God is getting you ready for eternity and he's watching how you respond to those situations.

God uniquely shaped you to serve others. I am a creative being, using my energy to co create a wonderful world. I know that I create my experience of life from within, and as I do so, I also create ripples of energy around me that echo into the world. My positive thoughts gather together with the thoughts and prayers of others, and together we create enough positive energy to heal not only our own lives but the world we share. I am grateful for the ability to co create peace in my life and in the world. You must have patience and know that God is not finished with us yet. When you feel like you are in deep water remember the one who walked on it. God sometimes take us into troubled waters not to drown us but to cleanse us. Any path you chose to travel along will always lead you where your Soul wants to go.

SPIRITUAL ASCENSION

The promise of Ascension is the hidden heritage and legacy of our human condition, the fulfillment of our evolutionary blueprint. The purpose of the Soul is to search for the inner connectedness with your Creator/ Source. This is when you move from mortality to immortality while still in this form. Mother Mary said to those who seek her" If you knew yourself as I know you, you could not help but fall in love with yourself". As Spiritual seekers we are told often to love ourselves. The Ascension is believed to be the returning to complete Oneness with God, raising the outer atomic structure of the physical, emotional and mental bodies into the electronic structure of the" I AM" Consciousness and becoming an ascended master eventually a Cosmic Being. This is our ascension into immorality through the reunion with Source. Your choice to never awaken to who you really are is entirely up to you. No one will make you do anything you are not ready for. You have free will and you can choose to participate in the Ascension or not. The first choice is to simply acknowledge that you are the part of your Creator. Choose to vibrate at your highest level possible choosing love over fear or hate. Strive to become the best that you are or just allow it to happen. Choose to open to the energies from above that are being presented to you every minute. Wake up to reality but don't be surprised if it is not what you thought. Choose to let these energies come to you through meditation and prayer and just allow them to talk to you. You have the power to make sense and decide it if it is right for you. Choose to let your relationships with yourself and Source becomes the most valuable relationship you have. Choose to let others make their own choices and you stick to yours. Work on cleaning up your body from trauma either past or present. Choose to let go of control. Look within and connect to the real you in order to follow you own Divine guidance. If you surrender to who you are, the world will have no choice but to accept you as you are. The new energy that you find yourself in requires that you can no longer sit on the fence anymore. You must choose to take the path of least resistance or you can boldly choose to take your power. Often taking your power requires the strength to swim upstream. You are always in control when you choose to ascend. You will always be safe. You are a beautiful being created of love& light. Send that light and love into the Universe and the Universe will return that energy back to you.

We are all born into a state of duality. We have an ego side and a Divine side. The ego side is not a bad or something wrong. It gives us the sense of our individually which is important to develop as we begin our journey. As we journey unfolds we lose the role of the ego and our sense of oneness emerges. Our Divine side or the true self is the Soul essence of each being; it is what connects us to Source. It comes from source and it is a part of that energy. It is the higher mind which we sometimes think that it comes from the mind where it actually come from is the heart. Our true self is designed to co create with Source. We have been creating automatically by design. We are awakening to the fact that our thoughts are what actually create our current reality. There are universal laws showing us how things really work in the cosmos. They cannot be changed. Everything must work by these laws. Two of the laws are critically connected to our current awakening process. The Law of Vibration states that everything that exists has a vibration. The Law of Attraction or cause and effect states that where we vibrate and where we put our thoughts will cause us to attract to ourselves things of like vibration. If we vibrate on the lower frequencies we feel powerless and will attract things that overpower us, if we feel joyful and vibrate at the frequencies we will attract happy people. Where we vibrate determines what we create. Each of these vibrations causes a thought either consciously or unconsciously and those thoughts become our reality. Most of what we attract is done unconsciously driven by our past experiences in this life. This is what we call karma and it needs to be cleared before we can consciously create what we wish to see in our lives. The people in your life have been invited to you by you. You have created the experiences you wished to fulfill. Listen to the way people talk to you it will give you an understanding on how you vibrate. The world is a mirror for your vibration. The vibration is determined by your energetic state. Clearing your energy field allows you to become a conscious co creator of your own reality. You can consciously choose to think in the positive ways to raise your current vibration.

We can direct our energy and intentions into activities that promote peace rather than using it to create opposition. Optimistic thoughts energize others, giving them hope and inspiring them to work diligently on behalf of what they believe in. Being for something creates a positive shift in the energy. Standing up for something is often more challenging because you may be introducing an idea to people that may scare them on a Soul level. Being for something takes less energy as it is already in a lighter form. We must learn to consciously use 100% of our Creative Power of thought, feeling and spoken words to create perfection, joy, and love in the world. Using opposing thoughts or feelings or words only create limitation and chaos in your own experiences and in the world. The Law of One is the original law of creation. This Master Law is the law of Omnipresence of all life and it is the supreme law over all laws in all dimensions. We are all one. All beings exist within and of one source. The Law of One is an energy reality, a conscious focus of knowing that I am all and we are one. As a Soul, you are born from the unity of consciousness, which is God. The Divine design of the creator is imbued within you. The "Law of One" acknowledges the value, interconnection and interdependence of all components of reality and the living God-Source or Spirit alive within all things. We are direct self-expressions of the One. No being can ever be outside of God-Source. Each expression of Source has the freedom to explore and experience directly the Laws of Divine Love and Creation. We have the Spirit of God within our being, and it is the force which exist in all things and it is the same force which can guide us through this journey we are now embarking upon.

DIMENSIONS OF CONSCIOUSNESS

A dimension is a state of consciousness and a means of organizing different planes of existence according to a vibratory rate of that which exists. Each dimension has a certain set of laws and principles that are specific to the frequency rate. All human beings are multi-dimensional beings of light with a visible dense physical body that have the potential to access the other dimensions. We are comfortable with our awareness being in the 3rd dimension but with a Spiritual practice either meditation or reflection and asking our guides for assistance we can access the 4th dimension usually referred to be the astral plane of time and some even can access the 5th dimension. Indigo and Crystal and Light workers and star seeds, can access the 4th, 5th, 6th, and 7th dimension. Some Crystal Souls can access the higher dimensions as well as evolved human beings or star people whose origin are from a star or star system. Human beings whom have applied themselves to a Spiritual practice can gain awareness of the 4th and 5d worlds or perspectives, within or outside our Galaxy. Many people are feeling a planetary shift in energy or consciousness; this is what is being called a cleansing. As we ascend to higher levels of consciousness we move further away from ego and closer to Source. This growth may feel uncomfortable as we are forced to disconnect from and release our attachment to this physical world. At our highest level of consciousness we are in service to all humanity and the Universe as we teach and prepare lower beings to return to the original source of God. The first three dimensions are about motions, be it physical, emotional or mental. 1st Dimension- physical time is the awareness as a point in space and time. It is the level of consciousness at which human genetic coding, water and minerals would resonate. For humans this level is unconscious to our five senses. 2nd Dimension is about the emotional feelings it is awareness as a point in line. This is a level of consciousness of plants and the lower animal kingdom live. The 3rd dimension is mental thought. This is awareness of point, line, width, height and volume. It is the conscious world as we know it. The 4th dimension is the awareness of point, line, width, and breath height, volume and time. This dimension is also referred to as the astral plane. When we are sleeping we are unconscious of the 3rd dimension and conscious of the 4th dimension. The consciousness of this dimension is in the astral body, also referred to as the higher human. This etheric body is home to our dreaming, intuition, physic ability, creativity and magic. The astral body is of a higher vibration than the physical body and is in form that is known as etheric. This is the unconscious mind. In this dimension feelings and thoughts create reality and at this level there is the awareness of the Universal Law of One, or unity consciousness, stating that whatever affects one affect all of us. Some humans are born in this dimension in the physical form such as Indigos or Crystals. Indigo Souls carry this awareness which is the key to multi-dimensionality and it leads them to be warriors for cause to heal the Earth. They realize that no one is greater than anyone else.

The 5th dimension is the awareness of point, line, width, and breath, height and volume time and spirit. There is no illusion of limitation. Some Indigos are born into this dimension. We are liberated to create a new paradigm of being, thinking, and doing as part of the universal one. There is a constant experience of oneness. This dimension holds unconditional love and unconditional acceptance. We hold no judgment, guilt or negativity towards the lower aspects of ourselves that are striving to remember our higher selves. The 6th dimension is one of crystal consciousness. Here, life is playful and magical and we surrender to the flow of our evolving spirit while continuing to create on an individual level. Some human that are born into this dimension are known as Crystal Souls. The crystal consciousness has access to their magical and Spiritual aspects, and has playfulness with life. Life is seen as magical and blessed. All life is directed and advanced through the work of spirit. The person in the 6th D awareness surrenders to the flow of Spirit's evolution while exercising the right to be a creator on an individual level. In the 7th dimension we are fully aware of the nature of the spirited mission of our Being. It is a field where we share our aura for the good of others as part of our planetary duty to heal and teach them about higher consciousness. The Crystal adult can connect to their Soul family and where many light beings gather to communicate with lower levels. In the 8th dimension we have complete control over the story of our lives. It is the place of eternity where the Soul is intangible, undefined and immeasurable. The 9th dimension is full cosmic consciousness and has full responsibility for stewardship of the planet; the 9th dimension incorporates with the 8th D. The next three dimensions are the Consciousness of our Creator. The 10th dimension is where we communicate with creation through sound and vibration. We become aware of all the planets that make up our consciousness and assume responsibility at a solar level. In the 11th dimension we exist as a ray of light. Our galactic level of consciousness is achieved. There is where the Twin Flame and the higher selves' Angelic beings inhabit. Twin Flames are a higher frequency because they are ultimate examples of the Yin/Yang energy. They are each two whole individual Souls on their own but they complement, understand and connect in a very in a very unique way. They are called twin mates because they emit the same frequency of vibration which accounts for a strong feeling of energies when they are physically around one another. If you have had someone in your life that you can't quit describe the connection there is a strong chance that's your Twin Flame. When we meet our Twin Flame in our current life there will be a high level of comfort, intimacy, understanding, of each other and a sense of peace, it's a feeling connectedness.

During our journey at times there are beings that come into our life's at the right time and says or does the right thing. They help us to perceive ourselves more clearly by words or actions. They help us cope and see us through difficult situations reminding us that all will be ok. Human Angels agreed to, before their births to make a commitment to be a positive contribution to the world at a particular moment. They come into our lives when we least expect them and when we can most benefit from their presence. Most are just going about their own lives until called upon to be in the right place at the right time. They are here to bring peace, joy, and help or to heal when they are needed the most. You may have already met one who gave you a piece of advice that touched your Soul and influenced your path, sometimes offering nothing more than a kind word or a smile, or when you can draw the most strength and support from their simple action. You can be a human Angel yet not know it. Your fate or intuition, may guide you towards others challenges or in distressed situations. Human Angels give of their inner light to all who need it, coming into our lives and often changing us forever. The Angelic human 9th dimension brings a message of awakening to your capacities to reveal and reflect an individual message held within the personal identity of each being. As we awaken to our messages the call of the Angelic human light draws from you the grace of your Soul. Angelic Realm, comes with unconditional love, providing guidance and assistance toward our highest good and always honoring our Free will. Angelic Humans know in their heart, and hears the message. The Angelic human posses with in their DNA a code. Known as the silicate Matrix. A "genetic package" imbued to present time humans. The Silicate Matrix contains the original 12-Strand DNA code structure of the original human. It presently exists within a number of humans as a latent genetic code sequence that must be brought into activation. Once activated, it allows for the progressive transmutation of form. Not all humans carry this code, and not all code carriers can endure full activation, but those who carry this matrix which is contained within the cellular material currently call junk DNA have the potential ability of accelerated evolution. Our junk DNA is not junk! But instead part of the heritage that will one day led you back to the wholeness of your identity. In the 12th dimension we return to Source and resonate in unison with the physical form of our Universe, we are beginning to feel whole. You become a full Universal Being with the understanding of universal level of consciousness. The Angelic human are here on Earth to bring about the transformation of the world and its people. Often refer to as Earth Angels they come now to make the invisible visible. Each Angelic human carries certain codes with in their DNA that opens a new paradigm of experience within life itself. Earth Angles know that it will take courage to know their brilliance and with integrity they bring completion to their message now. During portal activation many of the codes are set into activation. We are evolving!

As we seek and learn of things unknown, we will walk down many paths in life encountering just what we need to help awaken us to a higher destiny. Our journey will cover a lifetime as we gather a multitude of experiences that will help us to expand and evolve. The most important issue to the human condition is not to allow ourselves to become rigid and unyielding in our thinking. This is a common human affliction and causes many to shut down the gates to further exploration, settling comfortably within the confines of one belief system. Our Universe is expansive, vast and never ending and mostly unknown - anything at all is possible...and all things are possible. Everything in the Universe is made of energy and you too are an energetic Being. You are energetically connected to everyone and everything you love and these energy cords carry information that continually influences our physical reality. Being aware of your own energy nature and taking the time to recharge yourself through meditation will enhance your well-being. Ground yourself by visualizing an energy cord running from the base of your spine to the center of the Earth and feel all your anxiety and upset feelings drop down away from you and into the Earth.

Waking up at the same time at night might be a sign that you need to pay attention: Your energy body is connected to a system that is energizing different part of your body. If you wake up at night your energies in your body may be blocked. If you find that you have trouble falling asleep between the hrs. of 9-11 it may be a sign of stress from worry. Your sleep cycle is a time when you can dream and you will receive messages from the Divine about your path. You are being called at these times to pay attention and wake up because your higher power has something to tell you, just be aware of it. You start to understand that you really part of the unity consciousness and are being guided by the most highly evolved Spiritual Enlighten Beings you could ever have imagined.

INDIGOS/CRYSTALS/
STAR SEEDS SOULS

The Indigo children and adults have been coming into this planet for many years. They are considered to be Spiritual Warriors, the way showers or path cutters. They are coming in more now that before due to the fact that they are here to break down the old systems. There are changes that need to be made. They are creating a new path to human evolution. A lot of Indigos have been searching for the answers as to why the world is so different, so challenging and in many cases hell on earth. Indigo are Beings from another octave, a higher vibration, a higher awareness and an entirely different perception. The ways of the lower vibrations just do not work for these higher octave Beings and the more you try to make them conform to this lower scale the more resistance and frustration you get because it just will not fit into who we are. These Beings are very bright and psychic but many of them have been labeled by others as being different. Indigo have been sent here by their own choice to help change the planet working through the consciousness grid. Some of the qualities and challenges that the first wave indigos experience are that they are wired differently that other people. Often times knowing in their core that they are here on a mission but some don't remember what that is. They have an inner awareness that what is going in the world is just not the truth. Many have a strong sense of truth and ethics, justice and freedom. That is why the authority figures irritate and frustrate them. Many have a strong or unusual psychic and telekinetic abilities; they have extraordinary levels of compassion. This causes them to sometimes put others ahead of themselves. Indigos can be seen sometimes as strong willed, aggressive at times due to the fact they are Spiritual warriors. They have a need for peace yet often times cannot find that peace in the outside world. They are very intelligent but are often under achievers. They think outside the box and don't like to live within the norms of society. The need for meaning in what and where they place their energy is very important. They have a strong desire to be around their own kind and do not always fit in with others of a lower vibration. Others may perceive them as strange or weird so they keep their feelings to themselves yet when it gets too much for them they often time may speak out. They have often shut down their psychic abilities because it scares some people. They carry a strong bond to nature, and can relate to children, feeling more comfortable around others that are like them and uncomfortable with others those are not like them. Indigos carry a high capacity for love and therefore others may feel uncomfortable by that intensity. Very sensitive sometime hyper sensitive and may not be able to distinguish between the emotional field of those around them and their own personal emotions. Many experience periods of apathy and cynicism as a coping skill. They are very sensitive to energy from people sometimes misunderstand than is energy as their own. They are aware of parallel realities, and are well developed, with psychic ability. They are able to perceive things that are usually beyond the range of human senses. Also refer to as visionary, clear sighted, discerning, extra sensory, telepathic, spiritualistic. Their brains are wired differently; they can sense energy and have the ability to sense when things are not right. They may be an intense longing for their own kind, or Soul mates. They have an innate sense of oneness and connectedness to all of creation and enjoy physical touching, hugs and love to cuddle. Sometimes they may exhibit what is refer to as HDD-(Hug Deficit Disorder or cuddle syndrome). They need immense amounts of physical touching, hugs and cuddles. Because of being misunderstood they often feel betrayed and may develop trust issues and therefore keep their thoughts and feelings and opinions to themselves. They are often bored or frustrated with school. Indigos have a strong desire to know why and if they don't see the point or if it is not properly explained can feel it is not worth their time and energy and will resist or just blow it off and turn towards things that make sense to them. They have an evolved awareness of how things work and therefore the rigid rules make no sense to them. All first wave indigos have a healing gift making others feel better and understand that distance make no difference to the efficiently of their work. Because of their expanded perception unusual creativity and wanting to try new things and run way ahead of what is considered normal many are seen as having attention deficit disorder. They are extremely creative and express innate skills. Because of their feelings so foreign to this planet some are put on antidepressants to make them appear normal and fit into society. This is only a temporary fix and most often leads to other challenges. Because they feel so alien here many go through periods of severe grief, and loneliness and displacement and may search for a way out. A high percentage of Indigos are living through extreme hardships as children and teenagers and young adults. These Indigos had to figure out how to balance and keep their inherent integrity levels while being exposed to painful experiences. Indigos are considered the Cosmic Cleanup crew here to rid the planets of corrupted consciousness and physical energetic disease that are destroying and affecting all life forms. Many have been the recipient of walk-ins because of the deep empathic abilities. This often adds to the insanity of their lives. Connecting to nature allows them a sense of being alive which helps balance them. Many can have problems with depression or rage until they learn how to control these emotions they sometimes suffer. They know that they have a mission but sometime are unclear as to what it is. They understand that things that are being taught are not always the truth. They are aware of the hidden agendas and have a hard time accepting that. Their Spiritual path is about learning the life lessons and understand that they are working with the universal energy with an innate sense of connectedness with creation. They have a creative side to them and therefore may be interested in expressing those qualities thru a wide range of interest in many different things. They may deal with things differently but they are here to shine their light and help with the Ascension.

There are many people who undergo the experience of a rapid shift into multi-dimensional awareness, or, the shift from the Indigo state to the Crystal state of consciousness. There are people who make the transition in a relatively gentle way, but there are many who experience a crisis when this happens. Some have chosen to open up to the higher dimensions. This choice is not made logically by the rational mind, but is rather a Soul choice made in response to the available transitional energies of the Earth herself. So, sometimes a person is thrust into psychological, emotional and bodily changes for which they can find no logical explanation. This can cause a crisis. This transition often happens to people who have been on Spiritual paths and are better equipped to handle the shifts. Indigos, and Star seeds no matter what their state of Spiritual awareness, are particularly vulnerable to the spontaneous experience of transition or breakthrough to the awareness of higher dimensions. There are several experiences that some Souls go through. Sudden extreme sensitivity to people and environments. A person who has previously been sociable and active suddenly finds they can't bear to be in shopping malls or in crowded environments such as restaurants. An increase in psychic ability and awareness. This most often manifests in the ability to almost "hear" the inner thoughts and feelings of others. This can be disconcerting if the person imagines that everyone else can also read their thoughts and feelings. Also an extreme sensitivity to negative energy in certain environments or people, including the inability to tolerate certain people who had previously been close. This increased sensitivity can lead to panic attacks or anxiety attacks. These can occur at any time, even when the person wakes up at night. Often there is no valid reason for the attack, although the person will often seek to find a reason. The person might also find themselves zoning out for long periods of time, just wanting to sit and do nothing. This can be irritating to someone who has previously been very energetic and active. This is just the consciousness adjusting to spending more time in the higher dimensions and less time in the

3rd and 4th dimensions. Related to this is the need to rest and sleep for far longer than previously, and a general slowing down. This is because multi-dimensional consciousness can access all levels of the group mind, including that part which holds the fears and anxieties about the survival of the species. Also a fear of going crazy and being unable to cope with everyday life in the future. Again, psychologists and doctors seem able to offer very little help. This is often just the consciousness clearing out old layers of energy that need to be released. It is not necessary to process or relive the experience, just allow the body to release the energy. Have patience with the process and know that it will pass. Disrupted sleep patterns, often waking up to 3 times a night. Again this is just the consciousness adapting to new cycles of activity. Higher consciousness is often more active at night since the lower dimensions are quiet at this time. Feeling strange electrical energy waves through the body. The Crystal body is incredibly sensitive, and feels solar and lunar waves, cosmic waves, and energies from the galactic centre. Often these energies are assisting in the process of "rewiring" the body to carry higher energies. Speaking from experience, I know how uncomfortable this can be. But the body eventually acclimates to dealing with these energy waves. You will probably find them to be more intense around the Full Moon. The best way I have found of dealing with this phenomenon is to go outside and release all of the anxiety and imagine the energy running through your body and into the earth.

A whole range of physical sensations and experiences, usually related to detoxification. The Crystal body holds no toxins, but allows everything to pass through it. In fact the eventual trick to being Crystal is just to allow everything to pass through and hold onto nothing. The ultimate state of detachment. But at this stage the body needs to release years of "toxic" waste, whether physical, emotional or mental. This release is always through the physical body, which presents symptoms such as intense fatigue, muscle and joint pains especially in the hips and knees, headaches, especially at the base of the skull, and neck and shoulder pains. Dizziness or feeling spacy is because you are in higher states of consciousness. You need to get used to being at these levels and staying grounded at the same time. These sensations tend to increase with solar flares and full moons, and any retrograde period as well. Increased appetite and putting on weight or even losing weigh can happen during the releasing phase. This is because the body needs huge amounts of energy to power this process. We have the ability to see beyond the veils, that is, to become aware of Spirits, and Angels as a reality and to communicate with these. This can be very frightening if the person is not accustomed to this kind of other dimensional awareness.

The best advice I can give is to be accepting of the process and do not resist. I found that the key was acceptance. When you can except that you are the process of change you can then begin to explore the adventure or the positive side of this new state. Be at peace with what is happening to your being. You are becoming a Crystal Being. Another term for this is a "Christed Being", which refers to a multi-dimensional Being with full access to 9 dimensions, and beyond. Some people will only open to 5D, others go through to 6D. If you make it through to 6D then you will probably achieve full 9D awareness in this lifetime, if not in the very near future. What a privilege and a blessing!! Be kind to yourself and nurture yourself. Remember, as a Crystal being you carry an equal balance of the "mother" energy and the "father" energy. The mother says, nurture yourself as you would a new-born baby, for in fact that is what you are. You will need time to grow in strength and learn the skills of your new environment.

Avoid crowds and crowded places, in order to not spend too long in tiring and toxic environments. Gradually you will be able to tolerate more and more exposure to these environments. As you make your way back out into the world you may still experience times where you may just need to retreat back to nature, or any comfortable environment. The key here, of course, is to hold your own peace and harmony so strongly that instead of you being affected by the environment, you in fact affect the environment in positive ways. The Crystal person always holds and carries positive energy, but you will learn to use it in incredibly powerful ways once you have gained your balance and are able to move among people again with ease. The length of time is really up to you. Don't be surprise if you now see, that out there things are totally different then you saw before.

Stay grounded and centered. This can be very challenging for those who are acclimating to higher dimensional awareness. Try to pay full attention to the physical and grounded aspects of life. Spend as much time as you can in Nature. You will find spending time in fresh air and sunlight will assist to strengthen the new bodies. There is help out there to help support your processes. There may be a full range of the emotional spectrum, from spontaneous and instant crying to lack of expression, and may have difficulty expressing anger constructively. You may feel that you have gone to hell and back or rebel against system considered dysfunctional, broken, and ineffective. They feel a burning desire to do something to change and improve the world but may have trouble identifying their path. Many had few if any Indigo role models and support structures. They are highly intuitive and can be very psychic. You begin to go through a time of awakening and seeking a deeper meaning to life and try to understand where they fit it. Indigo's have an inherent sense of the connection to all things. Indigos have a deep longing to find others like them be it kindred Spirits, Soulmates, or Twin Souls.

The Indigos are indeed a new breed because they represent a new breed of consciousness now entering incarnation within our time. The Indigos are true representatives of consciousness once prevalent on Earth, and in their reemergence today they become the way showers of things to come, as our race evolves, it moves closer to its intended destination. Indigos are here by design and intention; their coming here because they were asked to come and they have come to fulfill their part within a much greater evolutionary mission. The phenomenon of the Indigo Children is both Spiritual and genetic, and their placement among us represents the beginning of the externalization of our process of evolution. Comprehending the nature of the Indigo Children, and the nature of human existence itself, requires first and foremost the acknowledgement of a Multi-dimensional Reality Structure.

Star seeds have agreed to participate directly during this time in the human species evolution as the Heavenly host of ascension. The mission of adult Indigos is to act as an energy bridge between the two energies purple and indigo. They are the initiators who are preparing the way for those that are still unaware. The indigo frequency differs in its vibration. As the incoming frequency is different and the physical body is neither prepared nor accustomed, our first three chakras the ones which connect us to the Earth, giving us stability become unbalanced very easily.

The Indigos have great learning and assimilation capacity. They have an inquisitive mind and have the ability to develop their natural gifts of healing, clairvoyance. Indigos have a healing mission. The most important thing we, the Indigos, have to do, has to do with using of energy and the ability to make certain tones that allows to serve as living conduits of frequency, a very specific frequency. They have a gift to bring to the planet that the human populations alone, the 12-strand DNA, cannot do, even at their best. Indigos can hold and anchor more frequency. All Indigos share the same fundamental contract which is to hold and run as much frequency as possible, nothing else matters and since it is so extraordinary crucial nothing in 3 D nature could possibly compare. Angelic Human and Indigo races were sent into this Time Matrix as a guardian, protector and healer force, intended to protect the living Time Matrix and to assist, if and when possible, in the reclamation and redemption. You are entering into your birthright. If you resonate to the majority of these characteristics you may be an Indigo, Star seed, or Crystal Being, who are just beginning to wake up. There are many Souls here to help you with this transition. You were born to SHINE! Celebrate your transition. You are becoming a Galactic human, the next step in human evolution! Deep down in your Soul you know who you are and embrace your destiny.

The human Soul and consciousness out of which all of us emerge can literally change the way our DNA operates. Our DNA governs the structure of our physical body and our physical body will determine what type of consciousness we are able to bring in to our conscious mind, and our relationship to its source and the Universe. Our DNA is now being coded in light by the Universe although this depends on each Souls effort and your willingness to preserve until you create a new foundation of Quantum Light. We can start to expand the potentials of our body, so we can bring more of our consciousness and awareness, as we bring more of our Soul into manifestation here. There is an intimate connection within Spirit your Spiritual aspect, your higher dimensional aspects and consciousness moving through the body. It is not only mystics that awakened and acknowledge the energetic nature of reality, but quantum science has come to the same conclusions. There is nothing solid 'out there'! Reality is comprised of wavelengths of vibration. Everything is Energy. The good news is energy is MALLEABLE! It can be created, shaped, directed, transmuted, transformed, and raised. You are made of energy, and you are generating energy through your thoughts, feelings, beliefs and intentions all the time. That energy is creating your reality!

Your frequency patterns are affecting your life, for better or worse. Are you feeling like the radiant magnificent being of love and light that you truly are? Constricting energy we may be carrying, old programs and the like, get in the way of that experience. Change your energy and you change your world. From a metaphysical perspective, reality is a hologram of the entirety of your consciousness. It is an illusion, a dream, and you are the dream-weaver, whether that is happening at a conscious levels or not. Your energy patterns are dictating your experience. They may exist at deeper unconscious levels, they may even relate to past-life. You can consciously clear, align and raise your energy, and release what is, un-serving or holding you back. In meditation you create the space for Divine healing and co-creative assistance from your Higher Self and guides, and in this space you create Divine assistance in the process of healing, renewing and aligning your energy system.

Source has created a network of communication by which it not only transmits energy from itself to itself, but by which it, in turn, receives communication back from each expression of itself. Thus, the leaf gives to the acorn just as much as the acorn gives to the leaf. This communication system of Source is known as Merkaba. Mer: God Force Movement Ka: God Force Expression Ba: Vehicle Merkaba: Expression of God Force in Movement in its most basic expression. This takes the form of two Counter-rotating spirals which continually expand and contract the perpetual supply of renewed energy, radiation into and out of manifestation out from and back into Source.

We have the ability to become free and powerful loving and wise. It is up to us to rediscover this promise and to reclaim our power as co-creators within the universal scheme and use it. God gives challenges to those with a strong character God will meet you at the level of your expectation, without a calling life has no purpose. You must define your greatness and dare to walk that path. Look for the vision that God wants from you. Walt Disney said "If you can dream it you can do it "Dream Big. Believe Big. Its Gods favour that pushes us forward, look back at how far you have come on your path. This is wisdom use this wise medicine, and laugh in the face of adversity, pain and sorrow. Be like a child in your innocence and purity. Learn discernment so as not to give away your energy or power to someone who would use it against you. During this powerful time, this ascension process, we are to look deeply within and find the love from the Creator there. In order to balance and be one with the Universe we must continue to carry a loving, forgiving heart and share it with others. We must step into our Divine and Higher Light Body, or allow it to merge with our physical body which is what this ascension is all about anyway. To do this we must purify our temples body/mind/spirit through and through. Claim your own Divinity Walk with unconditional love, and keep your heart open to love, for the world reflects what and who you are at all times. Allow the gifts of the Holy Spirit, to bring forth the transmuting violet flame and transform your old belief systems and patterns into unconditional love and light. Through this time of ascension be the flow.

Whenever you feel sadness or sorrow, or feel like the whole world is tumbling down all around you, just take a moment or two and look into a mirror. Look deep into your eyes, the windows to your

Soul, and reflect upon your reflection, for there standing before you is magnificence! Behind everyone's eyes there is a child somewhere inside always be gentle and kind. Our lives may be full of challenges, and many days you simply wanted to roll into a little ball and give up. And, if the truth be told, you may have done that on more than one occasion yet, even at your lowest there was this hope that kept flickering. There may come a day when the messages become so loud that you can no longer ignore these messages. Understanding the honor that is being offered to you, to make life work. This takes courage, daring to go beyond the damaging patterns that had defined our lives, taking a quantum leap from darkness into the light.

Treat the Earth and that entire walk upon her with respect, walk together for the benefit of all people. Give assistance and kindness whenever and wherever it is needed. Do what you know to be right, look after the wellbeing of your mind and body and Soul, and emotions be truthful and humble at all times. Take full responsibility for your action, let go of the outworn habits and attitudes that no longer serve you. These patterns can drag you down and hold you back from you highest purpose. You have to put the past behind you before you can move ahead. Go within and listen for the direction from your true self who knows and has always known what parts need to be attained and what parts must be let go of. Only that which fits into the right thought should be worthy of your focus. When we learn to put the negative memories of the past to rest they no longer have control over you, but honor them because they have brought you to this place in time and you are stronger due to those experiences. An ending is a new point of beginning, there is always time to change directions and be flexible and flowing to the universal energy that surrounds you. Have faith in the power that is greater than you trusting that it will protect you at all times and under all circumstances. Declare that there are no problems that do not have solutions. There are no questions without answers. Bullying, jealousy, hate, greed, lies, arrogance, self-absorption, destructive mentalities are wasteful pursuits and causes the human heart to fall to the ground. It is beyond healing, beyond human conscience when people fight with each other. We are here now it is our responsibility to bring peace, harmony and balance back to the world. This will not happen if we continue to find fault with ourselves and perpetuate it on each other. We are the foundation on which nations are built. If we are weak, the people are weak. If her heart is strong and her mind is clear, then the nation is strong and knows its purpose. If we wonder often, the gift of knowledge will come. We will be known forever by the footprints we leave. Everyone who is successful must have dreamed of something. Remember that your children are not your own, but are lent to you by the Creator. You already possess everything necessary to become great. You can't wake a person who is pretending to be asleep and one finger cannot lift a pebble. We all have the potential to do great things but we should not attempt them all alone. Ask for help and guidance as you travel down these paths. Awaken to the greatness that is in every one of us.

As you journey down certain paths you may come across an enlightened Being. You will certainly know because their carry themselves differently. They know what they want and trust in their ability to achieve it. They take time to meditate and connect with their higher self's for guidance. They will probably not follow crowds as they enjoy tuning into their heart energy and lives in that higher truth. They may require freedom from the ordinary to create the experience that they truly wish to connect to. If you are and old Soul you need to fulfill your inner dreams and follow the path where Spirit leads you. You may find that some of the trait of the old Soul is simplicity. Simple living and pleasure make you feel warm and familiar. Sitting in a deep conversation is what old Souls often crave. Old Souls are sometimes intensely Spiritual people and may need time to detach and meditate. These tools are helpful and are necessary for their own wellbeing. They come across as daydreamers but that is how they accept the connection to Source. Often times someone may need to bring them back to reality. Often times their consciousness remains in the higher dimension where they feel better in those realms than in their current situation. Old Souls have gifts that they work with getting a feeling that something is going to happen even before it does. They may not have all of the fact but the somehow know this. The thing you call intuition is your Soul speaking to you, TRUST IT. The wiser you become the more you will understand that's its ok to live a life that other don't understand. This is your calling not everyone will have the same calling. Allow others to show you who they are.

We are never victims of our reality. We are volunteers and when we feel specific oppression from someone, realize that they are including us into their reality and that we affect them on a deep level. Sometimes we will elicit a strong negative response from a person or family member that appears as if they are judging us, or hating us for something we have done. So, realize the honor you have of just being in other peoples' lives; they find the need to draw you into their lives for a beautiful healing experience. Peace exists inside every person, and it is up to us to make it flow freely, so that it can illuminate life with its presence, and give us the strength necessary to triumph over all obstacles. Reach for and lean into a higher expression of yourself. Look towards the light, feel that energy and become that. Take the higher road. Ask yourself the questions," How much Love Am I capable of" Someday you will forget the reason we cried and who we believed caused us pain. We will realize that the secret of being free is by letting go and letting things unfold in their own way and in their own time. After all what matters is not the first chapter of your life but the last chapter which shows how well we ran the race. Don't judge any one by the chapter of their life that you walked in on. You can't start the next chapter of your life if you keep re-reading the last one.

Every person is surrounded by a thought atmosphere. Through this power we are either attracting or repelling. Like attracts like and we attract just what we are in mind. This principle by which you attract into your life that which is in vibration alignment with your consciousness; your thoughts, feelings, beliefs and attitudes, whether you are aware of them or not. This is why the first step on the road to success and to deliberately manifest your desires is to become conscious of the thoughts and feelings that are creating your experience and to take responsibility for your reality. Taking responsibility for your life without self-judgment any perceived failures is both empowering and liberating. When you understand that you are source not subject of your world, you can change it. Your imagination is a gateway to the possible and a bridge to your unconscious mind. It is the boundless palate with which you craft your world and an integral key to manifesting your desires. Your subconscious mind does not know the difference between what is real and what is imagined. "Your imagination is your preview of life's coming attraction."

No matter what Spiritual path you have chosen to walk, in order to be more Spiritually aware, set aside time to strip away the unnecessary tradition or dogma. You know all things, each of you holds the answers and yet the fragmentation of yourself can set up barriers to becoming whole. It is this fragmentation that separates us from spirit and raises these kinds of Spiritual questions. Who am I? Why do I feel something is missing in my life? Is this all there is? Isn't there something better? Spiritual awareness or Spiritual awakening is the process by which we begin to explore our own being in order to become whole and reunite our Spirits with our physical bodies in a common search of purpose. We can overcome all doubt if we learn to trust in the Love of our Creator to help us through any seemingly insurmountable situation. Always keep your heart open to the Light and the intelligently coordinated co-creative power that lives within you, and works tirelessly to bring you into alignment with your life's plan. This is your individual map, which will afford you the greatest personality development and Soul growth. Remain as much as possible in this positive consciousness and receptive present now moment. This is the greatest tool for remaining connected to your Divine indwelling Spirit. A conscious elevated faith and wisdom-seeking attitude is required to transcend the fearful ego-mind. Your free-will decision to consecrate the higher reasoning mind can be synchronized with the highest and most loving Will. This is the Divine Will which follows the cosmic plan leading to light and Life, for both the individual and collectively for all humanity by the manifestation of Love. Human beings are the time-space evolutionary vehicles through which this co-creative process occurs. The experiential knowledge gained in the process is invaluable to the Creator and the gift each mortal offers. Between incarnations your Soul rests and gets ready for your next incarnation. Souls are educated in the energetic Archangelic realms. Each Soul will go through many stages of development, Infant Souls, Baby Souls, Young Souls, Mature Souls, Old Souls, and Infinite Souls. Old Souls strive not to harm others, they intuitively know that they are a part of a bigger picture and are connected to others on a deeper level. They understand and demonstrate unconditional love.

No matter whether you are just starting on your search or have been a traveler on the Spiritual awareness path, the answers you seek have always been with you. Perhaps in your seeking Spiritual awareness you have been interested by a process and simply have not allowed yourself the time to become aware. Put aside all restrictions and limitations and allow yourself to simply be. In this moment now look neither back nor forward and allow yourself to see your Spirit. It is you, there, awaiting your rediscovery. Spirit is always within us yearning to be once again given freedom to be and to become a whole part of each of us. It is not necessary to struggle, neither physically nor spiritually. It is your unresolved issues that leaves you confused and alone. Your purpose, which you seek, is here for you now. There are many paths to help you become whole but it is up to you to take the steps forward.

Becoming whole is simple, unique to you, and yet others have ventured along similar paths and may be of assistance to you as you travel just as you will be of assistance to them. You may choose to take the direction, listen to your own signs and those of people who have gone before, helping you discover your truths, or continue to struggle and repeat the lessons endlessly. Listen to your heart and the love you have for self and others and know your truth. Take time now to meditate, for in meditation you empower your Spirit to be. As thoughts arise, acknowledge them and put them aside but allow them no energy. You have the answers within and they may not fulfill your expectations. Put aside expectations and your spirit will fill you with love beyond all previous understanding. Your mind will not easily surrender to your Spirit just because you have chosen to increase your Spiritual awareness. You are your spirit; it is only your mind that is holding you back in fulfilling your truth and becoming all you want to be.

Have no doubt about who you are, what you want, or why you are here. We are all here for fulfill the Divine plan, even if at this time you are unaware what the plan is, we must continue to search for the light that is us. Keep looking and it will show up to create joy, peace, and love. It comes from within your Soul. When we search for God in this moment we realize that he is inside of you every minute of every day. Right here Right Now. When we accept this as fact we begin to let go of all the stuff that we don't need and exhale and really begin to breath. When we can let go of the past and be open to the now moment we can access another path for our lives to take. The path to freedom a way back Home! Returning to our original blueprint that God designed each of us to be, whole, being one with our Creator.

Having a great purpose in your life is essential, but that is not all. Besides that, you need principles. Principles are the guidelines of your life. They mark the way you are going to pursue your purpose in life. Your principles can reflect three possibilities: Your way, other people's way, or God's way. Among those there is no doubt; the best way is the way of God, for God's will represents not only what is best for you, but best for all. If you choose God's way, you must strive to lead your life based on truth, love and service. Someone who seeks truth, harbors love in his or her heart, promotes other people's lives through unselfish service, and has found the way of true happiness. Purpose and principles make up the core of your life's plan, but they are not enough if you are not a flexible person. Although you should have short-, medium- and long-term plans for your life, you must be open to make changes when necessary. In making plans for your life, you should be aware of three elements that invariably cause you to turn to them, as you live your life. These are: Unexpected circumstances, your interaction with other people, and the plans of the Spirit Within for your Spiritual development. These three, but specially the Spirit of God in you, with His Spiritualizing influence in your life, will make you consider changes to your life's plan and sometimes these changes will be of great importance. Life is much more meaningful when it is first thought out and then lived. That is called living awareness. Your life is your responsibility. However, there is plenty of help available for you, so you can conduct it to fulfill a great purpose. Mainly, be aware of the leadings of Spirit Within, guiding you according to the will of God, so, even in the midst of challenges and trials, you may, in the end, have grown Spiritually, which after all is what really counts.

Practice being grateful for whatever path you are on, knowing that this too shall pass. Ask for what you need also accepting that what you want and what you need may be different. We find that the reward is that we are who we are, standing next to what we are. Look inside yourself to find what is scared to you, find the joy, peace, and love that God s gift to each of us you just have to want it with all your heart. Then the Soul is ALIVE

When you honor your path to who you are you may be taken down a detour, there lies the challenge to get back on your path that which feels good. Look for purpose in all you do and walk towards love. Be true to yourself knowing what you are meant to do. Beware not to chase dreams that are not yours because this equals suffering. Your life has purpose find it and live it on purpose. Vulnerably opens doors to intimacy. Take the risk and open yourself up to enhance your Spirit. Spirit is hope, grace, and light, that part of you that makes you feel good. Have courage to see those parts that need healing and embrace that. Heal thy self. Remember to find your path and follow your calling, as the saying goes: Do not walk behind me; I may not lead. Do not walk in front of me; I may not follow, Walk beside me, that we may be as "One".

As you begin a new Chapter in your life, how will you write this one and the next one? Move forward without fear knowing that you have the power to create your life to the highest good, do that which is in highest vibration. Love is the highest vibration reach towards that and to your awakening and "Enlightment". Understand that you are the eyes, the mouth, the hands, the feet, and the expression of the Creator on the worlds, levels, and dimensions of the Universes. You ARE experience! And because you are the experiencer you are to be loved and nurtured and given all opportunities to progress. You become creators in your own right and to experience greater and more sublime adventures that unfold as you raise your vibration higher and higher to experience those astonishing levels of creation and triumphs that were designed for you to master. Think about these things that have stated for you, breath out in joyous anticipation that God has plans that have yet to be revealed to us, for we are alive in the worlds of light and yet we are only just beginning our astonishing journey and only just experiencing the power of Divine love that encompasses us, teaches us, and compels us to reach higher and to know more of Him, the Universal Father.

Spirituality is a primordial component of a human being. The influence of the Creator in one's life is a constant. People can choose to ignore this influence the advice and suggestions from the Divine In-dweller but the Creators work in inspiring us to become the best we can be never ceases. In our material life, some people have decided to separate spirituality from every other aspect of society. When we talk about Spirituality, we are not referring to a church, but to your simply having the goal to fulfill the will of your Creator in your life. The name you use for the Creator is irrelevant. What is important is that you think of Him as the highest Source of truth, beauty and goodness you can imagine. Those who kill and oppress their peers in the name of a vengeful God who prefers some people over others and who doesn't treat all His children in the same way, are not living the will of the Father. Those who believe in a God of love, who is the individual Source of each and every person in this world, and inhabits each one, can truly aspire to manifest His will and become a reflection of this Source. The attributes of our Creator is truth, beauty, and goodness. Anything that doesn't have all of these three attributes, doesn't come from our Creator. Those who walk this higher path, will set their standards high and aim for perfection, requires them to fill their life with freedom, and they are truly the masters of their own destiny.

The rules of the Universe can be summarized in one word love. We are inspired to practice love, the highest love we can imagine, without reservation or condition, and for all beings, with the supreme goal of expressing that same quality of love we receive from God. Think about this for a moment the measure of any Soul can be weighed by the moments where this quality was freely willed as a choice over all other alternatives. The meaning of its value becomes better understood as it is expressed and experienced and never does it become undesirable. All sentient beings require it in increasing amounts for healthy growth of mind, body, and spirit. This quality is the Divine vitamin from which all systems draw vitality. We as Souls know that it is the greatest of qualities.

Alchemy is the transformation of the self. We never really can understand anything unless we go through it ourselves and then it changes who you thought you were into a version of yourselves you have yet to experience. This happens when you are awaken. As we awaken to our new reality and done our healing, the Soul is returned to its natural state of receptivity into the light. Students on the path are rediscovering our birthright and unlearning the confusion of our past. Each one of you was loved before coming into this world and Gods love will remain a constant and well beyond your understanding even after all your mistakes, and all your achievements what you choose to do along your journey is entirely up to you. It matters not to whether you are a carpenter, an astronaut, a healer, a leader, or a follower. What matters, is working towards progression is your Spiritual growth. As long as you keep the truth in your heart, you are doing Gods will. Each time you choose to be the best you can be in every situation in life, you are doing what God intended for each and every Soul. If you keep this intent in your heart and mind, all the things that you do will lead to the goal of Spiritual growth, and you will live a fulfilling life. Many among you have felt the impulse to lovingly serve your peers and to do something positive for your world. A few of you will have the chance to occupy important positions where you will be able to have a more direct influence over what happens around you. Do not be discouraged in case your efforts are ignored by some people. Do not stop your love from being freely expressed, just because the results may not be evident in the here and now. All the efforts to make the will of the Father a reality in this world will always produce fruit and you can be sure that the Father and a host of celestial beings will know about your efforts and rejoice at your intent.

In this world, do not be discouraged by feeling that you will not be able to fulfill all your dreams and satisfy all your aspirations. If these dreams and aspirations truly posses eternal value, you will come back to them later in your journey. Often you will not be able to determine with clarity the importance of a lesson you need to learn, but rest assured that all those things that come to you during your life experience have a purpose, and can be used by you to grow in Spirit and wisdom. You will have more than enough time to explore and discover your hidden talents. Spiritual growth is not one more task, it is the main purpose of your existence.

When your goals are in harmony with the plan of the Creator, when your will is in alignment with the Creators will, your desires do start to become more real. The materialistic motivations of the past will not affect you so much and you will start to feel the inspiration to achieve greater things in the eyes of God, not in the eyes of others. You, are actually a part of this experiential God! You complete Him with your free-will experiences and your unique life! There is nothing ordinary about your life as you are needed, unconditionally loved, and cherished for your part in the whole of this requirement to fulfill the Creator's desire to have all-experience.

Each one of us have been given an assignment, a mission of supreme importance. Each of us now has the opportunity, the privilege, to make a difference in creating a world that works for all of us. It will require courage. You have the potential to make changes in the world, just take the time you need to reinvent yourselves every day and to always look up towards the Heaven and bring that version down here on Earth.

The Journey Begins With Just One Step

Imagine if you saw a vision of your future which you KNEW to be right for you, which inspired you wouldn't that be wonderful? Receiving the vision itself may have been a helpful stepping stone on your path. Working with the higher energies can help you receive the answers you may be looking for. God and the angels recognize that many are seeking guidance and direction in life, a sense of purpose, and to know where we are heading. There are Angles that are sent to each Soul here that are happy to provide this in many ways. Some of the ways include receiving answers in your dreams, or during meditation, or receiving messages or signs, any way that appeals to you can offer you hope and inspiration to lift your spirits. Open your mind and make a connection to your higher self and ask for guidance that you may receive the answer you are searching for. You may receive a vision or you may receive a message that you just need to relax and allow all that is of the highest good be presented to you. When you are ready, close your eyes and take a few deep breathes, to relax your mind and body, and make yourself calm and centered. Choose a time and a place that feels right, and relax and get yourself ready in whatever way feels appropriate. Imagine you are standing in front of a doorway, in your mind's eye see the doorway, now put your hand on the door knob and open it, take a few steps in, you have literally just walked into your future. See what your future looks like, and spend as much time in this space as you need before returning to the present. Each small step might represent a year into your future.

Allow yourself to walk into your future, to a time in the future when everything is going really well for you. Allow yourself to notice where you are, who you are with. Are you pleased or excited about what is happening? Are you happy where you are? Allow yourself to become aware of why this is significant in your life. If this feels good, allow yourself to remember these feelings. How far into the future does this feel? Allow a number, and whether it is months or years, to pop into your head. Allow yourself to become aware of what steps you took that helped you to get to this point.

As you take each step very slowly and deliberately, allow yourself to sense "Is this the time in my future that feels good and feels right?" Keep going until you have found the exact spot. When you have found the spot that feels right, stop there. Now that you are in the right place, allow yourself to tune in and sense what is happening at this time in the future, when everything is going really well in your life. Now imagine telepathically sending all these positive thoughts and feelings about your good future, back to you in the now moment. Now you have insights, and the energy and feeling of satisfaction and success, which helps draw this future to your faster. KNOWING intuitively this is possible, you gain greater certainty and positive energy if you choose to pursue this path. The positive, optimistic and happy thoughts and expectations will help to draw positive situations, people and opportunities to you to help you. Once you have learned the technique, you can repeat it again and again, to receive a further boost of positive energy and inspiration, and further ideas to help you.

What message would you like to give to the present day you? "Go for it" or "Have faith and believe you can do it". As you finish your walk into the future open your eyes, walk back to the present time where you started and turn and face your future, and allow yourself to receive all of the positive visions, feelings and messages from the future. If you did not receive much or anything, know that you may receive a vision at some point in the future instead, when the time is right for you.

Our ideas are as valid as we make them out to be. We may worry what others think and if we can believe in our ideas enough to back them up, others will be more likely to see the validity behind our notions. Even if they don't end up agreeing with us, they will still respect and see worth in our ideas. Many of the greatest ideas in the world came from one person's ability to articulate an idea in a way that hadn't been thought of before. One person's notion can be the next great invention, if only that person is brave enough to put their thoughts out there. Believe in your ideas enough to share them with others today, and you will be contributing to the collective consciousness. Be Beautiful, Be Happy, Be Awesome, Be Spectacular, Be Loving, Be Kind. Loving life is about welcoming the blind turns and the possibility that there is no such thing as coincidence and that empathy is incredibly sexy and that it is never too late to pick up a paintbrush or to make a new friend. Love this life it could be over at any second. We are not offered any guarantees in life, understanding this we make the conscious decision to live each and every moment to the fullest. In the NOW, counting our blessing along the way. The Universe responds to frequencies and as we shift into a positive higher state of Being we receive more of that same energy back. The feelings of excitement sends a vibration to the Universe that you are on the right path acknowledging the vibration you are receiving.

The field of consciousness where "the Will of God is known" is the center from which Love draws energy and life. When our individual will aligns itself with and cooperates with the Will that governs the Universe, that Universal Will then cooperates and puts at our disposal its own infinite energies. Under these conditions individual will is neither annihilated nor diminished. It becomes transfigured. Life is never what it seems, you are encouraged to look at what you need to let go of, so you can choose, allow in, and manifest more of what serves you and the world. Sometime we must drop to our knees before we can get back up and stand strong. Allow courage to be your guide. Light is an active energy, constantly in motion. Therefore, as we invoke Light, we can expect major changes in our own consciousness, attitudes and actions. These same changes will occur in all who are ready. We invoke Light and then may find yourself appalled at what is revealed in the dark corners of consciousness and in the world around us. But these places cannot be cleansed and redeemed unless their way is made visible, through exposure to the Light. Remember Christ promised us he would raise us from our sleep to awake to our truth.

The lifting of the veil allow us to see the world with a different view. As we see ourselves in this new found world of ours we begin again to witness Gods miracle in our life and the lives of others. As we give love and support we become a reflection of that which we were intended to be. Then we pass on this truth to each Soul we encounter. We are all an expression of the One energy but unless you make the conscious decision to change who you were you will never understand how special you truly are. Just start by putting one foot in front of the other moving along a path design by the Universe for you, this is the Grace of God the choice is yours discover why you were created then act on that.

In order to get what we want in life, we have to be willing to receive it when it appears, and in order to do that we have to be open. Often we go through life with defenses we developed early on in order to protect ourselves. These defenses act as barriers, walls we needed at one time to feel safe, but that now serve to shut out desired influences, like intimacy or love. So an essential part of being receptive to what we want is to soften these barriers enough to let those things in when they show up. For example, we may spend a lot of time alone as a way to protect ourselves from being hurt by other people, but we can see how this is now preventing us from connecting with other Souls. Becoming receptive involves a softening of our defenses and a willingness to remain open to possibilities outside our immediate realm of vision. If we are looking for love or friendship, it means first looking within ourselves to see where we are shut down, and second, not getting too fixated on where we might find the love we want. In this way, we become more open as individuals and more expansive in terms of what we see as possible.

Often, the things and people we want to draw into our lives elude us because we are unconsciously blocking them out, either with our defenses, or with tunnel vision that causes us to not see them when they appear. When this is the case, we can take action by exploring and softening our barriers, and expanding our vision to encompass new possibilities. These actions are the essence of receptivity. You may feel a little dissatisfied or unworthy today. If so, you could find yourself seeking things you believe could add more significance or depth to your life. Maybe you are making an effort to form new kinds of relationships or create new kinds of work that can give you greater fulfillment. You could even be thinking about new ways to spend your free time. Becoming more active in the world could help you reconnect with your life purpose. You may even want to do some brainstorming and write down what you'd like to have more of in your life. Pick one item off your list and make it happen today.

When we wish to manifest a more meaningful existence for ourselves, we can find the power to do so within. We are the Soul, creators of our destiny. Nothing has a more profound impact on the depth of the lives we live than our own thoughts and actions. Propelled by a longing for substance, we can decide which action to take to create more substantive connections between ourselves and the world around us. Each bond we consciously create or deepen with others, serves everyone and gives our lives more meaning. Go within today to discover what you can do to be more fully engaged with the world around you, and you will inevitably create a more meaningful life.

Many of us continue to undergo a major lifestyle change. Things that we thought that were important to you no longer are your perspective is now changing. It is a restricting as well as a deep cellular transformation. This is called the "Opening of the Seal". This opening has occurred because you have said yes to the Universe energy of LOVE. It can cause intense changes, physically, emotionally, mentality and spiritually, sometimes we are not always prepared for these changes. Keeping an open mine and open heart will help elevates some of the physical symptoms. Your physically body is blending with your higher self and the two will become one. The pineal gland is activating to the new energy released into your brain. This may sometimes cause lucid dreaming, ringing in the ears, seeing shapes, and symbols that you never could have imagines prior to the opening. At this time you may be experiencing what I call a download. New energies are downloading light source into your Being. This transmission you are receiving is your connection to your higher self. You may find yourself in isolated situations and are wondering what you are doing wrong but there is nothing wrong it is a beginning of a new way on living. You are become fully awake and alive, the veil you lived under before has been lifted. You are able to live from a higher perspective and can actively participate in a new way. Once you have cleared any debris that you may have stored in your Spiritual house you open to the freedom your Soul longed for. It is a returning to yourself. You begin to feel free once more returning to your Source of creation. You are home. There is a new foundation in which you begin to build your future. We now understanding that we no longer need to know what's next, we trust that we know that a new life foundation is being built. You can try to break free from the silence space but something will always push you back into the silence again. You are growing stronger and able to now receive the Power of Light. AS WE KNOW it, WE BECOME IT, and then life as we know it changes forever. You begin to see yourself as part of the larger order of things and accept your role. I am an integral part of the whole. I accept that it requires courage to walk my earth walk and wisdom to know when I need to make changes, each morning we wake to a new day upon which we can create a new reality for ourselves. There may be mountains that you have to move but I know that there are also great moments of Joy, Peace and Love waiting to be discovered. Remember it's not the destination but the journey that matters most.

Our goal is to walk towards the light of Love so that we can go to the Spirit world with clean hands and straight eyes. We will face our options, and make choices and depending on what you decide indicates whether you must return for another earth walk if there are lessons still for you to learn. Each day embrace more of your inner beauty because this is the essence of who you are, always do your best to walk the walk and talk the talk always in the highest good for all. Whatever you decide to be make sure it is the best you that you present to the world. It is not so important that you know of the distinction between you and your Spirit, but rather you acknowledge the partnership and feel the harmony. You will learn to recognize this harmony and the Father's voice will always speak in the terms of the highest values of unity. Love is the greatest unifier in creation and it can be applied to any situation or circumstance in a way that will have the greatest future value. In other words, the voice of love will always bypass the ego and show you a view from the mountain top, which leads to growth and progress even if the current circumstance would appear otherwise. Never will the Divine Leading tell you what to do, but rather will He speak of the way of love and the highest possibilities, but you must choose to act in harmony with your Creators Will.

When you begin to recognize this way of thinking, then you will understand the connection of Spirits voice within you. When you bring your attention to Spirit and intimately converse and share your deepest thoughts, desires, and problems, you will hear Spirit speak to your mind and it will echo back the wisdom of love as it is applied to your questions, thoughts, and problems. This is why it is so important to work on self-mastery. Self-mastery quiets the loud voices that drown out the still small voice of Spirit. Spirit is personal for each and every Soul and so they rely on the partnership with you and your personality. Fusion with Spirit occurs when the voice of harmony becomes a voice in unison and there is little distinction between you and the Inner Spirit of the Source. Fusion does not equate perfection, it only provides a much expanded consciousness for the continuing adventure. When you have traveled across the Universes of time to the center of infinity and you stand in finality before the Universal Father and receive the Divine embrace, you will know this unity to be like the Father for those that see you' will also see GOD.

The process of awakening allows you to emerge into a being of light, a human embodiment of the Christ Consciousness now here on earth. We now enter into an opportunity to join with others working in the light to help heal this planet. IT has been referred to as a changing of the guard. WE must enter the dark to truly know the light of GOD! Life offers you a second chance each and every day which we call tomorrow. Start each day with a smile knowing it is your life, create it as you wish. Remind yourself every day, I AM Blessed, I AM, Loved, I AM Healthy, I AM Creative. I AM Alive I AM AWAKE. Begin each day living your life on purpose and with meaning. Be the person who someone might one day say "I am lucky to have known someone like you who was so hard to say goodbye to."

We accept that our past experiences has brought us to this moment in time shaping you, molding you, to grow stronger. To give into the old patterns would dishonor yourself because you have been gifted with deep knowledge the inner knowing that hope was within your Soul. It may take years to accept that we had not made mistakes, but made decisions using the tools we had at the time which resulted in right and not so right choices. These are the lesson which propels us along in life. As you see yourself as part of the larger order of things and accept your role you will have no need for applause, because you are now an integral part of the whole. You accept that it requires courage to walk this earth walk and wisdom to know where you need to make better choices. Set your goal every day to walk towards perfection so that when you leave this world you may return home.

The world around us sleeps and you find yourself alone with Spirit, the invitation is to stay awake. It seems at night that we can hear the calling and it awakens us. Daytime diversion have a hypnotic power unknowingly we walk through the day in a make like trance, a world that seems that nothing is real. You find peace in the night time quiet. I think about dying and rising, shedding the past and new birth and letting go and trust that the fertile seeds submitting to the Universe through prayer with hope in the promise of a future life renewed. And I know that I too must do my homework and learn my lesson. I too must shed some and die some to let go and submit to the grace of God's mysterious ways. There is so much to see in the dark and it all looks really clear. We can attune ourselves to this realm of life even in the daytime for at night is not only a time but a place and we must find that place in our lives. And if you're faced with a choice, and you have to choose, I hope you choose the one that means the most to you. And when one door opens to another door closed, I hope you keep on walking till you find the one that leads you home. I wish that this life becomes all that you want it to be and that your dreams are big and your worries are small and that you never have to carry more than you can hold. I hope you know that somebody loves you and wants the best for you. I now choose to be beyond the problems, to seek the wisdom & guidance of that which is greater than me to provide solutions to any discord that may appear. Within me is a voice that speaks to me and the freedom of thinking beyond limitation and doubts. As you go inside, ask your inner guides to show you the way to manifest your dreams. Imagine you can do anything because in truth you can no matter what shows up on your path, the Divine, wisdom, and harmony with the Universe are around you and within you.

Napoleon Hill put it like this:" We do not have to wait for future discoveries in connection with the powers of the human mind for evidence that the mind is the greatest force known to mankind. We know, now, that any idea aim or purpose that is fixed in the mind and held there with a will to achieve or attain its physical or material equivalent, puts into motion powers that cannot be conquered." "He can who thinks he can. And he can't who thinks he can't". This is an indisputable law. You must find your Strength of Purpose and Energy of Will to obtain that which you came here to accomplish.

Your awakening brings ecstasy to your endeavors that begin bearing fruit. You'll discover that you are focusing on the positive aspects of your experience as it is unfolding in the present. The great news that has brought joy to your heart can only encompass a single aspect of the journey that has led you to this point. Exploring the challenges you faced in the now moment can help you learn valuable lessons. You may find you have become a stronger person because you bravely stood up to adversity. Or you may feel confident from the fact that it was likely your actions and decisions that allowed you to accomplish what is bringing you so much pleasure and joy.

Our experiences can only add value to our lives when we strive to comprehend how individual events have shaped our personalities or the adversity we have overcome has influenced the path we have chosen to follow. Life's lessons are conveyed to us through challenges we have no choice but to face, yet we are free to accept or ignore those universal lessons as we see fit. In recognizing that a certain experience has the potential to convey an educational message, we enable ourselves to receive wisdom from even the most unpleasant situations. We are changed the moment we realize we can experience enlightenment from simply Being. When you understand the scope of all you have learned in your lifetime you will understand that everything happens for a reason.

As you begin Soul searching trying to understand who you are on a deeper level you can turn to astrology and other Spiritual realms. Research your birth name, birth date, these all have special messages to help you on your way. Your birth date is no accident you were meant to be born on that vibration. Finding our frequency takes a willingness to make this part of your life's work. Although you have other areas that you must attend to you must make this your path. Seek wisdom, not knowledge. Knowledge is of the past, Wisdom is of the future. Tell me and I'll forget. Show me, and I may not remember Involve me, and I'll understand. Wisdom comes only when you stop looking for it and start living the life the Creator intended for you. No river can return to its source, yet all rivers must have a beginning. Whatever you do in life, do the very best you can with both your heart and mind. And if you do it that way, the Power of the Universe will come to your assistance, if your heart and mind are in Unity. Whatever we do affects everything in the Universe. If you do it that way that is, if you truly join your heart and mind as one whatever you ask for, that's the Way It's Going to Be. Life is meant to be enjoyed not endured. Our Creator intended each individual Soul to think for themselves and to grow into the Divine blueprint that was bestowed upon each living Soul. We are the center of a circle the circumference of which is determined by our self-imposed limitations. It is time to shift gears to begin your journey to our inner essence and remember the path of least resistance offers little opportunity for Soul growth.

As we seek so shall you find the answers to the questions that you are now experiencing. The outcome is up to you if you chose to make a Connection to the higher realms! The path that I am walking now asks me to allow positive experiences in my life as well as in others' lives. Let the power that be shine now!" All that was great in the past was ridiculed, condemned, suppressed only to emerge all the more powerful all the more triumphantly from the struggle." Nickola Tesla. "As we will it so shall it BE"! I do believe in an everyday magic where the connectedness we experience with people, seems somewhat strange at times, but it is synchronicity that keeps us moving forward towards our next adventure. This has been my experience, as we approach our destiny may we all find that connection to our Source and be grateful for the gifts we have been given. Give a little bit of your love to me, I'LL give a little bit of my Love to you, we are on our way back home!

LIFE IS BUT A DREAM

Whenever righteousness wanes and unrighteousness
increases I send myself forth.
In order to protect the good and bring Love & Light
and to make a firm foundation for future generations,
I come into being age after age

"Your visons will become clear only when you can look into your own
heart. Those that look outside, dream; those who look inside awaken"
Carl Jung

Namaste: My Soul honors your Soul. I honor the place in you
where the entire Universe resides I honor the Light, Love, Truth,
Beauty and Peace within you because it is also within Me, We are
United, We are the Same, We are One.

I AM "AWAKE"
Barbara Knapp

P.S. ARE YOU AWARE OF HOW AWESOME YOU ARE!!!

RESOURCES

Awakening into Oneness- Arjuna Ardagh-

Alchemy of Nine Dimensions-Barbara Hand Chow

The Law of Attraction- Esther and Jerry Hicks

Loving What Is- Byron Katie

www.Google

Awakening Intuition- Mona Lisa Schulz

Light Worker- Sahvanna Arienta

The information contained within this book comes from the guidance I received. All of the Light workers who have contributed to this message please accept my deepest gratitude as we work together to bring this information to light we grow closer to fulfilling our mission to connect to Source and help with Ascension. Blessed Be!!

Printed in the United States
By Bookmasters